Free Churches and Society

Free Churches and Society

The Nonconformist Contribution to Social Welfare 1800–2010

Edited by

Lesley Husselbee and Paul Ballard

continuum

Continuum International Publishing Group

The Tower Building	80 Maiden Lane
11 York Road	Suite 704
London	New York
SE1 7NX	NY 10038

www.continuumbooks.com

British Library Cataloguing-in-Publication Data
A catalogue record for this book is available from the British Library.

ISBN: 978-1-4411-5613-6 (hardback)
978-1-4411-0911-8 (paperback)

Typeset by Fakenham Prepress Solutions, Fakenham, Norfolk NR21 8NN
Printed and bound in Great Britain

CONTENTS

ACKNOWLEDGEMENTS AND EDITORIAL NOTES

The Editors and the Steering Group wish to express their gratitude to all who have contributed to the project and enabled the production of this volume.

- Those who shared their memories of community work: Keith Argyle, Ernest Crutchley, Maggie Hindley, Janet Lees, Adella Pritchard, Dennis Neville, Craig Russell, David Tennant, Brenda Willis.
- Ann Honey, Laura Collins and Jenny Crane who contributed to the thinking in Chapter 9.
- Those who attended the seminar in January 2010, offering stimulating discussion, fresh insights, and warm endorsement for the project.
- Colleagues, especially John Campbell, then Principal, in Northern College (Congregational and United Reformed), Luther King House, Manchester, who have provided encouragement and administrative support.
- The Coward Trust, Westhill Trust and Northern College for generously covering the cost of the seminar and editorial expenses.
- The authors who worked under considerable time constraints.
- Nicola Rusk and the editorial team at Continuum, who enthusiastically embraced the proposal and have facilitated the production process with professional skill and generosity.

The editors and authors have taken every reasonable care to observe copyright. Any inadvertent infringement should be drawn to their attention and the matter will be rectified as appropriate.

Endnotes are provided for each chapter. These provide detailed references to the resources and literature referred to under that particular heading.

The Select Bibliography for further reading brings together a shorter list of the more recent and other accessible literature relevant to the project as a whole.

Mention is made of a number of historically significant persons, some of whom may be unfamiliar to readers. Biographical information may, in most cases, be found in one of the following:

ODNB: *Oxford Dictionary of National Bibliography*, which can be accessed on oxfordnb.com

Taylor, John and Binfield, Clyde (eds) (2007) *Who They Were: In the Reformed Churches of England and Wales 1901–2000*, United Reformed Church History Society, Donington, Dyas.

Vickers, John A. ed. (2000) *A Dictionary of Methodism in Britain and Ireland*, Peterborough: Epworth.

Lewis, Donald M. ed. (2004) *Dictionary of Evangelical Biography 1730–1860*, Peabody, MA: Hendrickson.

CONTRIBUTORS

Paul Ballard, a Baptist minister, is Professor Emeritus at Cardiff University, where he taught practical theology. Recent publications include, with Malcolm Brown, *The Church and Economic Life* (Peterborough: Epworth, 2006), with Lesley Husselbee, *Community and Ministry* (London: SPCK, 2007); and, as editor, *The Bible in Pastoral Practice*, with Stephen R. Holmes (London: Darton, Longman and Todd, 2005) and *The Church at the Centre of the City* (Peterborough: Epworth, 2008).

David Bebbington was a research fellow of Fitzwilliam College, Cambridge before moving to the University of Stirling in 1976, where he is now Professor of History. He has also taught at the University of Alabama, Birmingham, at Regent College, Vancouver, at Notre Dame University, Indiana, at the University of Pretoria, South Africa, and at Baylor University, Texas. His publications include *The Nonconformist Conscience* (London: G. Allen and Unwin, 2nd edn 2010), *Evangelicalism in Modern Britain* (London: Routledge, 2nd edn 1993), and *Victorian Nonconformity* (Chester: Lutterworth, 2nd edn 2011).

Clyde Binfield is Professor Emeritus in History at the University of Sheffield. His research, reflected in his publications, has concentrated on English Nonconformity in the nineteenth and twentieth centuries, with particular reference to its social, cultural and political contexts. He is a past president of the United Reformed Church History Society, and of the Chapels Society. He is a Trustee of the Historic Chapels Trust and of Dr Williams's Trust and Library.

Peter Catterall teaches history and public policy at Queen Mary, University of London and for the Hansard Society. He is founder editor of *National Identities* and has recently edited for publication *The Macmillan Diaries: Prime Minister and After 1957–1966* (London: Macmillan, 2011).

Lesley Husselbee is a retired minister of the United Reformed Church. After local ministries in Coventry and Bourne End, Buckinghamshire, she served as Secretary for Training for the United Reformed Church and as Director of Church Related Community Work at Northern College, Luther

King House, Manchester. Recent publications include, with Paul Ballard, *Community and Ministry* (London: SPCK 2007).

Stephen Orchard is a retired United Reformed Church Minister who, after local ministries, served as Assistant General Secretary (Community Affairs), British Council of Churches, 1982–1986; General Secretary and Director of Christian Education Movement, 1986–2001; and Principal of Westminster College, Cambridge, 2001–2007, where he was an affiliated lecturer in Cambridge University and also served as President of the Cambridge Theological Federation, 2005–2007. He was Secretary of the Religious Education Council of England and Wales, 1991–2001, and also Chairman, 1999–2001. He delivered the bi-centenary lecture for the British and Foreign School Society, of which he is a former Chairman, in 2008. His most recent book is on the history of Nonconformity in Derbyshire.

Robert Pope, a minister of the United Reformed Church, is Reader in Theology at the University of Wales, Trinity St David, based in Lampeter, Cardiganshire. He has published extensively on Welsh Nonconformist history and thought as well as on aspects of contemporary theology. Relevant publications are: *Building Jerusalem: Nonconformity, Labour and the Social Question in Wales, 1906–1939* (Cardiff: University of Wales Press, 1998); *Seeking God's Kingdom: The Nonconformist Social Gospel in Wales, 1906–1939* (Cardiff: University of Wales Press, 1999). His most recent books are: *Lloffion ym Maes Crefydd: Ysgrifau ar Ddiwinyddiaeth Gyfoes* (Cardiff: University of Wales Press, 2007) and *Salvation in Celluloid: Theology, Imagination and Film* (London: T & T Clark, 2007).

David M. Thompson, Emeritus Professor of Modern Church History at the University of Cambridge, is a specialist in the nineteenth and twentieth centuries. He is also a non-stipendiary minister of the United Reformed Church, Moderator of its General Assembly in 1996–97 and is presently Eastern Synod Ecumenical Officer. He has been actively involved nationally and internationally in ecumenical dialogue. Recent publications include *Cambridge Theology in the Nineteenth Century* (Aldershot: Ashgate, 2008) and *Protestant Nonconformist Texts, Volume 4: The Twentieth Century*, with J. H. Y. Briggs and John Munsey Turner (Aldershot: Ashgate, 2007).

Kirsty Thorpe is a United Reformed Church minister, currently ministering in Wilmslow, Cheshire, and is a Moderator of General Assembly 2010–12. She has a particular interest in women's church history, writing, with Elaine Kaye and Janet Lees, *Daughters of Dissent* (London: URC, 2004), a history of women in the United Reformed Church.

INTRODUCTION
Kirsty Thorpe

This volume makes a significant contribution to a contemporary under-standing of social welfare in Britain over the past two centuries. From an early twenty-first-century perspective some may identify secularization alongside industrialization and urbanization as three of the most significant influences on people's lives during this period. There is another story to be told, however, of the impact Christian Churches have had in local neighbourhoods from the start of the Industrial Revolution onwards. Active Christians, working in their communities every day of the week, have contributed to the education, housing, social welfare, community involvement and wellbeing of the people living around them. Their ways of operating and of describing their activities may seem far away from those familiar to us today, seen through the disciplines of sociology and community organizing. The place these churches held in the settings where they witnessed may have looked very different from those now filled by their inheritor congregations in the era of post Christendom. Yet the under-lying inspiration and motivation that energized these people in their social outreach can still be traced through to the social involvement of many contemporary Christian communities now.

Establishing the existence of such a continuity of activity between nineteenth- and twentieth-century Free Church social welfare work and Christian social involvement today is one aim of this volume. Another is to redress the imbalance whereby some historical accounts of church engagement within local communities give insufficient identity and recog-nition to the particular contribution of Free Churches as distinct from that of the Established Church. These traditions were adept at planting new churches or projects in places where their members believed God was calling them to serve their fellow men and women. Free Church organiza-tional flexibility, and the scope this allowed for individuals to respond to need as they saw it, allowed a huge spectrum of social involvement to arise in a wide variety of settings as this volume will demonstrate.

It is one thing to see a missing element in an historical account, but quite another to establish a project which researches the untold story and tells it coherently. The existence of this book owes much to the staff at Northern College, Manchester. As part of the ecumenical theological centre at Luther King House the college trains minsters for the United Reformed Church and

Congregational Federation, as well as church-related community workers for the United Reformed Church. It specializes in teaching community ministry as well as the study of chaplaincy in all its forms. In delivering courses on these areas it had become clear that there was a serious lack of resources explaining the history of church social action and community work. Without such a reference tool it was difficult to give an adequate historical context for the church's involvement with addressing current social needs and concerns. As a result, students found themselves trying to understand contemporary issues without an awareness of the relevant history.

John Campbell and Lesley Husselbee raised this as a matter of concern with the College's Community Work Course Consultative Group, which included the United Reformed Church's national officers in the field as well as practitioners. John Campbell, principal of Northern College from 2005 to 2011, contacted the officers of the United Reformed Church History Society to enlist help with the gathering of materials to meet this need. A series of meetings took place and a Steering Group was set up to undertake the project. Administered by Lesley Husselbee, the group included Paul Ballard, Clyde Binfield, John Campbell, Ann Honey, Stephen Orchard, and Kirsty Thorpe. From these discussions the idea arose for a publication to examine the history of Free Church engagement in social welfare over the past two centuries. It was to be written from a perspective of interest to both social historians and contemporary community theologians, as well as many others. The decision was taken to tell the story thematically and a number of writers were each invited to research and contribute a chapter on a given topic.

It was acknowledged by the planning group that this was not the only way the project could have been undertaken. The story could have been told chronologically or geographically, through the towns and cities where episodes in this story had regularly unfolded. The group was also aware that compiling a book with a number of contributors could produce a very uneven narrative, with wide variations of approach and tone between them. To address this issue, and in recognition of the fact that a history of community ministry would benefit from the interaction, mutual learning and stimulus offered within a learning community, the group organized a three-day meeting in January 2011. Here the authors and the Steering Group were joined by others, such as community work practitioners, students and historians from a variety of Nonconformist traditions. The first drafts of the chapters were circulated in advance and at the meeting each contribution was given to discussion. In the light of this it was possible to draw up more coherent editorial guidelines and for the authors to revise their texts.

This volume represents the fruit both of the writers' initial work, of those face-to-face dialogues, and of the further writing and research which followed that meeting. It will still contain some omissions. One characteristic of community theologians seems to be their preference for activism over the keeping of records that would help future historians. There are also further stories to be uncovered, particularly about women and members of minority racial groups, whose contribution is hardest to identify and faithfully interpret. Nevertheless it is hoped that what is presented here will stimulate interest in and affirm the deep roots of social commitment among the Free Churches. The Steering Group also hopes that the resources uncovered by this project so far can be adapted for use in other ways, such as for use in training programmes or with study groups, to help encourage further the identifying of community church history and the practice of theological reflection on this among practitioners and in local congregations. If so, as the next generation of Christian social activists will begin to emerge, its exponents will be people who understand, value, and take pride in the Free Church traditions within which some of them will stand.

1

The Free Churches and their Nation

Stephen Orchard

The common thread of this book is to examine how the historic Free Churches, which are defined chiefly as Baptist, Congregationalist, Methodist, Presbyterian, together with the Quakers and Unitarians, expressed their pastoral ministry in the communities among which they were set. This common thread might be deceptive in the sense that the nature of religion within Britain changed a great deal over the four hundred and fifty years which are covered. A Baptist of 1600 has things in common with a Baptist of 2011 but is also a very different person. Other denominations have proliferated. There have been considerable economic, political and social changes which have also characterized the period. They have had an effect on religious groups just as they have had an impact on wider society.

The origins of Free Churches lie with those who stood over against the established church in the sixteenth century. After religious toleration was established in 1689 there was a modest increase in the numbers of those classed as Protestant Dissenters from the Church of England, that is, Baptists, Congregationalists, usually known as Independents, and Presbyterians. These congregations were in numerical decline again towards the end of the eighteenth century. At the same time the Evangelical Revival led to significant numbers of other Christians choosing to live their religious life outside the Established Church. Those touched by the Revival were still a minority and some remained in the Church of England. Some Evangelicals were attached to existing Dissenting congregations but a large number formed Methodist societies or independent Calvinist meetings. In the nineteenth century what we now call the Free Churches enjoyed unparalleled growth, which they would have ascribed to the truths of religion they

proclaimed, but for which sociologists might wish to find other, if supplementary, reasons. The context of this growth is what we shall go on to
discuss. In the twentieth century the same Free Churches have experienced
severe decline, along with other religious bodies, and their future in the
twenty-first century is, in the minds of many of their members, problematic.

To consider this rise and fall out of context, as church members are
inclined to do, is to miss the wider significance of what is past and to blight
the future. This book shows the contribution of the historic Free Churches
to the life of communities in Britain in the past, with a view to a balanced
assessment of what was achieved and why. It is for others to draw lessons
for the future. What is here is designed to redress the balance in historical
analysis, which has often overlooked the Free Church contribution. It is
also designed to remind those who still reach out to meet the needs of
their local community from a Free Church base, of some sense of the long
tradition in which they stand. For instance, the distinctive contribution of
High Church Anglicans and the Salvation Army in the East End of London
is well-documented. The work of Free Church missions and settlements is
harder to uncover. A thorough survey of church attendance in London in
1902–03 is recorded in *The Religious Life of London*.[1] If we accept church
attendance as some indication of involvement in the local community it is
striking to see that in the East London boroughs of Poplar, Stepney, Bethnal
Green, Shoreditch and Hackney, combined Free Church attendances
exceeded those in the Church of England. Baptist attendance was particularly high and exceeded that of the Roman Catholics. The Presbyterian
Church of England had better attendances in Poplar than the Salvation
Army. Yet it is only specialist historians who are aware of the strength of
Baptist churches and missions in the East End, or the overall Free Church
outreach there. The differences between Free Churches may turn out to be
a strength at the local level but they obscure the aggregate effect of their
work.

Some consideration needs to be given to the earlier history of what
we now call Free Churches. The sixteenth century was a time of radical
change in the Church in Western Europe. The search for an authoritative
base for change led to the Bible. In Britain this animated those whom we
have since called the Puritans. Looking in scripture for forms of worship
and church governance they came to radical conclusions and created
turmoil within the Church. The generality of Puritans did not question the
indissoluble connection between church and state. Some Puritans wished
for reform of the episcopacy to make it more pastoral. Some wanted to
go further and adopt a Presbyterian order of church government. Only a
few at the radical fringe wished to break the connection between church
and state altogether. They were regarded as either mad or bad and, even
when state policy was to avoid religious martyrdom, some of them were
executed; they were seen as every bit as dangerous to the settled order as
the papists. At this period everything that we might now consider as welfare

provision was located in the parish and administered within the churches. The Puritans who eventually left for North America were not only fleeing persecution; they were trying to find a place where they could practice their full understanding of the Gospel in a context of their own devising. It was not possible to address the questions of education, medicine and poverty in Britain without full involvement in the established national church.

The Civil War and the establishment of the Commonwealth changed the perspective. Urged on by the Scots, who materially assisted the parliamentary forces, the English and Welsh abolished episcopacy and legislated for a Presbyterian order in the national church. This emboldened the Puritans, although they were never able to consolidate the legislation into universal practice. Independents, or what we would now term Baptists and Congregationalists, also took advantage of the changed order of things, leaving only the Quakers to be as unwelcome as episcopalians in the new freedom. These changes were reversed at the Restoration of the monarchy in 1660 and a large party of Puritan dissidents withdrew from the Church rather than serve under the conditions proscribed. From 1662 to 1688 various attempts were made to suppress the dissidents and restore conformity to the Church in England and Wales. Some Puritans simply kept their heads low, in or out of the established church, waiting for better days. Some defied the authorities in the name of religious liberty. This was the period at which dissent became a defining characteristic of these Christians and it is to this period that subsequent historians, apologists and myth-makers have always returned in their characterizations of the older part of the Free Church tradition.

In 1688 a revolution was organized by Whig aristocrats. They invited William of Orange, conveniently married to Mary Stuart, to contest the throne with James II, whom they suspected of wanting to restore 'popery' to Britain, with all it implied of French domination. After a minimum of fighting on the English mainland James took flight, and subsequent attempts by him in 1690, his son in 1715 and his grandson in 1745, to regain the throne for the Stuarts, all failed. William had a pragmatic attitude to religious difference. A Toleration Act was passed in 1689 which gave Protestant Dissenters from the Church of England a legal standing, so long as they registered as such and licensed their meeting houses with the church authorities. In Scotland the overthrow of the Stuarts opened the way to settle the Presbyterian order of the national church. Dissenters joined in hailing the Glorious Revolution of 1688 and thereafter looked to the Whigs to preserve and, if possible, to extend their rights. The significance of this in the broader Free Church perspective is that a century later Methodists, though reluctant to part from the Church of England, used this legislation to licence their meeting houses and so avoid prosecution. The founding Methodists were reluctant to go down this road, since their object was reform of the national church, not the creation of an alternative. Ironically, after 1689 Dissenters in England made various attempts to unite with each other and to reach reconciliation with the Church of England, but had largely settled for the status quo by the 1780s. After the French Revolution Dissenters and Methodists went out of their way to show loyalty to the crown. All outsiders were suspected of radical sympathies and throughout the Napoleonic wars political conservatism prevailed.

In the early nineteenth century the growth of Wesleyan Methodism was paralleled by a growth in Independent and Baptist congregations in England and Wales. As the political pendulum swung from the conservatism of the long Napoleonic wars to the reforming Whig governments of the 1830s these non-established religious groups voiced demands to be fully included in civil society. Toleration was no longer enough; emancipation was the aim, whether it be inclusion in local government or admission to the ancient universities. The Church of England's virtual monopoly in marriages and burials was challenged. There developed a campaign against the payment of church rates. National unions of Baptists and Congregationalists were formed to promote their interests alongside the Methodist Conferences. They saw themselves as more legitimate churches than the established church, which they dismissed as a sect. With growth had come self-confidence, which often toppled over into vain-glory. By the end of the nineteenth century the Free Churches had achieved a quasi-establishment status, but they were already in decline; their continuing numerical growth was not proportionate to the growth in population. The formation of Free Church Councils camouflaged this trend, which was reinforced in two World Wars. By the 1960s Christopher Driver, a journalist and member of a Congregational church, was writing *A Future for the Free Churches?*[2] in which the accent was on the question mark. By the beginning of the twenty-first century membership of Free Churches had become rare in local communities and below the radar of social commentators.

Alongside these developments in organized religion Britain was experiencing economic growth. A combination of extended trade around what became the British Empire, and technical innovation which brought about mass production, vastly increased the wealth and population of Britain. Because wealth was not evenly distributed there was a corresponding increase in the numbers of the poor. The existing systems of parish relief collapsed and new ones, industrializing poverty in a new pattern of workhouses, were created. The dependence on trade for this economic growth had been brought home in the Napoleonic wars, which were fought in European colonies around the world as well as in Europe. War made poverty worse and, when protests were mounted, British governments were repressive. Individuals with a background in Dissent, such as William Hazlitt, railed against the restrictions placed on protest and free speech but the meetings and chapels kept their heads down, waiting for better days. These came at last, as we have seen, in the 1830s, though the widening of the franchise only really began in the 1860s. Wesleyan Methodism continued to be politically conservative as the nineteenth century unfolded, and dissident Methodists groups, such as the Bible Christians, were spawned. Other new groups, such as the Churches of Christ, grew in the 1830s and 1840s. Such groups overlapped the constituency of the Chartist movement and the emerging trades unions. They were primarily lay-led and run on a voluntary basis. Some Baptist congregations also followed this route. They depended on the new artisan class of skilled workers to provide leadership, rather than the paid ministers, together with the squires and merchants, of the older denominations. The aspirations of this group, reaching out for the franchise and a right to negotiate the terms of their labour, were also met by the Church of Jesus Christ of Latter Day Saints (Mormons) and, later, Jehovah's Witnesses.

Of course, the new prosperity was not confined by denominational allegiance. You did not have to be an old Dissenter to acquire wealth. However, it may be observed throughout history that groups on the margins of established society often engage in banking and manufacturing. Since inherited wealth is not going to deliver you from poverty the road of the entrepreneur or the new industry beckons. The nineteenth century rejoiced in the stories of the 'self-made man', or woman, for that matter. There had always been an artisan class, of village blacksmiths, or carpenters or mining engineers, for instance. The blacksmith continued but some who had the skills of the farrier raised themselves to the new status of veterinary surgeon. The skilled wheelwright continued to make wheels for horse-drawn vehicles but his skills were multiplied as the demand for railway wagons grew. When metal wheels replaced wooden ones new skills were developed on the back of old ones. The architectural profession grew to serve the new middle classes. The expansion of education vastly increased the number of school teachers, although some of them remained relatively lowly. Expanding literacy fed a new bureaucracy in business and local government. In the churches themselves a new ministerial class grew up alongside the clergy in England and Wales and, eventually, in rivalry to the Church of Scotland. This expansion of the artisan and professional classes alongside the old hierarchies of squire, parson, doctor and attorney proved fertile ground for the cultivation of chapel life. In her classic novel *Middlemarch* George Eliot[3] gives an unsympathetic account of the growth of Dissent in the country town, and its origin in metropolitan commerce. Her caricature, and that of other nineteenth-century novelists, reflects sufficient of the truth to be taken seriously. Dissent could be narrow-minded, but it could also be dynamic precisely because it stood outside the old order.

Enough of the newly wealthy were Dissenters to fund the building of meeting houses and chapels to house the new congregations arising from the Evangelical revival. By the 1830s it was the complaint of many in the Church of England that its procedures for making extra provision for worshippers were cumbersome and expensive compared with the ease with which a new non-episcopal chapel might be built in a growing neighbourhood. Where once a market town might have contained a parish church and a

Dissenting meeting house, half a dozen chapels might spring up, funded by generous individual donations and loans. Each of these would have its own distinctive truth to mark it out from its neighbours, even if it was prepared to co-operate with others in a Bible Society auxiliary, or some local charitable purpose. When a chapel flourished it was enlarged. If a chapel failed it could be abandoned or sold on to another group. A parish church had no such option. Moreover, the raising of a local church rate became more problematic. As Dissenters grew in confidence they challenged the monopolies of the Established Church in religious ceremonies, such as marriages and burials, and in civic power. By the 1840s their theorists were arguing for a separation of Church and State, dismissing the Church of England as an episcopalian sect. Chapel expansion was part of the argument; it demonstrated that an alternative church could be generally available. This new attitude to establishment, to abolish it rather than to broaden it, was only possible against the background of increased resources. For a time in the middle of the nineteenth century the heady combination of Free Trade economics and the strength of local congregations sustained the conviction that voluntarism was the answer to all the ills of society. It was in this spirit that congregations turned from being spiritual cliques to agents of change in the local community. Some spiritual cliques remained. The same changes in society which promoted Dissenters made possible other and more exotic developments, some so eclectic that their demise was built into their structure, such as the Catholic Apostolic Church, and some destined to expand, such as the various Pentecostal groups.

   Throughout human history society has split into sub-sets defined by a common interest. The medieval guilds were later joined by other professional and commercial bodies. The original Methodists were gathered in societies, auxiliary to the Church. Dissenters were gathered in groups bound by a religious covenant, embodying their distinctive understanding of Christian faith. Within the Church of England itself societies were formed to pursue particular ends, for instance, the Society for the Propagation of the Gospel. From the eighteenth century onwards societies proliferated in the area of specific social concerns. Matters which went beyond the local were not seen as essentially matters for national government to address. Societies for the care of orphans, or the promotion of education or health, were formed by private individuals. Some of these societies would go on to petition parliament for legislation to address particular issues, such as slavery, or the climbing boys sent up to sweep chimneys. Other societies simply addressed problems from their own resources. When the nineteenth century began, turning to national government for action was not the automatic response of people who wanted to bring about social change. When it came to forming societies the Free Church denominations had a head start; their whole ethos was societal. It followed that Christian societies were often formed across denominational boundaries but then fell into disputes which ended in a distinctive Anglican version being formed. In the case of missionary societies all denominations eventually formed their own. The Bible Society very nearly split on denominational lines in the 1830s. The London City Mission did split. Where the words 'British and Foreign' appear in the title of a society it is usually non-denominational, but may sometimes have no Anglican membership at all. Societies run exclusively by the Church of England usually incorporate that fact in their title. There were many societies bringing benefits to the community which were non-denominational. However, the moment an element of religious opinion entered into the work or the selection of beneficiaries, division was inevitable. It is obvious that this volume will concentrate on societies associated with the historic Free Churches, but this should not be taken to mean that they were the only or dominant societies in their field.

The development of modern democracy is often described in terms of the political institutions and their history. This overlooks the context of politics in civil society. The dissemination of ideas which underlies democratic choice is dependent on free flows of information and the exercise of influence. By its nature we can trace the growth of information alongside the political process. The analysis of influence is more difficult and may ignore the societies which belong in the church sector. It was no more true in the past than now that the pronouncements of church leaders represent the unanimous opinion of church members. There are several examples in the chapters which follow of individuals gathering a local group around them to form a society whose objects are adopted by national religious leaders some way down the road. The promotion of total abstinence from alcohol was not a policy adopted nationally and promoted by denominational structures, but arose locally, and was initially opposed by the Wesleyan Methodist Conference. The Brotherhood Movement began with local promotion and was accepted by denominations without ever being a specific policy. The nature of most historic Free Churches is undogmatic; ethos triumphs over law, even in connexional denominations. Annual meetings of denominations might rally round specific campaigns but rarely had the control of local resources and individual agendas.

This is vividly illustrated in the case of the Free Church conscience. A growing proportion of Gladstone's parliamentary Liberal Party were avowed Free Churchmen; many of them ministers, who, unlike their Anglican counterparts, were not barred from standing for parliament. While they could wring their hands over Parnell's adultery and help sabotage Gladstone's plans for Irish independence, they could not exercise political leverage to secure policies they supported, such as disestablishment. A tender conscience is not a political asset. People like their politicians to be principled but they also like them to get things done. The aspirations of Free Church politicians were modified when political realism took over. The majority identified with the Liberal party, and its promotion of Free Trade and what we would now term human rights. Slotting particular Free Church concerns into the broader party programme was always difficult.

Free Church people were historically anti-colonial but, like the Liberals in general, they tended to favour powerful intervention in other countries to counter perceived injustice. So, in the 1830s, they were highly critical of the colonial administration in the West Indies, which was promoting slavery by another name, after its supposed abolition. In the 1870s they rallied behind Gladstone's call for condemnation of the Bulgarian atrocities and in the 1890s they rallied also against the Turks massacring Armenians. In Imperial matters they were caught between suspicion of colonialism and embracing the opportunities it created for Christian mission.

Such coherence as we find in Free Church social policy, especially in the twentieth century, is of antagonism to change. For a large part of that time the Free Churches opposed any increase in government aid to church schools. Free Churches were prominent in resisting changes to Sunday legislation, opposed liberalizing the licensing and gambling laws and rallied to the defence of censorship. Against this, they differed from Anglican and Roman Catholic official views on marriage and birth control as the twentieth century unfolded. These were regarded as personal matters and in the post-war world after 1945 Christians seeking to re-marry after divorce could usually find a sympathetic Free Church in their locality. As a connexional Church, the Methodists took longer to adopt these liberal attitudes into their rules, but Baptists and Congregationalists regarded local option as fundamental to their view of the Church. In ecclesial policies, the Free Churches were more adventurous. The ordination of women was not generally acceptable in these denominations at the beginning of the twentieth century, but was increasingly adopted after the ordination of Constance Coltman[4] to Congregational ministry of Word and Sacraments in 1917. As the twenty-first century began all denominations who ordained women to sacramental ministry were observing a profound change in the proportions of men and women offering themselves as candidates. There may be a relationship between the ordination of women and the relaxation of some attitudes in sexual matters, since women are more often the sufferers when inflexible rules are adopted.

This is particularly noticeable in the development of genetics. The Free Churches remained generally committed to the principle of the sanctity of human life. However, having conceded the principles of birth control as a general social good and aid to gender equality they did not corporately resist abortion law reform so far as it saved the lives of women. This same logic supported genetic research with a view to controlling hereditary diseases and finding treatments for chronic conditions. These nuanced positions were not intended to endorse abortion on demand or what are termed 'designer babies'. Once first principles are abandoned the consequences are not always foreseeable. The Free Church position was undoubtedly influenced by pragmatism and its pastoral experiences, particularly those of women. The reality of the church demographic, in which women predominate over men, may register more quickly in the processes of Free Churches. That is clearly the case in the ordination of women. Could it also be the case in matters of ethics? More work needs to be done in this area.

The Evangelical Revival of the late eighteenth century was accompanied by a new interest in Protestant missions overseas. Large parts of the globe were coming under European influence and control. Evangelicals looked for a purpose in this beyond commercial exploitation. This often threw them into conflict with colonial administrators, whose interests were dominated by commerce and politics, and usually saw no reason for disturbing the religious status quo. Christian missionaries professed to be bringing eternal salvation to people who might otherwise be lost eternally. The development of world mission is not the subject of this study. However, what world mission threw into high relief was the difference between culture and faith. Britain had an historic Christian culture but that did not mean that Christian belief was universal nor that the practice of Christian piety engaged the whole nation. The 1851 religious census clearly revealed these assumptions to be false. In England only half the population attended church and only half of the attendance was within the Church of England. This raised questions for all professing Christians, who assumed that attendance at public worship ought to be universal. The Church of England saw its historic position eroded by other denominations and wondered how to bring the unchurched half of the population into the fold. The Free Churches saw that if they could claim the unchurched for themselves they would be entitled to demand disestablishment of the Church of England, which many of them saw as desirable. This fuelled the enthusiasm for Home Mission, which shared many characteristics with Overseas Mission. The provision of education, simple health care, employment, financial subsidy and shelter were all part of mission at home as much as abroad. In particular, foreign mission had highlighted arguments about millennialism. What was God's purpose in history and why was world evangelism necessary? The millennium was understood as the thousand-year reign of the saints on earth before the end of all things. If you took an apocalyptic view, that the sudden appearance of Christ in judgement would precede the millennium (pre-millennial adventism), then as long as you were faithfully engaged in the work of mission at the coming of Christ you had nothing to fear. If you judged that Christians needed to work to bring in the millennium as a necessary preliminary to the coming of Christ (post-millennial adventism) then there was every incentive to strive to bring in the Kingdom of God by human endeavour. Groups such as the Plymouth Brethren were not active in their local communities because they were pre-millennialists. Radical social change would happen when Christ came. The main Free Church denominations were largely post-millennialists in their thinking and committed to changing the world around them so that Christ might indeed come again. They would have sung enthusiastically with the Anglican Charles Kingsley,[5] of a coming age:

When ever blue the sky shall gleam,
And ever green the sod;
And man's rude work deface no more
The paradise of God.

These lines from the hymn, 'From thee all skill and science flow', speak of
this Christian optimism that with a better application of the gifts of God
the earth may be transformed. 'Noble thought and deed', properly applied,
frees people from drudgery, ill-health and poverty, and enables them
to enjoy the blue sky and green grass of the countryside or, at least, the
public park. This is Christian eschatology for the Victorian entrepreneur.
It finds its particular expression in the Christian Socialist movement of
the nineteenth century but its post-millennial assumptions are widespread
among all Christians.

These assumptions came under pressure not only from the changing
intellectual climate but migration. Migration brought plurality to the British
religious scene over and above Christian diversity. In the nineteenth century,
Jewish migrants established local communities, to which specific Christian
missions, backed by educational and welfare services, were addressed. In
the twentieth century other major world faiths, such as Islam, Hinduism
and Sikhism, became evident in urban areas, where their places of worship
were found in old chapels or, increasingly, purpose-built centres. The Free
Churches nationally encouraged local contacts between faith groups based
on mutual tolerance, rather than attempts at conversion. This may reflect
the tradition dating back to the eighteenth century of licensing religious
difference rather than attempting to impose uniformity. It is noticeable
that successive governments have extended to the various communities of
faith recognition comparable to that given to Free Churches. At the local
community level one may find instances of community services traditionally
provided by Free Churches now dependent on co-operation with people of
other faiths.

The early Reformers did not envisage a separation of Church and State;
rather, a new relationship. The old idea, that the Church was an arm of the
State, was a long time dying. By the beginning of the nineteenth century it
was in a critical condition. The rise of Dissent and Methodism in England
and Wales increased the numbers of people chafing at the control the established church exercised over what we would now call civil society. There
were also ancient church taxes to be paid, which were resented. In Scotland
the established church was Presbyterian in form but challenged by internal
dissent which finally resulted in disruption in 1843. In Ireland a British
Protestant government was forced to make concessions to the predomi-
nantly Roman Catholic population. The sermon Keble preached in Oxford
in 1833, arguing that the Church was in danger, is seen as the well-spring
of Tractarianism, but it was more than that. It recognized a movement
of the tectonic plates of society. Within Britain today a Church may be

Established in a legal or formal sense, but it is still fundamentally regarded by the mass of the population as a private concern, just as religious belief is a private choice. The historic Free Churches may have been absorbed by the establishment, and take their place alongside the Church of England, or Scotland, at national events, but the presence of both symbolizes historical influence rather than actual power. Private religion means that in today's world there is an element of surprise in a neighbourhood when a church takes initiatives in the community; a Victorian neighbourhood took it for granted that churches and chapels provided amenities over and above public worship. That expectation in the popular mind was replaced after 1947, as people looked to other agencies, such as the local council, the National Health Service, or even something as vague as 'the government', to meet their needs.

This change in social expectations needs to be set against the philosophical changes from the Reformation to the present day. Classical learning was prized by the Reformers and their seventeenth-century successors. The ideal Puritan minister could produce a Latin treatise on disputed points of doctrine. In the eighteenth century the general intellectual climate put a premium on rationalism and churches were not exempt from this. The Dissenters questioned the structure and practices of the Established Church on the basis of scripture and reason. The doctrine of the Trinity was not explicit in scripture and reasonable conjecture suggested alternative understandings. Pure rationalism led to deism, but even within the Church of England there were those moving to what we would now term a Unitarian position. Rational Dissent, as part of the dissenting body came to be called, opened the way to similar conclusions. Methodism, centred on 'heart religion', seemed to offer an alternative but, even there, its leaders bitterly disputed doctrine, leading to the break between the Wesleyan Methodist Conference and the various so-called Calvinistic Methodist groups. Reasoned argument can rapidly deteriorate into factionalism and did.

Whatever happened at the popular level, the training of both Methodist and Dissenting ministers involved systematic study of the classics as well as theology. Mathematics was studied to cultivate logical thinking. What was then termed 'natural philosophy', which we would regard as science, also began to find its way into ministerial training. At its simplest it cultivated a sense of an ordered universe, reflecting an omniscient Creator. This commitment to intellectual development contained within it great danger for traditional faith. As the nineteenth century advanced, dedicated study raised awkward questions about the traditional understanding of the created world based on the book of Genesis. At the same time a radical critique of the Bible itself was under way, led by German scholars. Unitarians were particularly open to incorporate this in their thinking. The authority of the Bible became a contested area leading to an upsurge of Liberal Theology, as it was termed, in the early twentieth century. This emphasized the practical outworking of the teaching of Jesus in society and human relationships. Scripture had to be approached in the light of this experience. This contrasted with the more conservative Christians, who continued their general charitable work in obedience to Scripture.

Literary criticism of the Bible text, combined with the new science of archaeology, raised questions for the faithful. These were reinforced by the experience of the devastating European war which began in 1914, pitting supposedly Christian nations against one another. On the one hand this gave the Church practical credibility through its pastoral services to troops; on the other hand its theological answers to the questions of suffering seemed evasive. There was a consequent loss of faith in a Christianity which seemed to sanction killing in ways at odds with its fundamental beliefs. There was also a growth in spiritualism, as those who believed their sons and husbands had gone to another world sought to make contact with them. All churches felt they were losing ground to scepticism and unbelief. Not only had Darwin put a large question mark over the Christian interpretation of human history but theologians had now to begin to contemplate the implications of Einstein's Theory of Relativity. The space-time continuum did not sit easily with the idea of immortal life in heaven.

A renewed Christian orthodoxy, however, began to challenge Liberal Theology as intellectually inadequate with a concern for systematic doctrine, closely argued. Perhaps the most influential theologian of the twentieth century was the Swiss Karl Barth (1886–1968). Although Barth claimed to be returning to the beginnings of the Reformed tradition his experience of Nazism in Germany and of Soviet Communism led him to a rejection of links between the Church and State, rather than to see them as complementary to each other. This view was especially influential among Baptists and Congregationalists. The effect on church life was to turn the attention of churches towards their inner life rather than towards the community around them. Of the Free Churches it was the Methodists who remained more committed to community initiatives – in their policy for central missions, for instance.

The Second World War had brought more horror to the world, whether in the indiscriminate bombing of civilians, the extermination camps or the unleashing of the atom bomb. Once more the churches had a role to play in pastoral support but the Christian doctrine of the just war was exposed to more scrutiny. Some Christians played a part in leading anti-nuclear protests but the majority of church leaders stood apart. Free Churches nationally proved no more eager than the Church of England to adopt policies opposed to nuclear deterrence. A brief revival of church attendance in the 1940s and early 1950s has been followed by steady decline ever since. Philosophies such as Existentialism have come and gone until the age of multiple religions and none is characterized as 'post-modern'. Christianity tries to offer an overall narrative for human experience in a Britain which has privatized religion and regards the claims of competing world-views as precisely that – there being no reason to discriminate between them. In the words of a song in the Lloyd Webber musical *The Amazing Technicolour Dreamcoat* 'any dream will do'.[6] In such a world the distinctiveness of Free Churches as against the Established Church becomes lost.

Another factor which needs to be taken into account is the ecumenical movement of the twentieth century. Although it takes as its text 'that they may all be one, so that the world may believe', the mission of the Church is often lost in the small print of trying to resolve denominational differences. In the 1980s there was a moment when it seemed that the main Protestant denominations in England might unite. Similar moments came and went in Wales and Scotland. In place of these national reconciliations between denominations a form of local ecumenism has grown up, strong in some localities, weak in others. Mutual service to the community, be it after-school clubs, counselling services or Christian Aid collection, to name a few examples, is often carried out through these local structures. Again, this means that a distinctive Free Church approach may not be evident today.

One of the surprises for the modern reader looking over the period covered in this book may be the virulence with which educational provision was contested by different denominations in the nineteenth and early twentieth century. Universal elementary schooling did not exist in Britain until the passing of the 1870 Education Act and, even then, it took time to implement. Until then there was an unequal contest between the National Society (Church of England) and the British and Foreign School Society (Interdenominational, but mostly Free Church) over voluntary school provision for the masses. Private schooling continued throughout this period, including independent fee-paying schools established by Free Church denominations or their members. It was the schooling of children amongst the labouring classes which was contested on religious grounds. When government subsidies were made available to support the building of schools it was done on a matching basis. There was always more money in the National Society than in the British and Foreign Schools Society (BFSS), especially in rural areas. Free Church educationalists resented the use of Church of England formularies for teaching children who came from non-Anglican backgrounds. The dispute rumbled on into the modern era. Only in the late twentieth century was a truce declared.

The same rivalry existed over Sunday Schools. These had begun as basic educational enterprises but after the 1870 Education Act their focus shifted to religious and moral instruction. They were largely lay enterprises and involved a large proportion of the child population. Indeed, if all the children who went to Sunday Schools in the early twentieth century had become regular worshippers in churches then attendances would have been very much higher. Until the 1950s it is estimated that half the child population attended a Sunday School. Not only did this keep children occupied on a Sunday afternoon but it entitled them to a whole raft of other benefits, such as outings, parties and books. A Sunday School teacher was an adult who professed care for you, which your parents may or may not have done, and operated without the stricter disciplinary system of a day school. Sunday Schools fell victim to the increased secularism of the late twentieth century, combined with prosperity and social mobility. It has also to be said that within the churches the attempt to bind Sunday Schools more closely into the worshipping life of the adult church was counter-productive. Churches came to regard Sunday Schools as recruiting grounds. Wider society saw them as educative in a broader sense.

Education was, of course, behind the growth of literacy through the period we are considering. Soldiers in Cromwell's New Model Army were issued with 'Bibles' of a pocket book size, containing a few of what were judged to be key passages. The general ownership of Bibles in homes had to wait for the combination of the Bible Society, with its distribution networks, and the coming of cheap printing. Although traditional type-setting continued, the mass production of Bibles, religious books and tracts was accelerated by the invention of stereotype in the early nineteenth century. By the 1830s the age of tract distribution had begun in earnest. Bundles of religious tracts were bought by religious societies and individuals for distribution on the streets and in house-to-house visitation. The message was usually exemplary, showing how a life of vice led to poverty and degradation, while a virtuous life brought its own reward. Ignorance, especially ignorance of the Gospel, was the enemy; it was combated by schooling, street preaching and tract distribution, as well as an ample provision of chapels where people might hear a saving word. Tracts and small portions of scripture continued to be distributed, though on a smaller scale, through the twentieth century. The prize for regular Sunday School attendance remained a religious book. A church magazine with a pious message at its heart was still produced, even by small congregations.

Text was supplemented by illustration as technology advanced. Not only could tracts and books be illustrated but photography brought with it the possibility of projecting slides by what was popularly known as the 'magic lantern'. The missionary meeting could now be enlivened with exotic scenes from around the world. Only the richest homes could own their own projectors. The church hall, like the Mechanics Institute or the Temperance Hall, became a place where the population at large had access to the new medium. Theatres introduced slide shows to their programmes and cinematic films when they became available. Although churches did acquire film projectors, they were secondary providers, unable to compete with cinemas. J. Arthur Rank promoted films with a religious message and, in the 1950s, made hundreds of cheap cine projectors available to Methodist churches, but the appetite for cinemas was already dimin-ishing with the coming of television on a wide scale. Beyond that lay the world of the internet and the personal choice of images on a small screen. Denominations which had been formed by great orators moved towards the twenty-first-century digital projection of words and images in worship itself, reproducing something of the world in which individual worshippers now found themselves. Buildings that were shaped by the nineteenth-century wish to gather to share in a spiritual drama, conducted by preachers and musicians, seemed ill-adapted for the revolution in information technology.

Originally in these Victorian buildings other illustrative techniques were also adopted. The first Puritans were iconoclastic. Their successors created meeting houses of a plain nature. By the end of the nineteenth century Congregational churches were rejoicing in stained-glass windows celebrating their own saints, such as Cromwell, Milton or Bunyan, none of whom would have relished such images. Memorial plaques, such as were common in parish churches, appeared on chapel walls to celebrate the exemplary lives of former members and benefactors. The communion table might now have an appropriate text carved into the frame. If there were to be a central arch facing the congregation it might carry a painted text on the subject of praise or salvation. Often an organ, with elaborately painted pipes, lay under the arch. Not only did new chapels, built in the great mid-century expansion, offer these features in Victorian Gothic style, but old chapels were rebuilt to mimic them. This not only represented a claim to stand alongside the Church of England and, in the mind of the deter-mined Free Church people, to replace it; such buildings reflected the best taste of the period and offered a more economic way to encompass a large space than the old classical style of chapel. Unlike the Church of England, whose parish hall, if it existed, might stand at a distance from the church, chapel architects were usually required to provide a suite of buildings suitable for Sunday School and mid-week use. By the end of the twentieth century these ancillary buildings were often deployed for pre-school groups and community activities.

The mention of the church organ reminds us of the changing musical and poetic tastes over our period. The hymn, as distinct from the metrical psalm, was first developed by Isaac Watts and Philip Doddridge among the Dissenters, and given even wider popularity by Charles Wesley. Though the Puritans eschewed the plastic and visual arts, they reckoned music a proper expression of religious sentiment. Methodists took to hymnody in their early alliance with Moravians. Dissenters and Methodists sang unaccompanied or with such instruments as were locally to hand. Congregational singing became the main vehicle for participation in liturgy and for expressing a common spirituality. The power of singing to move people to religious commitment or to deepen it was widely recognized. The nineteenth century saw the emergence of the modern pianoforte and its mass production. There was also a growth in the production of mechanical pipe organs for churches and the mass manufacture of reed organs or harmoniums. This made it possible for smaller congregations to afford an instrument. Even when a large instrument was bought it required only one person to play it. Organs were viewed with great suspicion at first and often introduced in the face of opposition and with restrictions on their use. This innate conservatism among congregations surfaced again in the late twentieth century when it was proposed to replace organs with bands and keyboards. This musical provision in churches is often underestimated. As with church drama and debating societies, it widened individual horizons and provided opportunities to develop talent.

If hard sciences, such as physics, had a critical part to play in shaping religious thought in our period, the soft sciences, especially psychology, also had a dramatic impact. Psychology at its simplest level raised the question of whether God was a construct of the mind. At more profound levels it examined all spiritual experience and its contribution to mental health. Psychology tended to advance the idea of a healthy balance of emotions within individuals and set out the norms of human relationship in different terms from Christian tradition. From the late nineteenth century onwards Christians sought to work with psychological insights, choosing those which marched most easily with Christian thought, for instance, Jung rather than Freud. In practical terms this meant the development of Christian psychotherapy as part of the mission of the Church. Free Churches were active in this. The Presbyterian minister, John Gray,[7] was the founder of the Marriage Guidance Council (now known as Relate) and Methodists, such as Bill Kyle who founded the Westminster Pastoral Foundation, in particular were associated with the development of counselling services, such as the Richmond Fellowship. In the late twentieth century psychology moved nearer to the hard sciences, particularly in the analysis of neural activity in the brain. The implications of this for traditional belief have yet to be realized.

Related to developments in psychotherapy has been the emergence of specialist chaplaincies in all denominations. Although this was a function of historic established religion, in providing chaplaincy to hospitals and universities for instance, it has expanded to include industry and commerce. The specialist chaplain may now give personal support to people in a particular environment. This work is supplemental to general welfare considerations in a commercial enterprise, but is valued. A more hard-edged approach invites chaplains to engage in the ethical critique of the business concerned. What is interesting from a Free Church point of view is that the tradition would have expected the leaders of business and civic life to have been regular in attendance at their local church in order to prepare themselves to carry out this ministry as lay people. Their displacement by specialists, both lay and ordained, represents a shift in the dynamic of the local church as well as the workplace.

Given the background of post-millennial adventism which we have already recognized, it is perhaps not surprising that issues to do with the environment and international development have been the predominant ethical issues in Free Church circles at the beginning of the twenty-first century. To pursue this agenda people become more concerned with personal response and commitment than engagement with the local community around the church. People tap into national resources and attend national rallies and protests. At the same time there has been a growth of independent congregations, not allied to the old Free Church denominations. Some of these are black-led churches; most of them have a much younger age-profile than is common in traditional denominations. They, too, take the international agenda seriously but these congregations are also often engaged in local community work, such as the creation of credit unions or provision of street pastors at night. This is not to say that some individual congregations in the traditional Free Churches are not also exploring these modern examples of community work. However, it is interesting to see that something which exhibits parallels with Free Church experience in the past is being newly created. It reinforces the contention that church growth is influenced by community context as much as any doctrinal rationale. Free Churches started on the outside edge of society, at odds with the established norms. Perhaps the more they are drawn into ecumenical co-operation and quasi-establishment status, the need for a counter-culture will be met from elsewhere.

The chapters which follow explore the experience of the Free Churches and the implications which this has had to their contribution to British society. They examine Free Church understanding of community, as expressed in their own differing forms of organization, and of the place of education in that understanding. They pursue their evolving sense of citizenship, its rights and its responsibilities, in the light of their experience in the commerce, trade, and industry of what was the world's first industrialized society; and they explore their perceptions about living conditions and the ways in which these should be improved, as well as apprenticeship in the political action which those perceptions made necessary. All these matters shaped contemporary society; all related to the Free Churches' understanding of how the Christian community related to the national community, in the light of its relationship to God, the supreme authority.

2

Congregations and Community
Robert Pope

I. Introduction

In 1881, a matter of weeks after its incorporation, the Revd J. T. Stannard addressed the members of Milton Congregational Church, Huddersfield, explaining that Congregationalism, 'like every other type of Church polity, is itself but a means to the highest of all ends, viz: the nearer and nearer approach to the true ideal of a Christian Church – a spiritual brotherhood whose hand and centre is the living Christ'.[1] Less than two years later, his open letter to the members demonstrated that his interests were not confined to the identifiably religious. The gospel was not merely for members of the church, it was also good news for the world. 'Christianity is a religion which seeks to save society as well as individual men,' he wrote. 'It is the true social science. It is also the true social secularism, having the richest blessings for the life that now is as well as for that which is to come.'[2]

Stannard's words draw attention to a number of historical and theological points relevant to the discussion about the Free Churches, how they viewed society and their involvement in social action. If limited by the linguistic convention of his day, Stannard clearly felt that he remained true to the principles and traditions of his denomination by advocating the ideal of the church as a 'spiritual brotherhood'. There was nothing esoteric about the adjective; the church was the place for mutual edification and support, based both on its divine institution in, and on the members' incorporation into, Christ. As such it formed a fellowship of those who held certain things in common, a community distinct from and yet also part of wider society. By Stannard's day, the realization had gradually dawned that the church existed not only to advocate that civil authority be honoured and obeyed, or merely to pray that social and political leaders should be wise, just and righteous. It also existed in order to promote lasting change for the better as well as offering a degree of relief to the poor and destitute. Like many of his contemporaries, Stannard had acquired a 'social' conscience. The Christian gospel went further because even if it did not explicitly urge the salvation of society, it implied such a goal in its call to live a moral life. In the Huddersfield congregation of the early 1880s, as well as in other centres throughout England and Wales, it seems clear that the church was itself to be a community in which believers (or members) nurtured relationships which were to be of mutual benefit; but the idea was also established that the church did not exist for itself. Instead it was called, under the provi- dence of God, in order to fulfil a purpose within the world that resonates beyond the confines of the strictly religious.

With hindsight it can be said that, by the 1880s, the tide within the Free Churches had begun to turn in the direction of a social as well as individual application of the gospel, a change which is – perhaps – partly revealed by the fact that most of the people at his previous charge at Ramsden Street, when he fell foul of the guardians of the church's Calvinistic trust deed, had followed Stannard in founding the Milton church.[3] But this shift would only become clear later. Widespread as ideas about the gospel's social impli- cations had become by the late nineteenth century, there remained those who resolutely opposed them and the so-called 'social gospel'. Indeed, to speak explicitly of the church's social responsibilities in the 1880s could still be considered novel – or worse 'modern' – and, as a result, Stannard's views were regarded as suspect by some, ultimately leading to the schism at Ramsden Street. There remained those who believed that the Christian's responsibility was to 'come out from among them and be ... separate' (2 Corinthians 6:17). It was argued that the church could 'gradually influence the world to moralize it and to revive it externally' through championing 'sobriety, self-denial and remaining spotless and detached from the world'.[4] The nurture of the faithful and pious Christian life would inevitably effect those around without direct involvement in any worldly cause. Stannard's views, by contrast, reveal that Free Church piety was not always other- worldly, even if social concern was in practice more of a theological conviction than a practical policy; many agreed with the principle of social involvement even if they had no idea about how any change might be achieved.

The source of this social conscience was two-fold. There was a Free Church ecclesiology, a deep-rooted sense that the gathered fellowship of believers existed as an alternative to the social groups which existed in 'the world'. While initially almost sectarian, over time these churches broadened their horizons. Domestic, social, and economic factors contributed to this, but there can be little doubt that the liberalization of theology over the course of the nineteenth century supplied a much needed ideological basis.

These two factors, alongside genuine and heartfelt compassion (which itself was partly expressed politically, a possibility denied the Nonconformists in earlier periods), explain how, over time, congregations developed a sense of their own existence as communities and then began to look beyond themselves to wider human society. Indeed, these factors explain how it was that the Free Churches of the late nineteenth and early twentieth centuries gave such prominence to what they knew to be a 'social' gospel. In what follows, a sketch will be drawn of what the Free Churches and their antecedents believed Church to be, partly in their ecclesiological debates, but primarily as a deduction from their praxis, an overview into how 'congregations' became 'fellowships' and began to serve the communities in which they existed.

II. The Congregation

Perhaps the single most significant aspect of the contribution to church life made by the Free Churches and their antecedents concerns the establishment of what Gordon Rupp[5] called the 'fourth dimension' to Christian nurture. While faith was said – most famously by the Calvinists – to be cultivated by the Word, by the Sacraments and by the exercise of godly discipline, from the seventeenth century emphasis was also placed on the church as *koinonia*, as communion of those who were committed to Christ and therefore also committed to each other. This 'fourth dimension' can be discerned in the Dissent of the sixteenth and more especially the seventeenth centuries when the political ramifications of the Restoration of 1660 prompted the creation of a recognizable and legally defined Nonconformity. It can also be observed in the Evangelicalism of the eighteenth century which both reinvigorated the Old Dissent and brought to the fore a new force in the British religious scene, namely Methodism which, in its Arminian form in England and its Calvinistic form in Wales, grew into the largest Nonconformist or Free Church groups by the middle of the nineteenth century. Both streams offer some insights into the formation of community, particularly in the way churchly life was organized. While the specific customs which gave these groups their unique flavour were not widely practised in the twentieth century, the Free Churches continued to promote identities which were forged a century before, thus remaining dependent on those historical forms and patterns.

The early Dissenters were primarily concerned with how the church on earth should be organized and secondarily (especially after the Act of Uniformity of 1662) with the relationship between the church and the state. The sixteenth-century Separatists, such as Richard Fitz who led the church at the Plumbers Hall around 1567[6] and James Tyman, goldsmith of the parish of St Martin's in the Field in whose home a church gathered from around March 1568,[7] as well as the seventeenth-century Dissenters

such as the pamphleteer Henry Burton,[8] William Bartlet, who established a gathered church in Bideford, Devon, in 1658,[9] and John Rogers,
leader of a gathered church meeting in Dublin Cathedral during the
Commonwealth period,[10] all upheld the principle of separation. For them,
the state, whether monarch or parliament, should not interfere in the life
of the Church, for the Church derived its authority directly from God and
therefore needed neither earthly rulers nor bishops or priests either for its
good order or for its wellbeing. They retreated not so much from the world
for they accepted, in line with Christian tradition which hailed back to
Augustine and even St Paul (see Romans 13:1–4), that the earth was fallen
and thus the abode of sin, injustice and violence. Such a world required
strong and unyielding civil authority to maintain a semblance of order but,
under the providence of God, that was the extent of its influence. Thus, the
Dissenters chose separation from the Church by law established because
they believed it to be corrupt and because the state had refused to allow
its full reformation.[11]

However, this is only part of the story. The early Dissenters were
motivated too by a vision of the redeemed in their association with each
other which involved both the commitment to live godly lives as 'visible
saints' and, in part, to share together in mutual edification and support.
To say this was a particular understanding of *community* would be an
anachronism, despite evidence of the use of the word in such a way during
the seventeenth century.[12] Nevertheless, gathering together those of similar
conviction in order that they may live the Christian life, be faithful in
worship, and grow in fellowship was the necessary background to the
emergence of the congregation. Though leaders were important, the ideal
was not of a priestly caste who vicariously performed the religious rights
and duties on behalf of others. Instead, the ideal was that of *koinonia*, a
community of believers, where, in the living of the Christian life if not in the
churchly tasks of leading, teaching and preaching, each one played her or
his part. These early Separatists and Dissenters sought not only to establish
a worshipping body of believers but also a social structure for the church
on earth by emphasizing that fellowship and support were the natural
responsibilities of Christian believers. And they highlighted the responsibilities in the church covenant which specifically advocated a view of the
ecclesial body as a community of the faithful whose duties did not merely
look God-ward but also looked sideways to their fellow Christians who,
as Calvin among others had taught, carried in their person the *imago Dei*.

Church covenants tended to have similar characteristics. They all
emphasized the basics of Christian belief as the foundation of the Christian
life. But they also outline, with varying degrees of detail, the commitment
required of those who sought to become church members. As a result, it
was in these covenants that the nature of the church as a 'fellowship' of
the redeemed was first given any real and coherent expression. Examples
abound which can illustrate the point.

Henry Jacob,[13] whose church at Southwark is generally considered to be the first in England to be established along congregational lines, incorporated the church in 1616 with a solemn ceremony described by the eighteenth-century historian Daniel Neal:

> Having observed a day of solemn fasting and prayer for a blessing upon their undertaking, towards the close of the solemnity each of them made open confession of their faith in our Lord Jesus Christ; and then standing together they joined hands, and solemnly covenanted with each other in the presence of Almighty God, to walk together in all God's ways and ordinances, according as he had already revealed, or should further make known to them.[14]

Although undeveloped, it is the commitment of the church 'to walk together' that highlights the communal nature of church life. The Puritan fifth monarchist Vavasor Powell, though something of a firebrand, and given more to outbursts of principled conviction than well-argued theology, similarly outlined the commitment 'to walke together as a Church, according to the rule of the Gospell, and to watch over one another, and continue in fellowship together, and be helpful to each other, as God shall enable us, according to our duties expressed in the word of God'.[15] For Powell, Christians were not simply to 'walke together' but also to 'watch over one another' in a way that could accurately be described as 'fellowship', where sufficient intimacy could be established in their relationship together that one could admonish or encourage or support the other.

The covenant signed by a group of believers at Norwich on 28 June 1643 contained five clauses. The first clause concerned theological matters, affirming God to have been in Christ. This was followed by two clauses about Christian discipleship, the first promising to try, by God's grace, to walk according to God's will as revealed in the Bible, the second promising not to be polluted by sinful things and to give no offence to others. The fourth clause concerned the fellowship of the church: 'we will, in all love, improve our communion as brethren, by watching over one another, and as need shall be, to counsel, admonish, reprove, comfort, relieve, assist, and bear with one another, humbly submitting ourselves to the government of Christ in His churches'. The last clause affirmed that this could only be achieved in the strength of Christ.[16]

The church covenant remained significant in dissenting church life throughout the eighteenth century when the tendency was to include more detail both to demonstrate theological orthodoxy and to highlight the commitment required of those who became members. For example, the covenant of the Baptist Church at Bourton on the Water, dated 1719–20, had thirteen clauses, but it, too, gave prominence to the duty of fellowship and support. Thus, the fifth clause confessed

> That we will sympathize & have a fellow feeling (to our power) with one another in every Condition, & endeavour to bear each others Burthens, where we are joyfull or sorrowfull tempted or otherwise, that we may be mutual Helps to one another, & so answer the End of our near Relation.

This was further developed in the sixth clause:

> That we will forbear, & bear with one anothers weaknesses & Infirmities in much Pity, Tenderness, Meekness, & Patience not daring to rip up the weakness of any to those without the Church, nor to those that are within, unless it be according to Christ's Rule & Gospel Order, endeavouring all we can for the Glory of the Gospel, & for the Credit of this Church willing to cover, & hide one anothers Slips & common failings that are not sinfull.

Although these words do not contain any claim about the church's existence *for* the world, at least there is, here, the admission that the church should do nothing that might result in non-members (or non-believers) having a critical view of the faith or of the gospel. But even more significant is the fact that the interest of the Gloucestershire Baptists was not merely in upbraiding their fellow Christians for falling into sin. They were to exercise what could be seen as a more holistic sense of care. This was incorporated in the final (thirteenth) clause:

> That We will make Conscience of praying for one anothers Wellfare at all times, but especially in Time of Distress, as Poverty, Sickness, Pain, Temptation, Desertion, or the like; & that we will pray for the Peace & Growth of the whole Church in general & for our Ministers & the success of their Ministry in an especial manner.[17]

The covenant described the ecclesiological ideal to which the churches and their members were to aspire. Thus the church was a place where believers 'give themselves up one to another' and seek 'mutual edification' and where 'immediate need' (doubtless understood primarily in relation to eternity rather than temporality) was to be met.[18] Worship was clearly linked to doctrinal belief, but holding to the truth of Christianity was not enough. Christian truth had to be lived. Thus to walk in Christ's way involved a commitment to godly living, usually expressed in moral terms.[19] But alongside moral uprightness, the covenants included also the promise to live in fellowship with other believers which constituted the creation of a 'godly society' in which each one was responsible to and for the other. There was clearly a sense in which concern over one's own soul was insufficient, for attention and care were to be shown also to others.[20]

Nevertheless, this 'community' would certainly have had its limitations. The basically Calvinist outlook of the Separatists and early Dissenters meant that they believed not only in limited atonement but in the primacy of election; the world was not usually in their purview, nor was the idea of creating a community or fellowship that did anything more than fulfil its religious and spiritual duties. But they realized that this was only possible when true believers promised to walk with each other. Fellowship, including mutual support and edification, was implicit in their congregational life and explicit in their covenants.

Having said that, there were a small number of quite enterprising Dissenters who recognized that duties did extend beyond the ecclesiastical community into the wider society. Thomas Gouge, prior to his ejection from St Sepulchre's, London, in 1662, had from his own pocket funded a scheme to purchase raw materials for flax and hemp spinning and then to pay workers for their yarn. The work ceased after Black Bartholomew's Day and Gouge retired to Wales to concentrate his efforts on schemes of education.[21] The Unitarian Thomas Firmin built barns to store corn and coals which he sold to the poor at cost price in times of economic hardship. In 1676 he built a warehouse which at one time employed 1,700 of the poor in the manufacture of linen. He undertook similar experiments in Ipswich and also lobbied the authorities to take up the scheme.[22] The existence of such examples is far more significant than either the number of them or their apparent success. It highlights the way in which Christian believers were challenged not to transform society but to exercise their duties in the situation in which providence had placed them. It was at least the recognition that those who had much also had a great responsibility towards those who had less or even nothing at all.

The Evangelical Revival strengthened the view of church as Christian fellowship. Building on the 'private devotional groups' (societies) which had emerged in London from around 1678, the Methodists developed societies which concentrated on the teaching of justification by faith, the practice of extempore prayer, 'confessing ... faults and communicating ... experiences to one another' and undertaking a degree of charitable work.[23] In his preface to the Hymn Book of 1739, John Wesley told the Methodists that 'the Gospel of Christ knows of no religion but social, no holiness, but social holiness'.[24] The form of this social holiness, from 1742, was the Methodist class meeting. Each society was made up of a number of classes, namely a meeting of those 'summoned' (from the Latin *classis*). All those who sought membership among the Methodists were allocated to a class, and each class would meet together under a leader who 'watched over the moral and religious life' of its members. This leader 'knew each member and dealt with the spiritual and moral condition of each in turn, also interesting himself in their temporal concerns'.[25] Members of the class 'were expected to give some account of their religious experiences'.[26] For example, at Mount Tabor Chapel, Halifax, it was recalled that all members were 'encouraged to speak freely of his or her difficulties, failings or triumphs, when the leader could discipline or encourage'.[27] For those whose faith was secure, there were also the Band meetings formed within the classes by those seeking perfection.

While it is true that the Methodist class was primarily concerned with moral and spiritual nurture, it is also clear that it became the means of building communities of like-minded people which upheld particular standards of personal, and therefore inevitably social, behaviour. As one commentator has suggested: 'As the network of Methodist societies spread over the land, so in every place one could find a cohesive body of people living under the inspiration of the same beliefs and hopes, and guided, urged or constrained, by the same detailed rules and regulations.'[28]

For the antecedents of the Free Churches, it is clear that the idea of the gathering together of believers for fellowship, which included the commitment to mutual care, was established from the seventeenth century. While it could be argued that its initial focus revolved around discipline, it is clear that, for their members, this was a 'steadying' influence.[29] Through their moral codes and spiritual expectation, the early separatist and dissenting congregations established an ideal for community living which recognized an intimate connection to exist between all those baptized into Christ. Elements of this were adopted by the Methodist societies, but the emphasis on the sharing of experiences – a practice which also entered into some congregations of the Old Dissent – tended to increase the warmth of the fellowship enjoyed by its members thus creating a community ideal that had as much to do with affection and care as it did with spiritual oversight and the exercise of discipline.

This community ideal which is evident in the Nonconformists' practice was religious and self-contained. It concentrated on those who professed belief and on building up their faith. While some acts of charity were recorded, the goal was individual conversion and commitment rather than social cohesion. Nevertheless this created a foundation for ecclesial identity and social practice which was further developed during the nineteenth century.

III. The Church as Social Centre

To some extent, social and economic factors combined to provide the environment in which, by the mid to late nineteenth century, the Nonconformist chapels in England and Wales could flourish. The Industrial Revolution transformed British society as great urban centres developed around the major industries. Hundreds of thousands of people left the countryside in the nineteenth century in search of work, and this mass migration offered the chapels an unprecedented opportunity to expand their sphere of influence. Indeed, Nonconformist growth was directly linked to urbanization and the change which occurred was dramatic. In 1801, any town with a population in excess of 5,000 people was classified as 'urban'.

Census returns for that year suggested that one in every four English people lived in such areas.[30] By 1851, this figure had increased to the point where just over half the population of England and Wales lived in London or one of the other 62 principal towns, with the figure kept in check only by the inclusion of Wales in the statistics.[31] 'For the first time in the history of any large nation – half the population was urban', and at least two-thirds of that population had migrated from the countryside.[32]

By 1901, classifications had changed, and towns populated with 10,000 or more people were considered to be 'urban'. In that year, 62.5 per cent of people in England and Wales were found to be living in urban areas. Although Free Church membership fell in proportion to the growth in population between 1870 and 1900, the truth was that the Free Churches had made the towns and cities their own. In 1901, for example, 67 per cent of Baptists, 66 per cent of Congregationalists, 59 per cent of Wesleyan Methodists and 47 per cent of Primitive Methodists (representing the four major denominations in England) lived in towns with a population of 10,000 or above.[33] Indeed, as far as Nonconformity was concerned, statistics suggest that 'all but 8.6 per cent of its strength came from that 67 per cent of society which fitted between the professional classes and the unskilled'.[34] Nonconformity in England was not absent from the rural areas, but it gained its strength and became influential because it seemed better suited than the parish church to stake a claim in the industrial areas.

Although in Wales the Free Churches were not populated to such an extent by the 'urban middle class', a similar population movement, particularly – though not exclusively – to the coal mining and iron and steel working parts of the south, had seen the chapel there, too, become the social centre of the burgeoning industrial areas. Perhaps more so than in England, Welsh Nonconformity found its strength in its rural heartland and its potency in the towns was the result of the immigrant workers bringing with them the familiar surroundings of rural chapel life. Between 1850 and 1906, one estimate suggests that half a million people made the journey from the countryside to the towns[35] and by mid-century a Nonconformist culture had emerged where the chapel appeared to dominate the social and cultural scene and began to stake its claim in political and public life. The Religious Census of 1851 appeared to support this. From a population of 1,163,139, the census recorded 976,490 attendances on Sunday 30 March, of which almost eighty per cent were found to be worshipping in one or other of the Nonconformist chapels.[36] Despite the fact that the statistics of the Report are exceptionally difficult to interpret,[37] and it is likely that some people were counted more than once, the census still appeared to confirm what Welsh Nonconformists already knew, namely that, in Henry Richard's phrase, Wales was a 'nation of Nonconformists'. Indeed, it gave force to the most powerful myth of the nineteenth century, that to be Welsh meant belonging to a Nonconformist chapel.[38]

'Belonging' is probably the operative word for nineteenth-century Free Church life on both sides of Offa's Dyke. Chapel membership became synonymous with devoting a great deal of leisure time to the various activities provided by the local Salem, Bethel, Mount Zion, Shiloh, Ebenezer, Libanus or Penuel. As a result, the notion of the godly commonwealth as a society almost entirely separate from the world, an ideal that had been fostered by Separatists and Dissenters, was further promoted by nineteenth-century Nonconformists by ensuring that cultural as well as religious activities were provided for their members. Chapels throughout England and Wales went to great efforts in order to engage their members and adherents in what were perceived to be 'worthwhile' activities. Lectures and debates were common, reflecting the idea that the chapel represented an intellectual, wordy religion as opposed to an appeal to any other of the senses. The subjects which came under scrutiny were not necessarily religious, suggesting a widening of horizons which would later be condemned by those who felt that this secularized chapel life and contributed to the decline both in Nonconformist influence and in the number of people attending Nonconformist chapels. Such a criticism may be deserved, though it does fail to recognize either that decline is itself a complex phenomenon or that the chapels' embrace of the non-religious was as much an attempt to nurture a feasible and responsible Christian stewardship as it was an attempt to claim its rightful status in society.

These activities were fairly wide-ranging. At Acocks Green Congregational Church, Birmingham, for example, debates during Autumn 1875 included 'Ought there to be a redistribution of political power?' and 'Is a republican form of government more conducive to the welfare of a nation than a monarchical one?'[39] Many chapels had a 'mutual improvement society', such as that at Paddington Chapel which defined its purpose as 'the cultivation of mutual sympathy, the intellectual and spiritual improvement of young men, and for the promotion of the cause of Christ generally'.[40] Some of the chapels' activities had national organizations behind them such as the Christian Endeavour Society, the Boys' and Girls' Brigades, the Bands of Hope and the Independent Order of Good Templars. But churches also formed their own societies. 'These might be social, educational, literary or recreational,' noted Tudur Jones. 'The result was that Camera Clubs, Lawn Tennis Clubs, Golfing Clubs, Debating Societies, Concerts, Literary Readings and Lectures by celebrities became prominent and essential parts of church activity.'[41]

In Wales, the vast majority of churches, as was indicated by the report of the Royal Commission into Disestablishment (1910), provided cultural, literary and debating societies alongside competitions, choirs, lectures, dramas and 'social' events.[42] The report demonstrated that most Nonconformist churches were incredibly busy. For example, apart from its Sunday services, Ebenezer Calvinistic Methodist Chapel, Holyhead, recorded holding 15 different meetings during the week while the overwhelming majority of the churches in the borough of Swansea held meetings each weekday evening. The town's Libanus Welsh Baptist Church recorded the following: Monday, prayer-meeting and temperance meeting; Tuesday, Band of Hope and Christian Endeavour; Wednesday, *seiat* (the fellowship meeting); Thursday, sisterhood prayer meeting and choir; Friday, Bible Class, Saturday men's prayer meeting.[43] The result was that 'belonging to a church meant membership of a warm and intimate social movement, which offered education and entertainment as well as spiritual edification'.[44] As Tudur Jones concluded: 'All things considered, it seems that the wide-ranging activities of the churches in this period touched all aspects of the social and cultural life of their members.'[45]

Although this activity was very different from that encouraged by the early Dissenters and the Methodist societies, for it incorporated the non-religious, in fact it was, in a different century and in a different context, the extension of the same vision that had motivated those antecedents of Nonconformity in the seventeenth and eighteenth centuries. Nineteenth-century Nonconformists were only too aware of the temptations provided by alcohol and gambling and the effect their abuse had on family life. They were also inspired by the ideal of personal responsibility. In their attempts to deal with both, it was clear that pastimes which were edifying rather than destructive had to be provided and the chapels' activities were geared towards moral and intellectual improvement. In this way, the chapel created for its members a society which provided entertainment as well as opportunities to grow spiritually and socially. E. E. Kellet, born in 1864 and raised a Methodist, was effusive about the chapel life of the late nineteenth century.

> It took, by itself, the place now hardly filled by theatre, concert-hall, cinema, ballroom and circulating library put together. Here were all things required for social intercourse: recitals, songs, lectures with or without the lantern, authorised games and talk. It was a liberal education. Politics were freely discussed, books criticised and lent, music, and that not merely sacred, appraised ... It may have been a small and narrow society, but it was one which pulsed with life.[46]

Throughout the nineteenth century, the chapels found themselves to be in a stronger position than the parish church to meet the needs of the urban proletariat and, as a result, they enjoyed an unprecedented popularity. Consequently, the chapels' vision was more comprehensive than previously. It was clear that, by mid-century, the Nonconformists had to some extent embraced the very same world from which their forefathers had tried to retreat. As one Baptist minister put it: 'We no longer consider retirement from the world a sign of holiness, but believe that all man's life and work can be dedicated to heaven.'[47] And the dedication of 'all man's life' constituted a recognition that the gospel imperative included responsibilities to the world around. In this there was a clear ideological logic: the individual was 'saved', he or she then watched over fellow believers in the society of the church. But there was also a sense of lived Christianity where faith was to find expression in the world of work to the benefit of all. There was, initially, no sense that structures themselves could in any way be sinful. Instead, the whole scheme revolved around the exercise of personal responsibility. What was new was the way in which this was seen to include duties in this world and not simply the responsibility to secure eternal salvation and personal holiness.

IV. Looking Outwards

The primary motivation lying behind the chapels' engagement in work in the local community appears not to have been narrowly theological but practical. Indeed, much of their activity was motivated by the realization that the chapel was the bastion of the middle classes and the working class had either been excluded or had excluded themselves. If the Religious Census (1851) had demonstrated that a large proportion of the Welsh attended chapel, it had also shown that 'a sadly formidable portion of the English people are habitual neglecters of the public ordinances of religion'. Indeed, 'the masses of our working population ... These are never or but seldom seen in our religious congregations'.[48] The report *The Bitter Cry of Outcast London*, commissioned by the London Congregational Union and published in 1883, appeared to confirm that despite their activity, not to mention their confidence that the ordinary people belonged to them, in truth the chapels were failing to reach vast numbers of the population.

From the middle of the nineteenth century, the Wesleyans expressed concern about 'those who are plunged in social degradation, how few are the individuals who ever stray, even occasionally, into any place of worship!'[49] The initial response was to make special appointments of Home Missionary ministers whose work was to be separate from that of Circuit ministry. This mission was seen primarily in evangelistic and moral terms. The missionary ministers were to preach out of doors on every occasion, to visit every house in the immediate neighbourhood where the scriptures were to be read and tracts distributed, but political topics or any other subjects which could irritate were to be avoided. Ministers were to report on vice, profaneness, intemperance and Sabbath-breaking and to record the number of visits, religious services held, and the numbers of adults and children persuaded to attend.[50] By the mid-1870s, there were 70 such successful home missions with more than 250 chapels built as a result of their activity.[51]

The Manchester and Salford Mission was in existence as early as 1872 and by late century it employed seven lay missionaries and in one year recorded 24,821 visits, 28,570 tracts distributed and 295 open-air services.[52] Charles Garrett established a mission in Liverpool in 1875 where four lay missionaries were employed and midnight meetings were held for 'fallen women'. A similar mission was established in London's East End in 1885 while, in 1887, the West London Mission was opened at St James's Hall off Piccadilly Circus. This became the most famous of Wesleyan mission halls partly because of its minister, Hugh Price Hughes, and his championing of the 'Nonconformist Conscience'.[53] Although the work of the West London Mission had its social dimensions, Hughes, as befits someone who belonged firmly in the Wesleyan tradition, was motivated by a sense of personal morality. 'How do you expect virtues and morality from people living in one room?' he declared.[54]

Nevertheless, this work constituted a significant development in the life of the Free Churches. These missionary ministers were not simply responsible for spiritual growth among the faithful. Their obligations extended to those who lived in the area around the chapel but who had no formal connection with any of its activities. While conversion to Christian faith – if not also drawing more members into churches – was the goal, the recognition soon dawned that those who lived in social degradation were not in a position to listen to any spiritual message. As one twentieth-century Nonconformist minister put it: 'a man's soul can hardly grow to its full potential in a slum any more than a geranium can grow to full bloom in a cellar'.[55] As a result, the recognition gradually dawned that there was a mission to human beings in their present predicament, where living and working conditions were to be improved in order to reach them with the message of the gospel.

By the 1880s, the Methodists were bemoaning the fact that town centre churches were emptying as their members moved out to the suburbs and were replaced by working-class families, a body of people described by Conference in 1884 as 'dense populations living in vice and indifference'.[56] While much of the activity of the central missions revolved around the usual churchly activities such as class meetings, bible classes, cultural and educational classes,[57] their close association with the working class made it possible both to offer some relief and to become a means of supplying useful information to other bodies which sought to identify genuine need. For example, in Leeds, it was found that, on Sundays, 'some parents were so poor that they kept their children in bed until afternoon in order to save a meal'. As a result, the mission hall served breakfast to children on the premises.[58] In 1886, the Manchester and Salford Mission was providing a men's home, a 'labour yard' to help men to find employment, a women's home, a maternity home and hospital, as well as a 'cripples' guild', choirs, orchestras, bands, visitation schemes, Sunday Schools, and Band of Hope. The Liverpool Mission provided two houses for the homeless and, during the severe winter of 1891, gave away 180 gallons of soup a day for nine days while 700 children had free breakfasts for a week. The Hull mission, established in 1891, gave away 15,000 free breakfasts during the first eight months of its existence as well as giving away clothing to poor children and providing furniture for poor families.[59] Some of the mission halls provided medical advice. Manchester had a nurse and was said to offer help to 1,800 patients a year while the Leeds Mission noted that, in 1904, 2,277 had been helped in this way. According to George Sails: 'without exaggeration, it can be said that wherever need was discovered, and whatever the need was, an attempt was made to meet it'.[60]

The aim was to establish a seven-day-a-week religion where the mission hall provided a variety of activities for men and women of all ages. By 1906, the Queen Street Chapel and Mission, Huddersfield,[61] was open each day of the week offering the usual 'religious' activities such as a Wesley Guild, Band of Hope, a Men's Reading Room, a Boys' Brigade, a Girls' Club, a Sunday School. The tone was religious rather than spiritual, and moralistic rather than political, with five open-air meetings being conducted weekly alongside six cottage meetings, open-air anti-gambling and temperance campaigns, a 'Guild for Crippled Children' and a Women's Home. On Sunday evenings, volunteers went to the local lodging houses to bring 'outcasts' to services, while there were 'Pleasant Sunday Afternoon' meetings for men and 'Pleasant Monday Afternoon' meetings for women.[62] When individuals were willing to make an effort to improve their own lot, they found the church ready and able to help. A goose club enabled families to save for Christmas, while a cinematograph was installed in the church offering the opportunity for the public airing of films of an edifying and educational nature. Perhaps more radically, a Labour Bureau was established which, in 1906, enabled fifty men and women to find temporary work, while the church also provided clothing for the needy.

Unlike the Methodists (Wesleyan or Primitive), English Congregationalists were considered – and sometimes considered themselves – to be more 'middle class' with a mission to industrialists, people of business and artisans rather than the labouring classes.[63] Nevertheless, within Congregationalism too there were examples of town centre and inner-city churches transforming themselves into 'institutional churches' in order to try to reach the working classes. Without the connexional structure to impose a definite policy on the local churches, Congregationalism tended to depend more on the personality and conviction of individuals. But when the right individual was found in the right place, then some success was recorded.

Between 1896 and 1902, Westminster Chapel became a 'Christian Social Centre' under the ministry of the Revd Richard Westrope. Westrope had 'left Belgrave Chapel in Leeds, when there were complaints about the "social gospel" topics he had chosen for his Sunday evening social addresses'.[64] He has been described as 'an advanced Radical holding strong socialistic views' and that 'his great desire [was] ... to establish at Westminster a "People's Church", institutional, having clubs for men and women, a labour bureau [and] people's lawyer'.[65] It is recorded that the result of this was the decline in the congregation and, after the resignation of the Revd Westrope, 'Sunday services were conducted in the corner of the great auditorium'.

His successor was the Revd G. Campbell Morgan and under his ministry a sisterhood was established in order to reach 'the people of the slums of Westminster and the sleek, outwardly smiling streets of Kensington'. By 1911, there were nine full-time workers employed by the church whose responsibilities extended from superintending the primary department of the Sunday School, through secretarial duties, visiting, leading a women's study circle and keeping a women's employment register.[66] The Men's Slate Club tried to inculcate in the men of the church 'the principle of thrift and providing benefit during periods of sickness'. A 'Coal Club' was established as a savings account and means of provision during the winter months, a 'Cripples' Parlour' provided education for the children, a 'Dorcas Guild' made clothes for the poor, while a Benevolent Society provided 'help among the sick and poor who live in the parish and immediate neighbourhood'.[67]

Within Congregationalism, then, there were examples of churches which sought to establish their community life not only around religious piety but around enabling social life in the world both for their members and for others. Paddington Chapel raised money to supply blankets, sheets, shawls and coal to the poor. An 'Infants' Friends Society' was established to provide for the needs of pregnant women: 'one quart of oatmeal, one pound of loaf sugar, one pound of tea, and a New Testament'.[68] On 20 November 1908, Newtown Congregational Church, St Helens, opened a Men's Institute. Here the local working man – and the unemployed – could play billiards, draughts and dominoes, read papers and magazines and generally pass their time in recreation which was governed by a clear code of conduct.[69] The result was 'Congregationalism and club-cum-business house for Christ'.[70]

Perhaps the most famous of the Congregational institutional churches was Whitefield's Tabernacle on Tottenham Court Road, under the ministry of C. Silvester Horne.[71] Horne had gone to Whitefield's in 1903 specifically to 'promote a mission modelled on Wesleyan Central Halls'.[72] For Horne, the institutional church was intended to 'help man to develop all his faculties'.[73] At the opening of Salem, Leeds, as an institutional church, Horne explained:

> The purpose of an institutional church was to reconstruct human society on the basis of brotherhood ... It was a church for bringing the influence of Jesus Christ to bear on every side of a man's life, so as to transform him ... The cardinal point is institutional methods, second to a tremendous belief in the fatherhood of God and the brotherhood of Jesus Christ, upon the belief in the sacredness of man.[74]

Horne here outlined the two primary factors that gave rise to this vision of congregational and community life. The first was methodological: the introduction of a full programme of activities intended to appeal to those who would not otherwise enter a church. The second was theological. The conviction that God was sovereign over all of life had, to some extent, inspired both dissenting ecclesiology and the Methodist societies. For both, divine judgement could only be avoided when members subjected themselves to discipline. However, by the late nineteenth century, theology had liberalized and the vision of God as judge had been replaced by God as Father who, in Jesus Christ, had drawn attention to the common bond that held all people in the same human family.

In Wales, there were few institutional churches – Lionel B. Fletcher's time at Wood Street Congregational Church, Cardiff, being a possible exception[75] – and the concept was virtually unknown among the Welsh-speaking denominations. Yet enterprising ministers could be found there who tried to meet social as well as spiritual needs. For example, the Revd Leon Atkin arrived in Bargoed in the Rhymney Valley in 1931 to be minister of a central mission hall paid for in part by a donation from Joseph Rank. He was enthusiastic about the ministry of the Central Hall in the community: 'With cinema seats for a thousand ... a cinematograph projection box; the last word in kitchens ... and enough extra rooms to provide a hostel for the homeless, the Central Hall realised the practical Christian's ideal of a seven-day religion.'[76]

The unemployed could have free shaves and hair-cuts while shoes were repaired for the cost of the leather. Meals were served, while 28 men were lodged in the Hall in order to avoid the means test which denied assistance to those whose families earned above the permitted minimum. This led to a threat of prosecution for 'obstructing the administration of His Majesty's Government' and Atkin lost the sympathy of his denomination. He resigned from the ministry of the Methodist Church and spent the rest of his life as minister of St Paul's Congregational Church, Swansea. The crypt at St Paul's became a haven for the elderly, the down-and-outs and for drug addicts, while Atkin pursued his practical Christianity as a Labour councillor until he fell foul of the local committee and opted to stand, successfully, as an independent. He courted controversy throughout his life and was the bane of the political and religious establishments whether local councillors, the local Labour Party, denominational officers or the deacons of his church. Nevertheless, his ministry undoubtedly brought light and succour to many who were otherwise ignored by church and society alike.

Bloomsbury Baptist Chapel in London's West End engaged in social work from its incorporation in 1848. It was said, within two years, that 'the whole neighbourhood felt the influence of the new church, which poured forth help for all manner of benevolent and educational work'.[77] A Cheap Clothing Society was established through which the women of the church provided cloth for the poor and in 1852 alone it was recorded that 928 items were sold.[78] The church also distributed poor relief to the sick, primarily in the form of fuel and clothing. Medical advice and medicines were also available. As with the Methodists noted above, these Baptists were not political except in the widest of terms. They responded to a growing sense of service and a conviction that the proclamation of the gospel had to be accomplished by practical help or else any attempt to reach the poor was doomed to failure. As a result, the church's social work was in reality a support for its pastoral work, for 'no relief is given without personal visitation' and the visitors employed by the church were careful 'to combine Christian counsel with the temporal relief afforded'.[79] The aim was to enable the poor to help themselves rather than to become wholly dependent on charity. It is hardly surprising, then, that the church remodelled itself early in the twentieth century as an 'institutional church',[80] and by December 1908 there were two hundred members of the Institute.

One of the remarkable features of Bloomsbury Church's social outreach was the employment of women to offer practical help and medical advice as a means of reaching the poor. And Bloomsbury was not alone. By 1860, for example, there were 134 'Biblewomen' who were selling Bibles in the London slums as well as offering practical help to those who lived there.[81] In 1890 the London Baptist Association established a community of deaconesses in Holborn. There were four deaconesses at the mission on Cross Street, Hatton Green, and a further nine who were based in churches throughout London as well as in Ipswich and in Newport, South Wales. Working under the direction of the Lady Superintendent, Sister Constance, the sisters visited local homes for five hours on five days of the week: 'homes of poverty, of sickness, of distress, and terrible wretchedness. And into these dark sad homes, comfort, good cheer, sunshine, temporal help, and above all God's blessed message of tender forgiving love is ever being taken'.[82]

Perhaps John Clifford was the most prominent of Baptist social gospellers. When the church at Praed Street, Paddington, outgrew its accommodation, a new church was opened at Westbourne Park. Clifford ministered there until his retirement, inaugurating an Institute in the church in 1885 which, by 1892, had 1,500 members. Early in his ministry, Clifford had confessed that his aim was twofold. 'We have a private object – the consolidation and help of each other in the endeavour after spiritual manhood. We have a public object, the decrease of the evils of society, and the increase of individual and social good by the dissemination of the Gospel of Christ.'[83] For Clifford, like many Victorian Nonconformists, the individual was all-important. As a result, he insisted that the church's mission was to challenge the individual to convert while society should be a place where each individual can flourish. Apart from that, he appears to have worked out no real ecclesiology or any detailed conception of social life. His vision was political, but it depended largely on personal involvement and commitment to the cause.

Other socially orientated work was undertaken by the 'Tabernacles' whose pastors had been trained by Spurgeon at his Preacher's College. Indeed, the Metropolitan Tabernacle had a total of 21 mission halls and 25 Sunday Schools by the late 1890s. Ministers such as Archibald Brown at the East London Tabernacle and William Cuff at Shoreditch tried to reach the working classes living around their churches by 'institutional' means.[84] Outside London, an institutional church was established in Bradford, but it was not a great success: it opened on January 1903 and soon drew congregations of around 500, but it seems to have come to an end by May 1905.

Whether officially 'institutional' or not, other Baptists were motivated by the gospel to develop a social mission. F. B. Meyer is remembered partly for his work with the Keswick Convention and revivalism generally. Yet he combined a personal piety which strongly believed in the need for individual conversion with a recognition that effective urban evangelism was dependent on a willingness to deal with the temporal needs of the poor. With a band of faithful members, he raised the funds to build Leicester's Melbourne Hall (formerly a mission hall for Victoria Road Baptist Church) which worked with released prisoners which eventually became the 'Discharged Prisoners' Society'. Meyer also inaugurated schemes to give work to the unemployed including the selling of fire-wood and window cleaning.[85] The ideal upheld by Melbourne Hall was that every member should be engaged in service in the local community as part of the commitment to spread the gospel. The Revd George Dawson, minister of Mount Zion Baptist Church, Birmingham, declared in 1884 that 'a common end of purpose ... to clothe the naked, to feed the hungry, and to instruct the ignorant' was the key to understanding the gospel.[86] Queens Road Baptist Church, Coventry, organized clothing clubs during the First World War and mock pubs on Saturday evenings. Perhaps most noteworthy was the way in which the church supported those arriving in the city in search of work in the automobile industry. Successive ministers would arrange board and lodging for them until employment could be secured.[87] Park Road Baptist Church, St Helens, supplied clothing and food for the local community in the days of economic depression in the late 1920s.[88] All these examples suggest that, certainly by the first quarter of the twentieth century, the Free Churches had recognized that spiritual and temporal need went hand in hand and to meet one meant that some attention had to be paid to the other.

V. Congregation and Community

In the years from around 1875 to the outbreak of war in 1939 Nonconformists of different denominational affiliation were inspired by a vision of sharing the gospel in the wider community. They all seem to have shared the conviction that this would only be possible if they also offered practical help and immediate relief. Sometimes, as in the case of Bloomsbury Chapel or Melbourne Hall, this was a commitment which seemed enshrined in the church's ethos. At other times it seemed to owe more to the personality of a particular minister. The importance of men such as Hugh Price Hughes, John Clifford, Silvester Horne and F. B. Meyer cannot be denied. They contributed much to the life of the local churches where they ministered by encouraging a social mission to the poor of the area, and they did much to promote the work through denominational networks. But there were also hundreds of ministers, such as J. T. Stannard, Richard Westrope and Leon Atkin, who held nothing other than local appointments who set about the task of building communities through social service inspired by gospel imperatives. Perhaps the major criticism to be levelled against some of these men is that they tended to act alone and in ministering to the most needy they might have failed to nurture the community of the church. When Atkin died, for example, St Paul's church closed. And there were other examples where social involvement expired when those motivating the activity moved on to pastures new.

While the rise of the labour movement as well as straightforward compassion must have played a significant part, some of the inspiration to act in this way was certainly provided by the theological transformation which occurred within the Nonconformist churches in England and Wales during the last quarter of the nineteenth century. The liberalizing tendencies which began with Schleiermacher's address to the 'cultured despisers' of religion, developed through Ritschl's appropriation of 'value' into an ethical understanding of the gospel encompassed in Adolf Harnack's three-fold definition of the 'essence' of Christianity as the Kingdom of God and its coming, the Fatherhood of God and the infinite value of the human soul, and the demands of the higher righteousness.[89] Nonconformist ministers such as Will Reason (who played a prominent part in the Mansfield House settlement),[90] T. Rhondda Williams, S. E. Keeble and Alfred E. Garvie emphasized the social implications of Christianity as an essential part of the faith of each individual where the love of God would issue forth in the love and service of fellow human beings.[91] They affirmed the central motif of human 'value'[92] as a direct result of God's fatherhood and the concomitant 'brotherhood of man'.[93] Many in the Free Churches came to believe that the salvation of the individual and the salvation of society were to be viewed as 'two sides of the same endeavour'[94] and the 'brotherhood' which resulted would create the new age which could only arrive through the sanctification of men and women to the moral task[95] which was to be revealed in the world and established in society through the adoption of a higher ethic and the practice of love.[96]

This 'social gospel'[97] prompted the Free Churches to look beyond the idea of attracting society's marginalized into the churches and to work instead to meet social need in a more direct manner. The Calvinistic Methodist Connexion in Wales, for example, established institutions to deal with specific social problems such as the Children's Home opened in 1902 at Bontnewydd, Caernarfon, and the Kingswood Treborth Home opened in Cardiff in 1908 which focused on offering support to young women. From 1911, Welsh Nonconformists organized the Welsh School of Social Service which gathered annually to discuss aspects of the social problem right up to the end of the 1930s. After the Great War there was a concerted ecumenical effort to supply a Christian response to social needs with the Conference on Christian Politics, Economics and Citizenship (COPEC), held in Birmingham in 1924, and the International Conference on Life and Work held in Stockholm in 1925. COPEC issued in at least one remarkable effort in Bangor, North Wales, when local people, with ministers and nonconformist lay-people prominent among them, raised sufficient funds to build a street of houses, let at affordable rents, as part of the campaign to clear slum-dwellings in the city.[98] These are specific and in some ways isolated examples. However, they demonstrate that by the first thirty years or so of the twentieth century, Free Churches had recognized that the nurturing of their own communities carried with it a responsibility to do something for wider society. The congregation was no longer their only interest, nor was individual conversion their sole concern. Clearly, by the end of the 1930s, a social mission was well established in Free Church thought and practice.

VI. Conclusions

From the seventeenth through to the late nineteenth centuries, important developments can be discerned in Free Church life whereby the initial establishment of a godly society consisting of believers covenanted to walk together and offer mutual help and oversight became a means to establishing an alternative society catering for all the social and cultural, as well as spiritual, needs of its members. As R. Tudur Jones noted, 'something was found for everyone to do; no interest was left uncatered for'.[99] But whether intentionally or by accident, the institutional churches and central halls created an environment in which service to the community and the meeting of material as well as spiritual need could be seen as a natural part of the chapel's work. Thus what was initially a closed society, intent on creating its own community and emphasizing mutual care and service, over time came to see that there was a wider humanity which needed to be the focus of attention. Although initially social work was perceived as a means to reach the masses with the gospel, and indeed some went so far as to deny assistance to those who had no Christian commitment,[100] it soon came to represent the heart of what many understood to be Christian service. It was part of their calling as Christians to make a difference through service in the wider community. What Robert Moore said of the Methodists in County Durham could be said more generally of the Free Churches nationally, where a 'development of the idea of service' can be discerned which entailed 'actual work on and in the fallen institutions of society rather than the diligent and private pursuit of an individual calling alone'.[101]

This all laid the foundation for further development in the twentieth century. Individual service remained important, as seen in the work of some of the Methodist deacons and deaconesses and the Church Related Community Workers of the United Reformed Church, as well as the men and women who made up the ranks of the ordained ministry in the Free Churches. Congregations did their bit, though international need possibly gained greater prominence than the local, a situation which arose partly because of the establishment of the Welfare State as well as the emergence of para-church organizations, such as Christian Aid, whose focus was clearly relief on a global scale. It is clear that the developments in the twentieth century have precedents and precursors in the history of the Free Churches. Service is prominent throughout, but more fundamental is a sense of *koinonia*, of fellowship, which, when mixed with a recognition of common humanity (expressed in terms of 'brotherhood' by the social gospellers), created a particular understanding both of the congregation and of the community and the way in which the one relates to the other. But, more fundamentally, this is how the Free Churches sought to express the divine economy in their everyday dealings and thus to realize, if only in part, the Kingdom of God on earth.

3

Conscience and Politics
David Bebbington

At the opening of the nineteenth century the three historic denominations of Protestant Dissent, the Presbyterians, the Independents and the Baptists, occupied an odd position in the British State. The inherited constitutional arrangements in England and Wales gave the Church of England a privileged position. For many purposes it was assumed in law that Dissent did not exist. The Act of Uniformity of 1662, which had provided that all should worship in their parish churches, was technically still in force. Its rigours were merely alleviated by the Toleration Act of 1689 which allowed Dissenters to pursue their deviant forms of religion in private. The three denominations, and even more their Quaker contemporaries, were regarded in theory as total outsiders. Yet Dissent wielded considerable political power. In many boroughs its local leaders exercised a decisive say in public affairs such as the choice of parliamentary candidates. In a few boroughs Dissenters virtually monopolized the municipal corporations even though, under the Test and Corporation Acts of 1673 and 1661, they were in theory debarred from becoming members of corporations at all. Some of their number actually sat in parliament, from which they had never been excluded. They naturally wanted to end their second-class status, and so between 1786 and 1790 there had been a campaign to repeal the Test and Corporation Acts. It proved unsuccessful because the cry of 'The Church in danger!' was raised and then the French Revolution of 1789 put an end to opportunities of significant constitutional reform for a generation. The Dissenters remained the victims of political discrimination.

The late eighteenth and early nineteenth centuries, however, witnessed a transformation in the fortunes of Dissenters. Whereas in the eighteenth century they had constituted only a tiny minority of the population (around 6 per cent in 1715–18), by the middle of the nineteenth century they formed some 17 per cent of the people of England and about 45 per cent of the people of Wales. In 1851 it was shown that they were nearly half the churchgoing population. The change was largely the result of expansion following the Evangelical Revival. The growth was partly due to the rise of Methodism, the so-called 'New Dissent'. Methodists began as members of a religious society within the Church of England and became a distinct body only gradually, the key stage being in the 1790s, just after the death of their founder, John Wesley. Not all Methodists regarded themselves as Dissenters even then. Most members of Wesleyan Methodism, by far the largest of the Methodist denominations, positioned themselves for many years midway between Church and Dissent, but as the nineteenth century wore on they increasingly came to see themselves as part of Nonconformity, the new name for Dissent that came into vogue around the middle of the century. Some of the breakaway Methodists, and particularly the Methodist New Connexion that split off as early as the 1790s, had few inhibitions about politics, but most initially shared with the Wesleyans a policy of 'no politics' because any partisanship risked plunging the denominations into discord. So for a long time the Methodists were less likely than the 'Old Dissent' to play a significant part in public affairs.

The Dissenters in the early years of the nineteenth century generally aligned themselves with the Whigs. Because of their marginal position in the state, Dissenters were concerned to maintain the principles of civil and religious liberty upheld by the Whigs. There was always the danger that Tory High Churchmen might remove some of the liberties that Dissent enjoyed under the Toleration Act. In 1811, in fact, the Home Secretary Lord Sidmouth, alarmed by the rapid expansion of religion outside the Established Church through itinerant evangelism, introduced a bill to stop Dissenting preachers from being allowed to register under the act unless they had a settled congregation where they ministered. The bill roused the Methodists, the chief target of attack, to defend their existence by petitioning against the bill. Although the measure was defeated, it showed the need for vigilance. Many of the Evangelical Dissenters, the great bulk of the Congregationalists and Baptists, were wary of political action in the first decade of the century. Like the Methodists, they saw public action as a diversion from their main task of spreading the gospel. But they were stirred to take action in 1813, when the charter of the East India Company came up for renewal. Dissenters, like the Evangelical Churchmen led by William Wilberforce, successfully demanded that the new charter should permit missionary work in India. The Presbyterians, most of whom had developed into Unitarians, also achieved a parliamentary victory in that year. William Smith, the spokeman of Dissent in the House of Commons, steered on to the statute book a Unitarian Toleration Bill that abolished the penalties for avowing Unitarian belief. There was a rising tide of political activism among Dissenters.

In the immediate aftermath of the Napoleonic Wars, from 1815 to 1819, an upsurge of radicalism made it an unpropitious time to press Dissenting claims. In those years a number of men on the fringe of Methodism took up the cause of parliamentary reform or even more drastic change, but they were rapidly disowned by the Wesleyan authorities. In the 1820s, however, as social tension eased, it became timely once more to call for the repeal of the Test and Corporation Acts. A United Committee of Dissenters under William Smith persuaded several Whig peers to support the measure, which was carried in 1828. Dissenters could now take their seats on borough councils without fear of legal challenge. The stigma of being less than full subjects of the crown was swept away. They were divided, however, over a similar measure to redress the claim of Roman Catholics to have their exclusion from parliament abolished. Some Dissenters thought it was logical that since their own chief political handicap had been removed, they should support the termination of the equivalent for Catholics. Others, however, believed that Catholics continued to be such a threat to the political welfare of the country that they ought not to share in its governance. A marked suspicion of Roman Catholics was to remain an enduring feature of Dissenting politics for well over a century. In 1829, however, relief of the main Roman Catholic disability was carried, preparing the way for further constitutional change.

The greatest alteration in the British constitution during the nineteenth century was the passing in 1832 of the Great Reform Act. A system of representation unchanged in principle since the fifteenth century was transformed so as to extend the franchise to a much wider section of the population. Dissenters were almost unanimously in favour, knowing that many in their ranks would be enfranchised. They commonly supported the organizations in cities such as Birmingham and Manchester which demanded parliamentary representation for the first time. One such Dissenter, who had virtually determined his borough's representation in parliament in 1831–32, John Bonham Carter, a barrister and inheritor of family wealth in Portsmouth, nevertheless redrafted the Reform Bill so that it passed. In 1835 Dissenters were delighted when the Whig government passed an equivalent measure for municipal corporations, ending the system of recruiting new members by co-option and opening the corporations to election by the inhabitants. Many chapel-goers became councillors, aldermen, and mayors of their towns over coming years. Of the 102 Congregationalists who became MPs during the nineteenth century, at least 23 also served as aldermen and at least 36 as mayor. Local politics, which still depended on personality rather than party, was an attractive sphere of public service.

Now that many of their number enjoyed political privileges, Dissenters wanted to achieve redress of their particular grievances. One disability they suffered was that the only extant legal record of birth was an entry in the registers of the parish church for the baptism of a child. This arrangement was a particular problem for Quakers and Baptists, neither of whom observed the baptism of infants. Another handicap was that since 1753 all marriages in England and Wales, except those of Quakers and Jews, had to be performed in a parish church. In this case the legal requirement bore especially hard on Unitarians, who were compelled to use formulae in the wedding service which acknowledged the Trinitarian doctrine they rejected. Burials in parish churchyards, often the only places available, had to follow the Prayer Book of the Church of England and were subject to charges for the benefit of the Anglican clergy. The ancient English universities had tests that excluded Dissenters from Oxford altogether and, while allowing them into Cambridge, prevented them from graduating without embracing Anglicanism. The most pressing hardship for many Dissenters was the system of church rates. If a meeting voted a local rate for the repair of the parish church, all ratepayers, of whatever denomination, were required to pay. Dissenters had to support a form of worship with which in conscience they disagreed. Local campaigns for the refusal of a church rate became a common form of Dissenting political activity in the 1830s.

At the same time some Dissenters were driven to propose a much more radical course of action. If they traced the disabilities they suffered to the underlying issue, they encountered the question of the relationship of Church and State. The Church of England could claim unique privileges because it was the Church exclusively recognized by the State. The monarch was supreme governor of the Church of England; bishops sat in the House of Lords as of right; the House of Commons served as the legislature of the Church of England. The specific problems might be swept away, some Dissenters began to think in 1834, if the Church were to be separated from the State by disestablishment. That would guarantee once for all that Dissenters would not be the victims of discrimination. Edward Miall, a Congregational minister in Leicester who had been radicalized by the church rate issue, launched in 1841 a newspaper, *The Nonconformist*, to campaign for disestablishment. Three years later Miall set up the British Anti-State Church Association, which in 1853, the year after he became an MP, became the Society for the Liberation of Religion from State Patronage and Control. Originally designed to take up only the question of Church and State, it gradually extended its coverage to all the grievances of Dissenters. The Liberation Society, as it was usually called, turned into one of the most powerful pressure groups in mid-Victorian Britain, enjoying an income greater than that of the Liberal Party.

How successful was its cause? There were two major waves of reform in favour of Nonconformists. In the 1830s the Whig government took up some of the grievances of a body of people who were often its most faithful supporters. In 1834 there was a bill to open Oxford and Cambridge to non-Anglicans, but it failed. Two years later, however, the Whigs carried a measure introducing civil registration of births, marriages and deaths for all in the country, thus dealing with the first of the grievances. In 1837 a Dissenters' Marriages Act gave them the right to hold weddings in their own places of worship. The second wave of reform came later, from W. E.

Gladstone's Liberal Party, which also enjoyed the support of the bulk of Nonconformity. Compulsory church rates were ended in 1868. University tests were abolished three years later. From 1880 burials in parish church-yards could observe Nonconformist rites. So Nonconformists put these issues of discrimination on the political agenda against strong opposition from most Anglicans and Conservatives. Yet it should not be assumed that Nonconformists were wielding power in their own right. Governments were enacting changes when they chose and often the concessions were only partial. Thus, for example, the abolition of church rates took fully three decades to resolve and even then was not the total ban Nonconformists wanted, but merely the ending of powers to make church rates compulsory. Most fundamentally, there was no progress towards the disestablishment of the Church of England in England itself. Its sister church in Ireland was disestablished by an act of 1869, but that measure was primarily designed to placate the Irish Roman Catholics. Nonconformists could not enforce changes on their own behalf. They were merely suppliants at the door of progressive politicians.

Meanwhile Nonconformists were playing a full role in wider politics. They were particularly prominent in Manchester at a time when the city, with its thriving cotton industry, was at the cutting edge of global indus-trialization. Many Nonconformists prospered in the cotton trade, whether as manufacturers or merchants, and they formed the vanguard of the 'Manchester School' of political opinion. Believing that the aristocracy wasted the resources of the country, they contended for sharp reductions in public spending. They held to the principles of classical political economy, asserting that free trade was the essence of a wise public policy. Their leading pressure group, the Anti-Corn Law League, founded in 1839, aimed to abolish the duty on foreign grain which kept up the income of the landed interest and so raised the price of bread for the employees of industry. The first president of the League was J. B. Smith, a Unitarian cotton merchant from Manchester. Supporters extended beyond Manchester to other indus-trial towns, so that the treasurer was Thomas Shaw, a Congregational woollen manufacturer from Halifax. Many in this circle were so concerned to defend the right of mill owners to regulate their own affairs that they opposed the extension of the power of the state into humanitarian legis-lation. Thus R. H. Greg, a Unitarian cotton spinner and merchant of Styal in Cheshire, wrote a book, *The Factory Question* (1837), to oppose the movement that was campaigning, often on the basis of a Christian conscience, for a bill to restrict the hours of labour to ten hours a day. The greatest triumph of the Manchester school of thought came in 1846 when Sir Robert Peel, Prime Minister of a Conservative government elected to defend the landed interest, conceded that the corn laws must go. It is true that repeal was capably managed by Peel so as to be undertaken at a time of the government's choosing. Nevertheless it was a symbolic victory of the rising industrialists, many of whom were Nonconformists, over the

aristocracy and gentry, the great majority of whom worshipped within the
Established Church.

There were other broad questions of domestic policy addressed by
Nonconformists during the middle years of the century. Although a number
of the ideologically driven members of the Manchester School approved the
new poor law introduced in 1834 to reduce public expenditure on the relief
of the needy, several opposed its inhumanity. The ending of financial relief
to the poor outside workhouses, for example, attracted critical comment
from John Fielden, a Unitarian cotton master in Todmorden in Lancashire,
who, unlike co-religionists such as Greg, was a leader of the ten hours
movement. Nonconformists were even more strikingly divided over the
enforcement of Sunday rest. Evangelical Nonconformists, Congregational,
Baptist and Methodist, believed with few exceptions that it was the duty of
the State to ensure that work and recreation stopped in order to honour the
Lord's Day, which was interpreted in the light of Old Testament teaching
about the observance of the Sabbath. Part of their aim was to ensure a day
of rest for the working population when there was no break on Saturday.
Such Nonconformists campaigned to end Sunday trains, to stop Sunday mail
deliveries and to keep museums and art galleries closed on Sundays. Most
Unitarians, however, interpreted the Bible as encouraging higher cultural
influences and not requiring respect for Old Testament Sabbath regulations.
They therefore pressed for the removal of restrictions on Sunday recreation,
eventually, in 1875, forming the Sunday Society with that object. Here was
a clash of social policies grounded on differing theologies.

The Sunday question was one of those that agitated the localities.
It was in their home towns, rather than in national politics, that most
Nonconformists made their mark. Apart from serving on local councils,
they often acted energetically in the range of voluntary organizations that
were a feature of nineteenth-century society. Those who were businessmen
often sat on chambers of commerce; others who sprang from the working
people held office in trade unions. Many founded or sustained schools,
especially the institutions of the British and Foreign School Society
that were frequently associated with particular chapels. They supported
Mechanics' Institutes, which provided evening lectures for the population
at large, libraries, museums and art galleries. Their philanthropy extended
to orphanages, hospitals, maternity homes, convalescent homes, asylums,
almshouses, zoos and parks. They were also prominent in distinctively
Christian organizations such as Sunday School Unions, the British and
Foreign Bible Society and the Young Men's Christian Association. The
prevailing motivation was expressed by T. C. Taylor, a Congregational
deacon who became MP for Batley, when he remarked, 'I was trained up ...
in the doctrine that "None of us liveth to himself", and that our whole life
should be a means of helping those less fortunate than ourselves.'[1]

Sometimes involvement in these various organizations led on to political
activity on their behalf, for instance when supporters sought local acts of

parliament to advance their interests. In any case the participants in these bodies were playing a prominent part in the civil society of the day.

In overseas questions there was a marked tendency towards promoting the cause of peace. Again there was theological underpinning, this time in the postmillennial hope that was widely shared, especially by Evangelicals of all stripes. The gospel, they believed, would advance by means of Christian missions so that the earth would be full of the knowledge of the Lord. Only after ('post') the establishment of the millennium, an earthly age of peace and plenty, would Christ return to reign. So work for peace seemed to be the adjunct of missionary preaching in establishing Christian values throughout the world. Its success seemed guaranteed by biblical prophecy. The peace campaign also appeared to be a counterpart of free trade, which required the abolition of war for effective commercial relations between different lands, and the reduction of public spending, which entailed as one of its leading priorities a decrease of expenditure on the armed forces. Hence Edward Miall was a speaker at a series of international Peace Congresses between 1849 and 1853. His fellow Congregational minister and colleague in the House of Commons, Henry Richard, was secretary of the Peace Society from 1848 to 1885. Alongside peace, freedom was a goal that appealed to Nonconformists. Religious liberty was one of their concerns. They defended the right of Protestants on the continent to spread their faith. Edward Steane, the Baptist secretary of the Evangelical Alliance and editor of its journal *Evangelical Christendom*, regularly urged the British government to defend the interests of Protestants abroad. Nonconformists also championed anti-slavery (which is discussed elsewhere), defended oppressed peoples abroad and favoured European national causes such as Italian unification. In each case freedom was their lodestar.

Freedom was one of the fundamental principles of the Liberal Party that gradually emerged during the middle years of the century. The Whigs, who were more traditional in their views and more likely to defer to the wishes of the aristocracy, steadily gave way to the Liberals, who wanted more legislative changes and were less inclined to follow the lead of their social superiors. The two labels were for many years used interchangeably by the same body of men, but the date when the party tipped towards Liberalism is normally taken to be 1859. Yet the Prime Minister over the next six years, Lord Palmerston, though strongly opposed to slavery and displaying many liberal inclinations, was a stern opponent of any further parliamentary reform. Almost all Nonconformists, by contrast, were eager for another widening of the franchise. In 1864 Edward Baines, the Congregational editor of *The Leeds Mercury* and an MP, put forward a motion in the Commons in favour of parliamentary reform. Soon Palmerston was dead and reform became practical politics. Its eloquent champion was the Quaker John Bright, a former leader of the Anti-Corn Law League, who during 1866 and 1867 led the Reform League in the call for a broader franchise. The Conservative leader Benjamin Disraeli passed a measure of reform in 1867 in an attempt to gain electoral popularity, but the Liberal cause triumphed in the general election of the following year. Far more Nonconformists now had the vote, especially in the towns, and almost all of them supported the Liberal Party. It was a genuinely popular cause with the bulk of working men, who, often themselves chapelgoers, were grateful for the reform that Liberals had demanded long before Disraeli had taken up the question. The Liberal Party of the later nineteenth century was built on the principles of peace, freedom, retrenchment and reform; and Nonconformists, as Gladstone once remarked, were the backbone of the Liberal Party.

During Gladstone's first administration, from 1868 to 1874, Nonconformists looked at the Prime Minister with respect but also with a critical eye. Gladstone was a High Churchman who staunchly defended the interests of the Church of England and at times seemed to show suspicious sympathies for Rome. Some of his policies also appeared dubious or worse. In particular the Education Act of 1870,[2] continued to allow public money to go to Anglican and Catholic schools, a breach of fundamental Nonconformist convictions. At the 1874 general election there was little enthusiasm for Gladstone's programme in the chapels, a factor which helped Disraeli to return to power. Two years later, however, an issue arose which transformed the relationship between Gladstone and the Nonconformists. Irregular troops in the Turkish Empire put down an uprising among the Orthodox Bulgarians with great cruelty. W. T. Stead, the Congregational editor of *The Northern Echo*, raised an agitation on behalf of the Bulgarians, and Gladstone came to its support with a powerful public speech. Over the next four years Gladstone persistently harried the Conservative government for its support of the Turks. Nonconformists rallied to Gladstone's side, voting eagerly for Liberal candidates in the party's triumph at the polls in 1880. Thereafter Nonconformists were, in general, Gladstone's loudest adherents, praising his Christian fibre. During Gladstone's three further administrations of 1880, 1886 and 1892, they were bound into Liberalism by a powerful personal loyalty to its leader. When Joseph Chamberlain, a prominent Unitarian from Birmingham, led a revolt against Gladstone's policy of Home Rule for Ireland in 1886, other Nonconformists compared the dissident's betrayal to that of Judas against Jesus. On Gladstone's death in 1898, some Nonconformist parents named their new babies after him. Despite his distance from them in churchmanship, William Ewart Gladstone was their political hero.

A good example of the political stance of a Nonconformist of the later nineteenth century is that of Charles Haddon Spurgeon, the great Baptist pastor of the Metropolitan Tabernacle in south London. Spurgeon is remembered for his powerful sermons, but he had few inhibitions about expressing his political views. At the 1880 general election he issued an address to the local electors. 'Are we to go on slaughtering and invading in order to obtain a scientific frontier and feeble neighbours?' he asked. 'Shall all great questions of reform and progress be utterly neglected for years? ... Shall the struggle for religious equality be protracted and embittered? Shall our National Debt be increased?'[3] The first question was a protest against the recent imperialistic ventures of the Conservative government. The second called for measures of change that would benefit the common people. Religious equality, the subject of the third question, was the distinctive aim of Nonconformists, and the reduction of the national debt, the subject of the fourth, would mean a decrease in public spending. Peace, reform, religious equality and retrenchment – these were the core of Spurgeon's politics. He had also denounced American slavery, consequently supporting the North during the Civil War; he supported measures to ensure the observance of the Sabbath; and he defended the place of the Bible in the schools created by the 1870 act. Like Chamberlain, Spurgeon found Gladstone's proposal of Irish Home Rule distasteful. It would entail, he believed, a surrender of the Protestants of Ireland to repression by the eighty per cent of the population who were Roman Catholics. Although diverging from Liberalism on the Irish question during his later years, Spurgeon reaffirmed his personal esteem for Gladstone. The preacher embodied much of the political spirit of Nonconformity in the high Victorian years.

Gladstonian Liberalism made a particular impact on Wales. There some eighty per cent of the population had a loyalty to chapel rather than church in the later nineteenth century. There was even a denomination, the Calvinistic Methodists, which hardly gathered any support outside Wales and yet, inside Wales, enjoyed the support of more attenders than Anglicanism. Most Welsh Nonconformists resented the continued status of Anglicanism, an 'alien church', as the established form of religion in the Principality, but only in the 1860s did they begin to show it in their voting patterns. The Liberation Society, realizing that the Welsh formed an untapped reservoir of support for religious equality, sent an army of agents into Wales to rouse the people in support of the anti-establishment cause. The result was the transformation at the 1868 election of an overwhelming Conservative majority in Wales into a preponderance of Liberal MPs. Although only three MPs, including Henry Richard, were Nonconformists, the election was remembered as a turning point in the political history of the nation. Wales became a hotbed of Liberalism with a radical edge. Thus David Lloyd George, who was, during the First World War, to become Prime Minister of the United Kingdom, entered parliament in 1890 as a politician urging greater recognition for the national identity of Wales. The kernel of this radicalism long remained the campaign for disestablishment, which turned into the supreme national question in Wales. So powerful was its clamour that, despite stiff resistance from the Church of England, Welsh disestablishment was carried in 1914 and, though its implementation was deferred because of the First World War, it was put into practice in 1920. Wales became the only part of Britain to enjoy full religious equality.

The cause that, apart from disestablishment, came to be seen as most typical of Nonconformity was temperance reform. The temperance movement had begun in the 1830s as a campaign for self-improvement among artisans and had soon turned to the advocacy of total abstinence from all alcoholic drinks. At first Nonconformists had often looked askance on what seemed a rival enterprise proposing teetotalism as an alternative to the gospel, but gradually, beginning with the Primitive Methodists, they began to recommend taking the pledge to avoid strong drink themselves. By the 1860s many chapels ran Bands of Hope, evening meetings designed to alert children to the evils of fermented beverages. Their efforts concentrated on moral suasion, urging people to give up the bottle. From 1853, however, there existed a pressure group called the United Kingdom Alliance which campaigned to prohibit the sale or manufacture of alcohol, and pressure mounted for the government to tackle the problem of excessive consumption. Temperance increasingly became a political issue. In 1872 Gladstone's Liberal government carried a bill enforcing licensing hours for the first time. The chapels gave it their support and steadily thereafter they became committed to the battle against the bottle. In 1879 only a minority of Congregational ministers were total abstainers, but by 1904 about five-sixths were. Nonconformists often took local action, pressing corporation licensing committees to decrease the number of public houses permitted in their areas. In national politics their aim was the local veto, the right of local authorities to ban alcohol altogether. Nonconformists were delighted that measures to restrict the consumption of alcohol were proposed by Liberal governments in 1893, 1895 and 1908, but frustrated when the House of Lords, dominated by Conservatives, threw out the measures. Although many Anglicans in these years shared a desire for temperance reform, it became a hallmark of popular Nonconformist politics.

So did a concern for what was called social purity, the defence of Christian sexual standards. In the middle years of the nineteenth century churches of all types undertook a good deal of rescue work for prostitutes. Women who were exploited for sexual favours were welcomed to meetings where they would be urged to accept help to give up their way of life. In the 1860s policy towards prostitution entered national politics. A series of Contagious Diseases Acts[4] was passed providing that prostitutes living near military or naval establishments should be regularly inspected to ensure they were free from venereal disease. The women were often treated poorly, their male clients were tacitly condoned and the state seemed to be endorsing the legitimacy of sexual immorality. Accordingly a campaign began in 1869 to have the acts repealed. Its most prominent figure was Josephine Butler, the wife of an Anglican clergyman and schoolmaster, but it soon gathered solid Nonconformist support. The Wesleyans, for long the section of Nonconformity least likely to take up political action, formed a society exclusively to demand repeal. Under pressure from public opinion, parliament suspended the acts in 1883. Social purity became a priority for Nonconformists. They insisted on the enforcement of the new age of consent, they demanded prosecution for disseminating indecent literature and they called for any politicians found guilty of sexual misdemeanours to be excluded from political life. In 1890 their pressure helped ensure that Charles Stuart Parnell, the leader of the Irish party that was in alliance with the Liberals for the sake of obtaining Home Rule, should leave his post on the grounds of adultery. A Wesleyan minister writing to *The Times* declared that nothing less than Parnell's immediate retirement would satisfy 'the Nonconformist conscience'. The phrase that labelled the Nonconformist sense of responsibility for public affairs was coined in the campaign for social purity.

Many other issues preoccupied Nonconformists in the quarter-century before the First World War, the era when their conscience had to be a major factor in the calculations of politicians. In 1883 the Secretary of the London Congregational Union, Andrew Mearns, published a booklet entitled *The Bitter Cry of Outcast London*. It was primarily an appeal for increased evangelistic effort in the capital, but it pointed out the appalling overcrowding suffered by many of the inhabitants, especially in the East End. The cramped housing conditions, he contended, made the sexual abuse of children virtually unavoidable. The revelation of sexual immorality roused a storm of indignation led by Nonconformists; that led to a Royal Commission on Housing; and the result was a national attempt to address the problem of urban accommodation. In 1889 a strike in the London docks, then the nation's chief avenue of international trade, stirred church leaders to try to mediate between employers and workers. Because Nonconformists found themselves upstaged by Cardinal Manning, the Roman Catholic leader in England and Wales, some of them resolved to try to settle industrial disputes. Up until 1892, when the Congregational Union held a session on 'The Church and Labour Problems', redressing the ills of capitalist society seemed a pressing Christian duty. Neither housing nor industrial questions, however, became permanent crusading issues for the mass of Nonconformists. They appeared too complicated for simple moral analysis. A further issue, on the other hand, which did occupy a long-term place in Nonconformist political attitudes, was gambling. Here was an area, like temperance and social purity, in which reprehensible behaviour could readily be identified. Wasting money for the sake of personal gain seemed categorically wrong. From 1890, when an Anti-Gambling League was set up, Nonconformists regularly campaigned locally and nationally for tight restrictions on various forms of betting. Social policies became popular when they could be seen as moral.

Some prominent Nonconformists, however, took their analysis to greater depth. Hugh Price Hughes, from 1885 the founding editor of *The Methodist Times* and from 1887 first superintendent of the Wesleyan West London Mission, was a pioneer of thinking about social problems from a Christian perspective. His journalistic skills had been honed as the editor of the magazine of the Wesleyan society seeking repeal of the Contagious Diseases Acts and ever afterwards he retained a capacity for the outspoken denunciation of wrong that was the hallmark of that movement. From 1881 to 1884, however, he had been stationed as a minister at Oxford, where he had fallen under the spell of the socially constructive Liberalism of T. H. Green while pursuing a London philosophy MA. He therefore combined passion with erudition. From his London pulpit he urged the reconstruction of society on a Christian basis. The key to understanding his thought is his firm attachment to the postmillennial hope that the gospel was steadily transforming the world into the kingdom of God. 'The day is coming', he announced, 'when justice and love and peace will reign with unchallenged supremacy in every land; and when men will literally do the will of God on earth as angels do it in heaven.' Hughes showed great optimism that evil could be eliminated if only Christian people stood together against it. The essence of what he called the 'Social Gospel' of Christ was the replacement of Egotism with Brotherliness.[5] He criticized a Christianity that was too individualistic, insisting in particular that greed must cease to govern social relations. He was capable of criticizing those who wanted merely to be saved from sin as selfish, and yet he did not abandon his Methodist heritage of preaching for conversions. Hughes remained an Evangelical while expounding his social message, bequeathing a legacy of combining gospel passion with social action that, despite his early death in 1902, was to leave a lasting mark on twentieth-century Methodism.

Another broad Evangelical was John Clifford, minister of Westbourne Park Baptist Church in west London. He belonged to the General Baptists who insisted that Christ died for all; he edited their magazine and helped them to steer them into full merger with the Baptist Union in 1891. Clifford took a succession of London University degrees during the early years of his London ministry in the 1860s, making him open to fresh currents in the intellectual world such as Darwinism. He could discern no gulf between religion and politics, so that by the 1890s he was happy to address political rallies on a Sunday. Political activity, in his view, was a Christian responsibility. Clifford drew inspiration from Oliver Cromwell, led the Nonconformist critique of the British part in the Boer War of 1899–1902 and campaigned against the Conservative Education Act of 1902 that made Nonconformists pay the local tax for schooling in the doctrines of the Anglican and Roman Catholic churches. He became famous for his advocacy of Passive Resistance, a refusal to pay the offensive local tax and a willingness to have his property seized by the courts as a result. In 1903 Clifford received the highest vote at the election for the executive of the National Liberal Federation, the Liberal Party's central organization. Yet he was willing to take steps unusual for a Liberal. He acted as president of the Christian Socialist League from 1894 to 1898. He also became a member of the Fabian Society, an organization which existed to promote greater state intervention in social problems and which helped to found the Labour

Party. Clifford even wrote two tracts on behalf of the Fabians, *Socialism and the Teaching of Christ* (1897) and *Socialism and the Churches* (1908). This commitment to collective action on behalf of the weaker members of society was an expression of what he, like Hugh Price Hughes, called the 'Social Gospel'. While never wavering from his belief that the gospel challenged individuals, Clifford added the conviction that it also had the potential to transform society.

The spread of this opinion was one of the effects of the period of the Nonconformist Conscience. Previously Nonconformists had generally relied on voluntary action, believing that people need to be helped in person. The temperance movement, however, had induced many to reconsider. Its members continued to accept, as it was often said, that it is impossible to make people moral by act of parliament, but they realized that legislation limiting access to strong drink could make it harder to be immoral. They began to believe that national and local authorities had a part to play in advancing public welfare. The power of the State could close down brothels and limit gambling. By supporting this action Nonconformists supposed that they were extending rather than restricting their idea of liberty. Perhaps only when people were rescued from temptations could they enjoy true freedom. To help them to realize their potential through better housing and industrial conditions might also enhance their freedom even though the agency was the State. Nonconformists increasingly supposed that collective action was a friend rather than a foe. The higher estimate of the potential of the State at home was paralleled by increasing sympathy for the exercise of State power abroad. During the 1890s, the decade when Clifford was turning to socialism, many Nonconformists were beginning to drop their earlier peace preferences in favour of supporting the use of British power for righteous purposes overseas. The residual slave trade could be suppressed, massacres of Christians by the Turks could be ended and good governance could be extended to the ends of the earth. Nonconformists had generally objected to Disraeli's zeal for empire, but now many of them shared in the outburst of popular jingoism that marked Queen Victoria's Diamond Jubilee. At the time of the Boer War Nonconformists were deeply divided between those who, like Clifford, saw the conflict as unjustified aggression and those who, on the contrary, believed it to be a righteous struggle. Over the next few years the proportion favouring the Liberal imperialists rather than the little Englanders increased. The effects of greater trust in the State were therefore two-sided: an inclination towards collectivism and an endorsement of imperialism.

A popular development of this period, acting as a vehicle for the new enthusiasms, was the emergence of the Free Church Council movement. During the 1890s Nonconformists expressed dissatisfaction with their normal label. To be a 'Nonconformist' sounded negative and they wanted to project a positive self-image. They began calling themselves 'Free Churchmen' instead. A Free Church Congress was held in Manchester in

1892 to consider how the various denominations could best co-operate in addressing social questions and, at least among some of the participants, to move towards reunion between the churches. In its wake local councils sprang up spontaneously over much of England and Wales. Their objects varied. Social work and interdenominational co-operation were normal aims, but evangelistic work and religious equality efforts were also common. The education controversy from 1902 onwards pushed the councils further towards politics. Only by means of concerted action, Free Churchmen believed, could they hope to ensure that the Liberal Party won the next election and so reversed the legislation that discriminated against them. The National Council of the Evangelical Free Churches turned into an electoral machine, negotiating with the Liberal chief whip and putting up candidates at the 1906 general election. Fuelled by Free Church fervour, the Liberals won their greatest ever victory at the polls. More members of the Free Churches – as many as 179 were definitely committed – sat in this parliament than in any since the Commonwealth. Yet the triumph was largely illusory. The Free Churchmen in the Commons were divided on many questions and could muster only about a third of their nominal strength for strategy meetings. The House of Lords was able to reject successive attempted solutions to the education imbroglio and the act of 1902 remained on the statute book. The Free Church Councils proved able to put men into the House of Commons, but not to secure the legislation they desired.

One cause that eventually proved more successful was women's suffrage. The chapels, though served by an all-male ministry, almost always had more female than male members, often by a ratio of around two to one. Women held positions of responsibility, staffing the Sunday Schools, doing the bulk of the home visiting and raising much of the money. Among the Quakers and in the new Salvation Army women were actually allowed an equal place in ministry. So it is not surprising that some Nonconformists considered that there was no reason why women should continue to be excluded from the franchise. At least seven of the Unitarian MPs elected during the nineteenth century publicly backed the right of women to vote. The cause mobilized Congregationalists as much as the members of any other denomination. William Woodall, a Burslem potter, for example, was chairman of the Central Committee for Women's Suffrage, proposing an amendment to the 1884 Reform Act and introducing women's suffrage bills in three subsequent years. Dr Richard Pankhurst, the husband of Emmeline who became the leader of the Suffragettes, was another Congregational champion of votes for women. The Suffragette movement itself included women of character such as Jessie Yuille, the wife of the secretary of the Baptist Union of Scotland. She was typical of the Free Church participants in the campaign in believing that if women could play an equal part in politics, policies would be more family-friendly. As president of a branch of the British Women's Temperance Association, she particularly expected tighter restrictions on drinking to follow female enfranchisement. Women over the age of thirty who were local government electors or who were married to local government electors duly received the vote in 1918 at the hands of Lloyd George, a professed Baptist, and younger women gained it ten years later. The Free Church support, though by no means decisive, had been considerable.

The rise of the Labour Party in the early twentieth century owed even more to the Free Churches. Methodists were particularly strong in the trade union movement that was the seedbed of Labour. At least half the attenders at the conference of the Miners' Federation of Great Britain in 1890 were local preachers. When, in 1908, the miners' MPs in the Commons transferred from the Liberal to the Labour whip, it was a crucial step in shifting the party allegiance of many in the chapels. Early Labour branches in mining areas were often founded by Methodists. In Durham, for example, Primitive Methodists were to the fore. The chief architect of the Labour Party, James Keir Hardie, had once, in 1884, taken the lead in forming Cumnock Evangelical Union Church in Ayrshire, where he was agent for the county miners' union, and though he became critical of the churches he did not renounce allegiance to Christ as a social reformer. At the same time the growth of support for greater state involvement in social reform led naturally towards support for Labour, though a further move into outright socialism could mean, as it often did in South Wales, a renunciation of previous chapel attendance. The ideology of the early Labour Party, however, was often far from dogmatic. The party was overwhelmingly concerned with the bread-and-butter issues of the home and workplace, so that it was easy for Free Church voters to change their partisan allegiance without altering their political outlook. The postmillennial dimension of the theology purveyed in most of the chapels, giving rise to confidence in better times to come, chimed in closely with the hopes of the Labour Party for an improvement in the lot of the working people. The ethical socialism of early Labour, in fact, was close to the altruism that was preached as Christian duty from many a Methodist pulpit. So it was easy for erstwhile Liberals to slide almost imperceptibly into the nascent Labour Party during the first two decades of the twentieth century.

Specific events exerted a similar effect. The decision of Lloyd George to enter the 1918 general election in alliance with his wartime Conservative coalition partners jolted many Free Church voters out of a lifetime's loyalty to the Liberal Party. At that election John Clifford, the veteran Baptist leader, chaired a Free Church rally in favour of the Labour programme. As many as 22 Free Churchmen were returned as Labour MPs in that year and from 1922 the bulk of the Free Church representatives in the Commons sat for Labour. In the interwar years the party drew enormous strength from its chapel roots. Nearly half the Labour MPs of the period and about a third of the members and officers of the party's national executive committee were at least chapel attenders. One of Labour's greatest figures in this period was a distinguished Wesleyan who always kept a portrait of Hugh Price Hughes above his desk. This was Arthur Henderson, secretary of the Labour Party from 1911 to 1933, Home Secretary in 1924 and Foreign Secretary in 1929–31. At local level Labour was even more reliant on Free Churchmen. The achievement of Peter Lee, a Primitive Methodist local preacher, in County Durham is a case in point. Serving first as chairman of the Labour group on the council from 1919 to 1933, he steered it into undertaking idealistic but practical measures for the welfare of the people. The boldest was the creation of a reservoir in a Pennine valley to supply fresh water to the crowded districts nearer the coast. Lee's work was so valued that a post-war new town, Peterlee, was named in his honour.

At the same time alignment with Conservatism became much more of an option for Free Church voters than in the past. There had been a handful of unusual Nonconformists in the nineteenth century who had been Conservatives. One was Edward Ball, the Congregational MP for Cambridgeshire between 1852 and 1863, a farmer who saw the Conservatives as the natural protectors of the agricultural interest. The number of non-Liberals had been increased by the divergence in 1886 of Joseph Chamberlain's Liberal Unionists from Liberalism, insisting on the paramount need to defend the union between Britain and Ireland. Over subsequent years there was an active Nonconformist Unionist Association co-ordinated by the Wesleyan lock and safe manufacturer George Chubb which trumpeted the message that Nonconformists need not vote Liberal. In the 1906 parliament there were 14 Free Churchmen who sat as Unionists. The rise of Labour, however, troubled many of the more prosperous members of the chapels. They feared that socialism of a more full-blooded kind would lead to heavier taxes, threats to property and even revolution. Because of Lloyd George's electoral alliance with the Conservatives in 1918, many of these well-to-do Liberals found themselves voting for Conservative candidates and never lost the habit. In 1929 it is symbolic that Stanley Baldwin, the Conservative Prime Minister, was the guest of honour at an official Baptist Union dinner, something unthinkable in a previous generation. In the 1930s the rally of many Liberals to the National government, dominated by Conservatives, reinforced its attractions for Free Churchmen. Although the number of Free Church MPs had greatly fallen since 1906, in 1935 as many as 10 out of the 65 who claimed a chapel allegiance were Conservatives. Many Free Church voters had drifted to the right as well as to the left.

Yet there was a persistent tendency for Free Church people to vote Liberal during the twentieth century. Free Church newspapers often continued to voice a preference for the Liberals at elections. In 1923, for instance, *The Baptist Times* endorsed the reunited Liberal Party under Lloyd George, extravagantly claiming that his speeches in the campaign had outshone Gladstone's greatest oratorical triumphs. In rural areas there was little inter-war growth of Labour, and so the choice was still between the

Conservatives and the Liberals. In much of the West Country, for example, the Free Church–Liberal bond persisted. It was stoutly championed by Isaac Foot, a tireless Plymouth solicitor and eloquent Wesleyan local preacher who secured Bodmin for the Liberals in 1922, 1929 and 1931. Foot maintained the traditions of a former age, founding a Cromwell Association to perpetuate the union of religious and political values he championed. In the wake of the Second World War, however, when the Liberals in the Commons were reduced to a rump of six, Arthur Porritt, a Congregational journalist who could remember every general election since 1880, lamented the complete eclipse of the party. There was nevertheless a Liberal predisposition among Free Church folk that survived even that debacle. In particular middle-class Free Church voters remained far less likely to be Conservative and far more likely to be Liberal than their neighbours of other religious persuasions. Liberal leaders continued to appeal for Free Church support on the basis less of their current policies than of the historic affinities between Liberalism and Nonconformity. Individuals from the chapels continued to stand as Liberal candidates. Some such as Alan Beith, MP for Berwick-upon-Tweed from 1973, were keenly conscious of their Free Church heritage. Beith was a man who did see a natural fit between his Methodist values and Liberal politics. Although the link was for many a matter of history, for a few it remained vital.

Although members of the Free Churches were much more politically divided than in the past, certain causes continued to drive them into politics. The quest for peace was prominent among these issues. After the First World War, when hopes of world peace rested on the League of Nations, many chapels formed branches of the League of Nations Union. Divisions gradually emerged between those who, like the Quakers, held that war was an absolute wrong in which Christians should never engage and those who believed that, though an appalling calamity, the use of force was an essential reserve power in international affairs. This tension between between pure pacifists and conditional pacifists was acutely felt in the Free Church denominations during the 1930s as some declared that the outlawing of war was the only way to avoid another bloodbath like the First World War and others warned that the power-mad dictators of the continent could be contained only by being prepared to resist them. The Methodist Peace Fellowship, committed to the pacifist position, had enrolled as many as 5,000 members by the spring of 1940, many since the outbreak of war. Yet the great majority of Methodists believed the struggle against Hitler was justified. As the Cold War emerged in later years, there was again vigorous debate between the sections of opinion holding that either Communism or nuclear destruction was the greater threat. Agitation against Britain's independent nuclear deterrent was strong in the 1950s and again in the 1980s, but did not command a majority in any denomination until in 1983 the United Reformed Church adopted a resolution urging that Britain should renounce the use of the bomb unilaterally. By that time, however, it was becoming more common for debaters to consider such questions in terms of just war theory, a style of analysis previously confined to the Roman Catholic and Anglican churches. That theory specifically rejected pacifism in the name of realism about the conditions of a fallen world. Just as the Free Churches were far less united than in the past about their party preferences, so they had no common mind on questions of peace and war.

On social issues there was similar shared ground about diagnosis without any certainty about prescriptions. Free Churchmen, with the Congregational theologian Alfred Garvie at their head, joined Anglicans in the Conference on Politics, Economics and Citizenship (COPEC) in 1924 to thrash out Christian views, but there was little agreement on matters of policy beyond broad generalizations. In 1926, when the General Strike coincided with the Baptist Union assembly, a group of ministers who tried to put together a Christian solution abandoned the task as fruitless. The scourge of unemployment in the 1930s aroused deep sympathy and many local relief initiatives, but the churches normally did not feel they possessed the competence to propose specific remedies. Occasionally preachers would address such matters from the pulpit, one of the most inspiring being Ingli James, minister of Queen's Road Baptist Church, Coventry. The Methodists, deeply influenced by their Labour contingent, came closest to formulating policies on a variety of social questions. In 1959 the Methodist Church issued a compendium of its conference resolutions on a variety of questions. Their most eloquent spokesman on such matters was Donald Soper, long Superintendent of the West London Mission that Hugh Price Hughes had established. Soper was known as an outdoor speaker, famously dealing adroitly with hecklers at Speakers' Corner in Hyde Park. Alongside a commitment to pacifism, he developed a powerful critique of capitalism as a system based on greed. He acted as the conscience of the Labour movement, recalling his party colleagues to points of socialist principle, and in 1965 was created a peer so that the House of Lords became his soap-box. He also lent his support to various causes, serving, for example, as president of Shelter, the national campaign for the homeless. Soper was the leading Christian socialist of his generation.

Soper, like most Free Church people of the period, remained committed to the temperance cause. The campaign against drink was stronger among them in the earlier twentieth than in the later nineteenth century. In 1929 an election article in *The Baptist Times* gave as its sole reason for recommending readers to vote Liberal the fact that the party alone had a temperance plank in its programme. Four years later the repeal of the prohibition of the manufacture or sale of alcohol in the United States came as a cruel blow to hopes of enacting a similar policy in Britain, but the United Kingdom Alliance, led by the Baptist layman Robert Wilson Black, continued to campaign for restrictions on the sale of drink. In the second half of the century teetotalism, and with it pressure for limitations on alcohol, slowly faded away. Another traditional Free Church cause, the defence of Sunday, also enjoyed continuing support for many years. A Nonconformist-influenced newspaper in Wales memorably commented in 1939, when Welsh nationalists set fire to the Lleyn bombing school, that bombing ought not to take place on Sunday. As late as 1985–86 Free Church people joined other churches and trade unionists in the Keep Sunday Special campaign against the deregulation of shop opening hours, gathering sufficient backbench Conservative support to defeat Mrs Thatcher's government at the height of her popularity. But after deregulation was carried, remaining sabbatarian inhibitions in the mainstream Free Churches disappeared almost entirely. A third issue that reflected the older convictions also remained on the agenda long into the twentieth century. In 1953, as President of the Methodist Conference, Soper caused a stir by denouncing the devotion of the royal family to horse racing since the sport encouraged gambling. Later in the same decade, in 1957, there was strong opposition from the Free Churches to the introduction of Premium Bonds. The issues that had galvanized the Nonconformist conscience at the opening of the twentieth century still found expression many years later.

The moral landscape of Britain was remoulded by a cultural earthquake in the 1960s. The received norms of social life were challenged by new ways, some of them favoured by authority and others thrown up by the vibrant counter-culture. In some respects Free Church opinion endorsed change. In 1961, for example, the Methodist Church was the first religious body to call for the decriminalization of homosexual acts between consenting adults in private. It was a sensitive matter because four years earlier the Conservative government had refused to implement the Wolfenden Report that made this recommendation on the grounds that it was ahead of public opinion. The Methodists also supported the relaxation of the law against abortion in 1967 and the Free Churches, unlike the Church of England, generally acquiesced in the liberalization of the grounds for divorce two years later. Yet there was a growing feeling that the Western world was becoming less congruent with Christian values. A backlash against the permissive society attracted church people of all persuasions, but especially the most Evangelical. In 1971 there was a semi-spontaneous Festival of Light, largely Evangelical in inspiration, that naturally appealed most to the Baptists, the Free Church denomination with the largest Evangelical constituency. The continuing campaigns of CARE, chiefly designed to resist change on moral questions in the public sphere, drew backers outside the Church of England mainly from the same quarter. At the same time, however, the more and less Evangelically inclined were united in wanting to press assistance to the third world as a Christian cause. The relief of world poverty became the chief overseas issue agitating all Free Church bodies. They were delighted when, as one of the first acts of New Labour in power in 1997, a cabinet minister was assigned to international development and when, soon afterwards, the churches' Jubilee Campaign persuaded the government to take up the cancellation of third world debt in the international arena. The Free Church voice was still being heard even when it was part of a wider chorus.

The story of the Free Churches' engagement with popular politics is therefore an account of rise and fall. In the early nineteenth century Dissenters were the objects of discrimination and politically marginal except in a few specific places. They began to seek redress of their grievances from their patrons the Whigs, very slowly receiving concessions but aspiring to do no less than disestablish the Church of England. In broader public affairs they were inclined to pursue a common programme of retrenchment, free trade, peace and reform. They became the shock troops of Liberalism, heroizing Gladstone and applauding his policies. The peak of political involvement came in the era of the Nonconformist conscience around the opening of the twentieth century, when temperance, social purity and anti-gambling were among the key issues. Hugh Price Hughes and John Clifford, backed by active Free Church Councils, spoke out as prophets of righteousness. Free Church people promoted women's suffrage and, believing the state should do more for public welfare, turned in increasing numbers to the emergent Labour Party. Others adopted Conservatism or else retained their Liberalism and so the Free Churches became politically divided. Subsequently Free Church people normally supported peace and social welfare but disagreed among themselves on specific policies. They retained a fondness for their traditional issues but found responding to moral change in the late twentieth century a demanding task. Only on international development was there a common voice that was heeded. The high degree of unanimity in the nineteenth century was largely replaced by fragmentation in the twentieth. That diminishing political homogeneity, together with falling numbers in the later twentieth century, goes a long way towards explaining the decline in the role of the Free Churches in popular politics.

4

Providers and Protagonists in the Nation's Education

Stephen Orchard

One of the unintended consequences of the Act of Uniformity of 1662 was to divert hundreds of Nonconformist ministers into what we would now call 'teaching'. They did this in various ways. There was nothing corresponding to a modern system of schooling. Rich landowners educated their children at home. So some ejected ministers supplied private tuition in those families who were sympathetic to their cause. The better-off trades people and farmers might send their boys to a grammar school. Posts in grammar schools were open only to conforming clergy. When Nonconformists opened private schools in competition with them the response was often a prosecution. After schooling the pupils of such Nonconformists might progress to a Dissenting Academy, which was a substitute form of higher education for those who would not conform. It was essential to be a communicant member of the Church of England in order even to attend Oxford or to graduate at Cambridge. The alternative was to go to a Scottish university, since the legislation covered only England and Wales. The early Dissenting Academies were on a domestic scale; a few pupils boarded with a minister and followed a course of learning similar to that of the universities, based on the Latin and Greek classics and theology. All this education was for the select few. Notions of general education in the Nonconformist communities were no different from the population at large. Ordinary people might be expected to know their catechism and memorize Psalms and Bible stories; they should have some grasp of arithmetic to enable them to buy and sell goods; but universal literacy and numeracy was thought neither possible nor desirable.

All this changed during the eighteenth century. Philosophical ideas about human nature and human rights took a new turn during the Enlightenment. The growth of population, marching with the rise of mass manufacture, created new educational challenges, beyond the capacity of traditional methods to meet. The Scottish Presbyterian, Adam Smith, in his all-encompassing *Wealth of Nations*, was one of those arguing the case for universal education.[1] It was, he maintained, in the interests of the State to subsidize schools. Smith had grown up with a system of parish schools across Scotland, so he believed it was possible to offer education on a wider basis. He had ideas for the curriculum. Obviously, from his point of view, children needed basic literacy and numeracy. If one added to this knowledge of geometry and mechanics it would make people more serviceable to the needs of employers. He had a citizenship agenda also. Cultivating patriotism and discipline would make people more able to serve in the militia and thus reduce the need for a large standing army. It is instructive to see a tidy mind, like Smith's, struggling to sustain his social and economic analysis in areas where he knows inconsistency beckons. On the one hand he believed in market solutions, a lesson his twentieth-century disciples drank in with enthusiasm. On the other hand, he recognized that private and charitable systems were inadequate to meet the huge demands of a universal system of education.

However, the first recognizable moves towards a general system of education began in voluntary and charitable ways at the end of the eighteenth century. First popularized by Robert Raikes in his Gloucester newspaper, the Sunday School movement grew rapidly in the 1780s and 90s. In 1798, a considered assessment was made by an unknown writer in the *Evangelical Magazine*, widely read among those we would now call Congregationalists.[2] It recognized that not all Sunday Schools had been successful, but called for new commitments to create them and offered helpful advice on how to go about it. The first step was to raise subscriptions or arrange for the preaching of Charity Sermons. There is no hint that public money raised from parish rates or general taxation should be used for schools. The aim should be ambitious, admitting as many poor children as possible, aged five and upwards. It was a missionary opportunity as well as an educational enterprise. Parents of the children could be given tracts and introduced to religious ideas. Boys and girls should be taught separately and young people kept apart from children. Teachers should be employed in a ratio of one to fifteen children, though more children could be managed with voluntary help. The article does not anticipate the growth of specialist buildings for Sunday School work. It talks about using houses or vestries, preferably near a place of worship. Although it would be good to use an entirely voluntary teaching force, the inevitability of needing to employ some teachers was recognized and a rate of pay at two shillings a day recommended. Middle-class members of churches might not be willing to be teachers but they could have a role as visitors, in the official sense of that term. They would not be concerned with the routines of learning letters and numbers, but with the spiritual and moral tone of the school. The visitors could also learn from the good practice in Nottingham Sunday Schools and follow up on absentees.

The advice never lost sight of the fact that this was school on Sunday. Some kind of devotional activity should begin the day and the lessons go on until the time of public worship. The etiquette of worship would have to be taught to children who were unfamiliar with church services. The teachers should ensure the children kept their eyes closed for the prayers but wide open and fixed on the minister for the sermon. Their ears would also need to be open because during the afternoon classes they could be tested on whether they remembered the text. As well as truants the children who were sick should be visited, as was the practice in Stockport. 'But how encouraging to a teacher to see one of his pupils dying happy in the love of God, and to hear him breathe out his last prayer for his benefactors.'[3] By the standards of the time this was not a severe regime. The children were not to be beaten, since it was reckoned that such punishment was unsuited to the Lord's Day. Much better to give rewards, including money and clothing, as a means of regulating discipline. The benefits of Sunday Schools to the whole community were obvious. 'Peace and quietness is enjoyed in many a parish, where noise, riot and mischief before prevailed. Many thousands have already learned to read the Scriptures, who would otherwise have remained in heathen darkness.'[4] It is interesting to see that keeping the peace was set as a goal before that of religious conversion which was not seen as the chief aim of Sunday Schools. Once the nineteenth-century conventions have been stripped out the article is couched in the terms in which churches today advocate community ministries or social service projects as part of the Church's mission.

Sunday Schools were not the preserve of any one denomination. However, the old Dissenting congregations and Methodists were growing in strength and they became prominent in the development of the movement. All this was charitable work and it was obvious to educational reformers that it could only meet part of the need. True, Sunday Schools did not interfere with a child's work on the other six days of the week. But factory work, even when it was dignified with the title of apprenticeship, could equally well be said to interfere with a child's capacity to learn a greater range of useful skills. Some religious people considered that learning numeracy and literacy on Sundays contravened the keeping of the Sabbath and wished to see teaching on other days. Whatever the motive, there was enthusiasm for extending popular education beyond anything the Sunday Schools could offer. But even with the help of volunteers, where were the teachers to be found if teaching was to be daily and with an optimum class size of fifteen?

As the eighteenth century closed the so-called 'Madras system' of the Anglican, Dr Andrew Bell, and the monitorial system of the Quaker, Joseph Lancaster (actually similar in their methodology), offered a cheap and efficient way of meeting the need for mass elementary education. From Bell we may trace the National Society, a body exclusive to the Church of England, and from Lancaster the British and Foreign School Society (BFSS), a non-denominational body, bringing together Low Church Anglicans, Dissenters and Methodists, together with some free-thinkers. In their original philosophy these were both voluntary societies, raising funds by subscription. Like Sunday Schools they relied on local groups to raise money and set up management systems, while the national bodies represented their interests and provided resources. The National Society was always larger and better funded than the BFSS. Children in National Schools would learn the church catechism and their religious education would be within an Anglican frame of reference. In BFSS schools the pursuit of non-denominational education, avoiding distinctive doctrinal formularies, would lead to a Bible-dominated religious education.

The BFSS was formed to support the work of Joseph Lancaster, who had begun a school for poor children in Southwark. What he did was effectively to bring mass-production methods into education. He taught up to one hundred children in a large schoolroom and believed with a bigger room he could teach more. The children were arranged in rows, with the least able at the front. At the sides of the room were various charts to assist learning, in the absence of text books. The more able pupils were appointed monitors. They would lead their row of pupils to one of the learning points and take them through the prepared format for that activity, such as spelling. Above the pupils, in nets slung from the ceiling, were various cheap toys which were offered as rewards to the most successful. The monitors wore silver badges to mark them out. The front-row pupils learnt to trace their letters in a long, narrow and shallow box of sand which ran in front of their bench. It was a simple matter to smooth this out with a block of wood to start a new lesson. Once the letters were learnt then pupils moved back a row to learn simple spelling and reading. Arithmetic was introduced once reading had been established. It was rote learning, carried out in silence. Lancaster had the charisma to carry off this teaching *tour de force*. His schoolroom became one of the sights of London, visited by assorted philanthropists and royalty. He was given money to develop and spread his ideas.

Educational innovators are not necessarily good managers of resources. Lancaster had grand ideas and grand expenditure to match. That was why, as he lurched from one financial crisis to another, his friends decided to form a Society to support his work. The first minutes of the very first meeting of the Society, on 22 January 1808, is worth quoting in full.

At a meeting held at Mr. William Corston's, No 30, Ludgate Street. Present: Messrs William Corston, Joseph Fox, and Joseph Lancaster. It was unanimously resolved, 'that, with reliance upon the blessing of Lord God Almighty, and with a single eye to His glory, and with a view to benefit the British Empire, the persons present do constitute themselves a society for the purpose of affording education, procuring employment, and, as far as possible, to furnish clothing to the children of the poorer subjects of King George III; and also to diffuse the present providential discovery of the vaccine inoculation, in order that at the same time they may be instrumental in the hands of Providence to preserve life from loathsome disease, and also, by furnishing objects for the exercise of industry, to render life useful.

That in order to prevent any impediment to the prosecution of this grand design, the persons present do constitute themselves managers of this society, to plan, prepare and direct all its future operations; and that no business shall be brought before any meeting of subscribers who may probably come forward in aid of this society but what has been recommended by this committee of managers.'

Corston was appointed treasurer and Fox secretary. Behind the noble objects lay the practical necessity for Corston and Fox to underwrite Lancaster's considerable debts, in order that the work might carry on. In fact, over the next seven years the debt doubled as the work expanded. Corston was a City figure, the owner of a large hat-making business, and was the person who introduced Lancaster to the royal family, to whom he was a supplier. Fox was a surgeon-dentist at Guy's Hospital, with capital of his own, which he brought into the Society, along with his enthusiasm for vaccination.[5] Corston was a Moravian and Fox a Baptist. However, it was with the advent of two wealthy Quakers in July of 1808 that the new Society began to have hopes of survival and growth. William Allen of Plough Court was a manufacturing chemist and Joseph Foster, married to a Lloyd, a prominent banker. William Allen was an old friend of Fox and took over from Corston as Treasurer.

In Allen the Society had acquired one of the most dynamic philanthropists of the early nineteenth century. He brought to the Society the same entrepreneurial flair he brought to his business. His personal connections and travels were exploited to further the Society's ends. Unlike some other parts of Europe the English did not move quickly to adopt public funding for education or establish a government department to supervise it. The role of the Society was to provide advice to local committees of supporters trying to set up schools on the Lancastrian system, often known as British Schools. They also took forward Lancaster's work at Southwark in training monitors and teachers. Their Borough Road College became a national institution and the pattern for further colleges run by the Society. Lancaster became increasingly independent of the Society, which developed the committee structures and bureaucracy required by all nineteenth-century voluntary enterprises, but which are inimical to the genius of a person like him.

Consider an example of how British schools were founded in the nineteenth century. An advertisement in the *Derby Mercury* for 15 November 1810 announced, under the heading, 'Royal British System of Education', that:

> Joseph Lancaster, Inventor and Superintendant [sic] of the Plan for Educating poor Children, under the patronage of the King, Queen and Royal Family, Intends to deliver a LECTURE on his NEW AND ORIGINAL SYSTEM OF EDUCATION at the OLD ASSEMBLY ROOM, FULL STREET, DERBY, On the Evening of the day called Friday, Sixteenth of the Eleventh Month (November), 1810 at 6 o'clock. The object of this lecture is publicly to explain the manner in which one Master may govern and teach One Thousand Children, with as much facility as Twenty, in Half the usual Time, and at one-Third the common Expence. The principle of Order, the method whereby One Book will serve for Five Hundred or One Thousand Children, and the manner in which Five Hundred Scholars may spell at the same instant of time, will be elucidated by the exhibition of a number of Drawings representing the Interior of a large School on this Plan. *Tickets to be had at Mr. Drewry's, Bookseller, Derby.* Front seat 2s 6d – back seats 1s 6d.

The price of tickets indicates that this was not a lecture the poor themselves were expected to attend but something for the middle classes. The description of the date illustrates Lancaster's Quaker sympathies. Writing to Joseph Allen from Nottingham on the 18 November, Lancaster says that about 150 people attended, notably the Strutt family, 'who are almost lords of the town'. The Strutts were prosperous mill owners, a Unitarian family, and leaders of the Derby Whig party on behalf of the Dukes of Devonshire. Sir Robert Wilmot, another local magnate, was also present. Joseph Strutt was then busy raising funds for the new Derby Infirmary, but assured Lancaster that the school would be his next project. George Strutt received Lancaster at his house in Belper on 1 December. Lancaster gave another lecture to 200 people there before pressing on to Leeds. The Strutts were as good as their word and former industrial premises in Full Street were secured for a boys' schoolroom in Derby in 1812. When the school opened in 1813 pupils were required to attend a local church or Sunday School as a condition of admission. By 1815 there were 234 boys on the roll, of whom 95 were from the Church of England.[6]

One of the pupils in 1822 was a man called Richard Tennant,[7] whose family moved to Derby from Mansfield. The BFSS archives contain a copy of some memories he jotted down on both sides of a newspaper wrapper addressed to him at his house at Ipstones, near Cheadle, circa mid 1880s. Richard refers to his famous older brother, James Tennant,[8] Professor of Mineralogy at King's College, London, a friend of Michael Faraday and Angela Burdett-Coutts.[9] Richard believed his brother paid his school fees.

Certainly James was later a promoter of technical education. Richard writes about being a monitor in the school and describes in detail the operation of Lancaster's sand tray built into the desks. A memorable moment of his school days was the visit of an Egyptian mummy, bought by the Strutts, which eventually found a home in Derby Museum. The Lancaster school moved in about 1824 to purpose-built premises in Orchard St, and schools for girls and infants were added. James Gawthorn, the long-serving Congregational minister in central Derby, spoke at a meeting for the school in 1818, subscribed to it every year and was appointed joint secretary in 1834. By this time the school had 360 boys on the roll, of whom 138 were connected with the Church of England. The school ran its own subscription library for the benefit of the boys. This being the nineteenth century, there was a separate Ladies Auxiliary, which raised funds to keep the school going. This pattern was repeated up and down the country, though BFSS schools were always more likely to be found in urban than in rural areas.

These voluntary methods brought education to only a fraction of the poor. There was a government grant to encourage voluntary school development in Ireland between 1814 and 1831, when a Board of Commissioners of National Education in Ireland was formed and took over the funding. After the parliamentary reform of 1832 the Whig government voted a £20,000 annual grant for the building of schoolhouses in England and Wales. This money was allocated *pro rata* to the school societies. In the first year £11,000 went to the National Society and £9,000 to the BFSS. The scheme was only for school buildings; a preference was given to urban areas; and the money could only be given where it had been established that voluntary effort was inadequate for the needs, although even then the government grant had to be matched at least pound for pound by the locals. The only politicians advocating state funding of education in general were the Radicals, a small group in Parliament, influenced by the utilitarian ideas of Jeremy Bentham. Some of these had supported Joseph Lancaster's original plans but were alienated from the BFSS by its religious emphasis.

Denominational rivalries and the ideological commitment to voluntarism led to a vigorous campaign against proposed educational reforms in 1843. Sir James Graham promoted a Factories Bill which regulated the conditions under which children worked in factories. Among the provisions it was proposed that children should not be eligible to work in factories unless they were also engaged in some form of schooling. The employer needed to hold a certificate for each child, vouching that this was the case. In order to supplement existing provision, District Schools, funded out of the Poor Rate, and controlled by trustees, would be created to provide suitable education and certification. This wholly admirable intention to improve children's lives was then caught in the denominational struggles which characterized the period. At a public meeting in Derby, summoned to rally opposition to the bill, James Gawthorn, the Congregational minister, spoke at length about the threats to civil liberty and religious freedom which it constituted. On the particular matter of certificates this is what he had to say.

No person under 13 years of age can work in any factory without a school certificate. Now, there are only five parties who can give a certificate: the masters of these District schools [the schools established by the Act], of schools provided by the owner or occupier of a factory, of National schools, of British schools, and of Roman Catholic schools. A private schoolmaster of the best character and the highest qualifications, and pre-eminently successful in instruction, cannot give a certificate. This will seriously injure, in many cases ruin an excellent man who has devoted his life to the instruction of the young. No certificate can be given from a parochial school. A pious clergyman and his flock, a Dissenting minister and his flock, a Methodist minister and his flock, may establish a school; the master may be of the first abilities, the instruction and order of the best description, but no certificate can be given from such schools, no child in any such school will be allowed to work in any factory; but from a Roman Catholic school a certificate may be sent! Mr Gell, Mr Macklin, Mr Abney, [local Anglicans] or any other clergyman, may have an excellent school, but no certificate shall be accepted from them; Dissenters, Methodists, or other Protestants may have excellent schools, but no certificate shall be received from them; nor can any child in any of these schools be allowed to earn a farthing in any factory. But from Mr Sing's [Roman Catholic] school a certificate shall be valid; the children in his school may work in factories. Why this partiality and preference to Popish schools? Protestants, I appeal to you, is this fair, is this right?[10]

At the heart of Gawthorn's objections was the fear that the new District schools would be controlled by the Church of England and that they would supplant the voluntary schools, even those of the BFSS, because they could command funds from the Poor Rate. His anxieties were echoed at hundreds of similar local meetings around the country and endorsed by national meetings of Dissenters. At a meeting of the Committee of the Congregational Union of England and Wales, held on Tuesday, 4 April 1843, the resolutions were unanimously adopted in opposition to the Bill and brought to the May Assembly. They deplored the built-in disadvantaging of Dissenters. For conscientious reasons no Dissenter could teach using the formularies of the Church of England, nor could they act as trustees for such schools, where they would be compelled to use 'that most erroneous formulary, the Church Catechism, in which the doctrine of sacramental religion and salvation is so plainly taught'. They would have to pay for such schools through local rates and then raise funds to support their own schools. Even then, such education would not form a legal qualification for factory employment. It was further alleged that the system would be controlled by clergy, who could not be historically shown to be friends of the education of the poor. At heart there was a resistance, not only to the Church of England, but to the principle of state compulsion in the matter of education. It was a classic anti-Establishment position.

As Friends of the Poor, especially of the Dissenting Poor – they object to the education of their children being made a matter of the stringent compulsion enforced by this law, – as in many cases there will be no choice of schools for their children in the power of parents, – in all cases there will be heavy penalties on parents or non-attendance of their children, – a school certificate will be made a legal qualification for factory employment, – and, in the government schools, the children of Dissenters will be compelled to learn the Church Catechism, which they cannot recite with truth, or to be registered and separated as Dissenters in the view and scorn of all the school, and of the hostile clerical trustees.[11]

Edward Baines of Leeds spoke powerfully at the Congregational Union Assembly of 1843 in support of these arguments. It was many years later, as a member of parliament, that he conceded that universal primary education was beyond the scope of voluntary provision. In 1843 his first instinct was to challenge Congregationalists to follow the lead of Wesleyan Methodism and make school provision a priority. It took John Angell James, of Carrs Lane, Birmingham, to remind the Assembly that in addition to providing local schools congregations would have to support the BFSS with subscriptions because its college, at Borough Road, Southwark, was needed to supply trained teachers and to promote good practice.

In any event, the strength of the protests led the government to abandon the educational clauses of the Bill. The Dissenting cause had been advanced but the need to protect children from exploitative employers was only partly met. The question of how the state can legislate to provide general education without coming into conflict with those religious communities who reserve to themselves the right to determine what is true remains to the present day. This ideological commitment to voluntarism and local control does not correspond to modern community work practice. Local middle-class committees did good to the poor without involving them in the planning and management of schools. On the other hand, local churches of all denominations provided the infrastructure on which local voluntary efforts were built.

Somewhat in the spirit of Joseph Lancaster, another man with an idea travelled around England in the 1830s calling together local meetings to promote public welfare. This was David Nasmith, a Scottish Congregationalist, influenced by the pastoral ministry of Thomas Chalmers in Glasgow who had promoted the welfare of the poor in his parish. Nasmith is credited with the formation of the London City Mission although, like Lancaster, he soon parted company with his creation on ideological grounds and relied on the support of rich friends to continue his work. The term 'city mission' is accurate to describe his interests, but only if interpreted in the very widest sense. Nasmith fired off ideas in all directions. While still in Glasgow he promoted young men's societies, which some see as a prototype of the YMCA. However, he wanted young men to band together for more than their own self-improvement. They were to concern themselves with infant schools, prison visiting, welfare of seamen, sabbatarianism, 'instruction of people of colour', sick visiting, relief distribution, temperance, and tract distribution.[12] In short, to address social problems that remain until today, though our terminology and methods of dealing with them have changed. In terms of education the most relevant part of Nasmith's agenda was that which lay beyond the formation of young men's societies, that is, the promotion of technical education on a part-time basis. He had first-hand experience of the Mechanics Institute founded in Glasgow in 1824. The spread of such institutes throughout Britain was driven partly by the needs of industry to raise the level of mechanical competence in the workforce and partly by the good intentions of church people who wished to offer the benefits of education, especially as an alternative to the public house.

Nasmith's broad-brush approach to promoting causes may be illustrated by his two-day visit to Derby, at an unspecified date soon after he left Glasgow in 1828. He addressed 1,200 Sabbath School children in the principal Congregational chapel on Brookside and also 100 mothers and young ladies on Monday morning at the same place. This was the chapel of James Gawthorn, supporter of the British and Foreign School Society. Nasmith addressed a Sunday evening service in another chapel and there met with 150 young men. On Monday evening he held a ministers' meeting with a Unitarian, an Episcopalian, two Independents, a Baptist, and two Methodists. As a result he reckoned to have formed a Town Mission, a Young Man's Society, a Maternal Society and a Young Ladies Society. However, so far as we know, Nasmith never revisited the town and in the absence of his papers we do not know if he even corresponded with these people again.[13]

Whether he was the originator or not, Derby soon had a Mechanics Institute, founded by the Strutts in 1828 and moving into its own grand building in 1832. For the middle classes themselves, the Athenaeum Rooms in Brookside, re-named Victoria St, were created, to display pictures and curiosities, including Strutt's Egyptian mummy, and provide a venue for lectures. Later philanthropists created the Museum, Art Gallery and Library, and the Technical College and College of Art on these foundations. In the modern era the local authority takes forward the museum and library services and central government funds a university and further education colleges, which began as voluntary spare-time self-improvement classes. However, the only hint of the churches' role in creating all these enterprises is the incorporation of the former diocesan teacher training college in Derby into the university. What is true of Derby is true of other towns and cities throughout the country.

Mechanics Institutes and public libraries supported a form of education characteristic of the nineteenth century above all others, that of autodidactic learning. Various people were celebrated for raising themselves by their own boot straps, perhaps none more than David Livingstone, the Scottish Congregationalist who became a national hero. Self-help was a celebrated virtue, peculiarly suited to the Free Church ethos. Many people were members of such churches precisely because they were not prepared to be guided by the established authorities but wished to learn for themselves and take their own decisions. The missionary linguists, who started from scratch to devise an orthography for a local language, were those in the church context who mirrored technical innovators like George Stephenson, who overcame the limits of their education. In chapels around the country people were challenged to extend their capacities and their horizons. They were not free of the class system but they were offered the means of social mobility by winning the approbation of their peers, who in the outside world might be their social betters.

As the nineteenth century went by the government grant to the school societies increased. The training of teachers also concerned government. Student bursaries were created, together with direct grants to teacher training colleges such as the BFSS's Borough Road. By the 1860s it was evident that the limits of the existing provision were being reached. Even determined voluntarists such as Edward Baines, now an MP and a member of a parliamentary committee of enquiry on education, reluctantly accepted that a new framework, underwritten by government money, was needed. A National Education League was formed in 1869 by the more radical Liberals, to promote 'A system that shall secure the education of every child in England and Wales'.[14] It was centred in Birmingham and its leaders included the Liberal politician Joseph Chamberlain, a Unitarian, and R. W. Dale, minister of Carrs Lane Congregational Church. The League wanted to see schools run by local authorities, supported by government grant and local rates, so that the pupils paid no fees, and unsectarian, which effectively meant that none of them were to be controlled by the Church of England. Critics said that the League wished to go further and secularize education altogether.

It fell to W. E. Forster, a member of Gladstone's Liberal government, in 1870, to promote a comprehensive Education Bill. The thrust of the Bill was to create local elected school boards to superintend the existing schools, drawing on public funds, and to provide new schools so that universal primary education would be available. The government's argument was that it needed to retain the existing denominational schools because it did not have the resources to create an entirely new system for all children. The school-leaving age was set at 13 but there was room for local option on compulsory attendance. During the passage of the Bill there were heated arguments on the subject of religious education. These were partly resolved by a 'conscience' clause, sponsored by William Cowper-Temple, which allowed for withdrawal from religious instruction.

The denominational rivalries which dominated the political arguments before the Bill was passed continued into the election of the new school boards. In some places the denominations negotiated the make-up of school boards in order to avoid the expense of an election, but also to secure their own positions. In other places elections were fought with denominations sponsoring particular candidates. Others stood as critics of the way religious arguments were dominating the creation of a universal system of primary education. In Derby there was an election, with six officially nominated candidates from the Church of England, three of whom were actually elected, along with two other Anglicans, two Wesleyans, a Roman Catholic, a Congregationalist, a Baptist and a Primitive Methodist. There were no members of the board without an identifiable denominational affiliation.[15]

The reality of establishing primary education for all the children of Derby soon overshadowed any denominational differences. The first problem which was identified was the absence of accurate statistics for the number of children of primary age in the town. It was then pointed out that some parents had already made schooling provision for their children and it was only the remaining children who needed new board schools to be provided. It was thought that the enumerators in the forthcoming census might be paid extra to identify the homes with children and then a system of visits could establish which of them needed school provision. Beyond this an even more fundamental problem became evident. Unless the borough could get all houses to display proper numbers it would make the work of visiting unduly challenging.[16]

The 1870 Education Act was resisted by some Free Church interests. They foresaw what would happen – the gradual replacement of inadequate voluntary schools by new board schools. The BFSS reluctantly moved from the promotion of voluntary schools to concentrate on its other interest, teacher training. Local BFSS schools held on religious trusts remained in being under the school boards until the Education Act of 1902, when most of them, though not all Methodist ones, were invested in the local authorities. In both 1870 and 1902 the religious provision for pupils was a matter of acute controversy.

On the positive side it may be said that the Free Church insistence on non-denominational worship and religious instruction paved the way for modern ideas of religious education. The politicians of the 1980s were happy to use the notion of 'other denominations' to incorporate world faiths into the curriculum. A larger question remains from the controversies of the nineteenth and early twentieth centuries. How can a local school, publicly funded, be representative of common values and social attitudes? The board schools after 1870 and council schools after 1902 were still run by the middle classes, whose children were in private education, on behalf of the poor. It cannot be said that they were community schools except in a geographical sense. It is true that at that time most teachers lived in the places where they taught. A large proportion of school children also attended Sunday Schools and met their teachers on church premises as well as at school. However, only the Church of England and the Roman Catholic Church, with a small minority of Wesleyans, could maintain the old direct link between the church and the school. From now on the Sunday School is a much more important community activity for Nonconformists. However, the days were gone when the Sunday School might be the only educational provision a child utilized. Sunday Schools were thus released to concentrate on religious and moral learning. They were also places where children found opportunity for cultural expression and sport. Cultural expression was particularly important in Wales, where it was a place in which the Welsh language was widely used and where classes for all ages were continued.

In his paper, 'Sport and the English Sunday School, 1869–1959', Hugh Macleod discusses the significance of sport in local Sunday Schools during that period.[17] He links the growing popularity of sport in this period with the need of Sunday Schools to address the problems they were finding in keeping young people over the age of 13 in membership. Children who had left school at 12 or 13 were not inclined to continue in Sunday School. Running football or cricket teams, or organizing boxing matches, was one way to keep their interest. Free Church Sunday Schools worked under the handicap of not wanting to play on Sundays, while a good number of Anglican Sunday Schools took a more relaxed view of the Sabbath. Nevertheless they participated in Sunday School leagues, from which international players might emerge. Len Hutton began to play cricket at Fulneck and famously said of the Moravian minister that he could remember him taking a fine catch but not a word of his sermons. Most churches regarded the engagement with sport as a necessary part of their mission in the local community; a few regarded it as compromising with worldly values and exposing church members to temptation.

The other response to the needs of young people was to recruit them into a Bible Class, as distinct from the Sunday School, though it might meet at the same time. Like the Sunday School these classes were largely lay led. The gender politics of the time kept young men and young women in separate organizations. The young men's Bible classes were more likely to have as their aim the development of people who could lead public prayer and preach; the young women were in preparation for Sunday School teaching or taking their place in the women's meetings which knitted and sewed for church funds. Arthur MacArthur[18] recalled how when he became minister at North Shields Presbyterian Church in 1950 there was still a Men's Bible Class with over fifty members. In the 1930s it had two or three hundred members, serving not only Christian education, but providing a means of sustaining spirits during the lean years of the economy. In Derby the Young Men's Discussion Class that started in the last years of James Gawthorn's ministry at the Brookside chapel blossomed as the nineteenth century closed into a Mutual Improvement Society, admitting women as well as men. In 1904 this further developed into a Literary and Debating Society. Such societies not only drew on local resources but were the windows through which members saw the wider world. In Derby famous Congregationalists such as Joseph Parker and R. J. Campbell lectured to the society, as did politicians and even E. T. Reed, the *Punch* cartoonist.

A high proportion of young children were involved in Sunday School throughout the late nineteenth and early twentieth centuries. A smaller number of young people would attend Bible classes. Although some church members were recruited from the children of Sunday School when they reached a mature age, this was always a minority. There are examples of churches opening branch Sunday Schools which subsequently became congregations in their own right but even there only a minority of children took up church membership. Many children went through Sunday School and entered the church building only for special services. They left at 12 or 13 and might regard themselves as 'belonging' to the church associated with their Sunday School, but did not see church membership or attendance at worship as something they would wish to do for themselves. Only in Welsh-speaking Wales did the Sunday School engage older age groups. The preservation of the language and culture was the distinguishing feature there.

Throughout Britain Sunday Schools and the linked para-church organizations, such as Boys Brigades or Bands of Hope, were places where children had opportunity to develop musical or dramatic gifts. Even at the end of the twentieth century an older generation of actors could speak of getting their first opportunity to perform in a Sunday School play or anniversary celebration. The morally improving stories told in Sunday School lessons might lead to unanticipated results. Thus Henry Moore would tell how the Sunday School lesson about Michaelangelo 'discovering' his statue of David in a rough block of stone first set his imagination to consider sculpture. There was also a long tradition of Sunday School 'treats', when children were taken into the country or to the seaside for recreation and a meal. This reward for regular attendance was further reinforced by prizegivings, when children were given Bibles and books at the end of the school year. All these activities were calculated to raise the aspirations of children as well as to supplement their education.

As far as formal education is concerned the Free Churches moved away from the provision of schools following the 1902 Education Act. The same constituency which had resisted the introduction of school boards now sprang to their defence. This was partly because the school board regime ensured a good provision of non-denominational schools. Free Church interests had learnt to work with this system and secured places on school boards. Their schools, fewer in number and not so well funded as those of the Church of England, had often closed but they were satisfied with their influence over the non-denominational board schools. The shift to local authority control weakened their hold on the management of such schools. Moreover, it was now proposed to fund church schools, including Roman Catholic ones, from the general rating system. The Free Churches wished local schools to have a Christian ethos but not one determined by the formularies of the Church of England or the Roman Catholic Church. It is not fashionable in these ecumenical days to dwell on the bitterness of this argument. At its sharpest, the protests evoked ultra-Protestant slogans, decrying 'Rome on the rates'. Large numbers of protesters refused to pay that part of their local rate which went to church schools. Some suffered distraint of goods; others went to prison. This campaign of passive resistance, now largely forgotten, but fully equal to the anti-Poll Tax campaign at the other end of the century, resulted in 190 people going to prison in 1907 alone. These included up to 60 Primitive Methodists, 48 Baptists, 40 Congregationalists, 15 Wesleyans and 25 from smaller denominations.[19] The Wesleyan numbers are particularly piquant, since they had schools which received public money under the terms of the 1902 Education Act, against which they were protesting. There is a possibility that Mahatma Gandhi was aware of this campaign when developing his own version of passive resistance.

The BFSS included both those opposed to the Act and those who regarded it as the best practical way forward. Like many modern charities, the Society found itself necessarily in partnership with government, from which it received substantial funds, yet being urged to campaign against government policy by large numbers of its own supporters. In the event, at a special meeting in January 1903, about half those present abstained from voting. A resolution encouraging local committees to co-operate in implementing the new Act was lost, in spite of support from three vice-presidents, including Sir Joshua Fitch, the Chief Inspector of Schools, whose brother was headmaster of the British boys' school in Hitchin. Fitch was a member of the Church of England, which may have dented his credibility with Free Church members. A more critical resolution, recommending local committees to delay handing over their schools until they could be satisfied of government intentions, was carried. The consequence was that BFSS staff were involved in supporting local committees during the period when local education authorities were being constituted, especially in seeking assurances that existing trusts and their provisions for religious liberty would be respected.[20]

Although conservatism delayed the handover of schools to local authority control, with the exception of some Wesleyan Methodist schools, Free Church interest in the direct provision of schools ended with the 1902 Act. The 1944 Education Act made provision for Free Church places on local education authorities. The 1988 Education Act strengthened the legal requirement for non-denominational religious education in non-church schools. However, subsequent legislation removed Free Church places from education committees and by multiplying the categories of publicly funded schools diluted the religious education requirements. At the beginning of the twenty-first century the churches were being challenged to resume a role in managing local schools under the Academies programme followed by the so-called Free Schools legislation.

One survivor of the old denominational controversies over education is the local authority Standing Advisory Committee for Religious Education (SACRE) in England and Wales. This has a duty to monitor religious education and collective worship in local schools. From 1902 local authorities began to develop Agreed Syllabuses for religious education, some of which were adopted by others. The 1944 Education Act gave local authorities power to establish SACREs and a corresponding Standing Conference to devise a religious education syllabus. The 1988 Act made SACREs mandatory, with power to call for a revision of the local Agreed Syllabus. In England each SACRE had what were effectively four caucuses to determine its policies representing the local authority itself, teachers, the Church of England and other denominations. In Wales the SACRE has only three components, since the Church of England is not represented there. After 1988 the legislation was taken to include other major world faiths in the 'other denominations' category. The local authority could not block a request for syllabus revision if it had been agreed by the other categories. On the other hand, once a Standing Conference has been established for syllabus purposes it can only proceed by unanimous agreement between the various categories. The purpose of this elaborate arrangement is that religious education should be governed by consensus. In practice it has led to dialogue between faiths as well as dialogue between religious interests and the secular authorities. More recently national guidance has been made available to SACREs to counteract any local idiosyncrasies. The legislation has also provided for the continuance of the conscience clause allowing pupils to be withdrawn from religious education. This has been the only part of the curriculum which, in theory, engaged the community in determining what should be taught and provided for conscientious withdrawal.

After the 1902 Act the chief institutional interest of Free Churches in English education was through teacher training. Congregationalists controlled Homerton College, Cambridge as trustees; Methodists had various colleges, including Westminster College, Oxford, and Southlands College, which later became part of Roehampton University. The BFSS ran a number of colleges, including its flagship Borough Road College in a new location at Isleworth, and co-operated with the Froebel College. Baptists, Congregationalists, Methodists and Quakers ran Westhill College at Selly Oak in Birmingham, originally to support Sunday School work but broadening into general teacher training and youth and community work. Around Selly Oak, encouraged by Quaker generosity, a group of colleges with a Free Church ethos was developed, providing adult and vocational education. In the 1970s the expansion of higher education made demands on colleges for expansion, soon to be thrown into reverse by a policy of bringing smaller colleges together in more economic units. The Free Church colleges, like the Church of England ones, either threw in their lot with universities or closed and moved their assets into educational trust funds.

At the local level churches have continued to provide auxiliary services to schools and children. Many church buildings have been used for pre-school provision, though not always using church volunteers. After-school clubs, with supplementary learning and mentoring for individual pupils, have also grown up in churches. Local churches, usually acting ecumenically, have supplied volunteers to support collective worship in schools or contribute to religious education classes. This work has been paid for by local subscription. There were moves afoot to provide training and accreditation for such work in schools.

The Independent sector of education is also indebted to the efforts of Dissenters in the early nineteenth century who wished to secure a good education for their children without subscribing to Anglican views. Schools were formed on trusts which embodied Nonconformist principles. They also raised endowments to provide boarding education for the children of ministers and missionaries. There were two categories of schools: first providing for the sons and daughters of missionaries and secondly providing for the children of ministers and missionaries as well as lay people. Quakers, Methodists and Moravians all had their own schools. Congregationalists and Baptists were conscientiously opposed to endowed schools but recognized the need to educate the sons and daughters of missionaries and ministers and they collaborated in providing schools for lay people for whom the best known is Mill Hill School which celebrated its bi-centenary in 2007. Until modern times these schools worshipped in their local Free Churches and were seen as part of the local church community.

Education is highly dependent on good interpersonal relations. It is also has community dimensions. It is a natural activity for Christian churches and embodies many Christian values. At a basic level, gathering people in communities to learn brings economies of scale. Beyond that it provides stimulus and support for the individual learners within the group. What we might term 'learning communities', of which churches and schools are examples, have expectations that learning will take place within them. Other forms of community, such as neighbourhoods or workplaces, may be expected or required to provide learning but primarily in order to carry out tasks or to keep the rules. The dynamic of the latter is rather different, since the object of the learning is more obvious than learning for the sheer fun of it. A local church may be a place, as in the creation of the Sunday School movement, which identifies a learning need and addresses it in a systematic way. Equally, a local church may, as in the case of a parliamentary election, offer a one-off opportunity for learning, by bringing the candidates together in an attempt to draw out their opinions and values. Churches are predisposed to believe that learning is a virtue, and that it is worth learning things for learning's sake; this may not be the case in their surrounding neighbourhood.

A case could be made for our Free Church predecessors making a contribution to educational innovation, though it might be difficult to distinguish what was particular to them and what was general to all Christians. Temperance Gell, a Presbyterian, endowed a school for girls at Wirksworth, Derbyshire, in the eighteenth century, but her kind of Nonconformists also worshipped in the parish church. The development of a broad curriculum for girls was also a feature of private schools established by Dissenters in the nineteenth century. Women had voting rights in church meetings and began to take up what had been regarded as male roles in church life rather earlier than in Anglicanism or Catholicism. Nonconformists are sometimes credited with the introduction of economics and natural sciences to the curriculum of higher education in their academies, though the case may be overstated. There seems to be an overall willingness to take up new ideas. Methodists were influenced by the Moravians who, in turn, followed the example of Francke of Halle, for whom schooling was part of total community development. John Wesley formed Kingswood School on these principles and there were also schools in Moravian settlements. In the nineteenth century the Congregationalist, Andrew Reed, pursued some of the same principles in improving the provision for orphan children. The theories of Montessori and Froebel were taken up by the BFSS, who offered some of the first training in kindergarten methods in England. It could be argued that all these were part of a Free Church ethos, though it is equally likely that large numbers of Free Church people were as conservative in educational matters as the population at large.

Equally, in considering Free Church people who were influential educators, it is difficult to distinguish their Nonconformity from their originality. In the twentieth century, Basil Yeaxlee, 1883–1967, Principal of Westhill College from 1930, was the first proponent of 'life-long learning' and established the study of educational psychology in Oxford. Although he was a Congregationalist he was equally a member of the group of ecumenical movers and shakers who coalesced around the Student Christian Movement. Another of that group, Roy Niblett (1906–2005), a member of the United Reformed Church, was an influential policy maker. John Hull of Birmingham, originally an Australian Methodist, trained with Congregationalists at Cheshunt College, Cambridge, to become an internationally recognized Christian educator. The same could be said of others. What might be claimed as distinctive, especially in the historic Nonconformist denominations, is an ecclesiology which set great store on the participation of members. This is sometimes mistaken for popular democracy. It is actually something more profound – a belief that the will of God is best discerned by the church members collectively, rather than by delegation. In order for people to take on these responsibilities there needs to be understanding as well as spirituality. Therefore education is a priority if the Church is to be the Church.

5

Industry, Philanthropy and Christian Citizenship: Pioneers in Paternalism

Clyde Binfield

I. Introduction

England was the world's first urban nation. The census of 1851 showed that more people lived in England's towns than in its countryside. There was also a religious census in 1851, a snapshot of those counted in to church or chapel on one generally dismal early Spring Sunday. It demonstrated that, on that Sunday at least, a disturbing number of people were absent from public worship and a surprising number of those who were present had chosen not to worship with the national church. These statistics, generally available from 1854, apparently pointed to an unexpected degree of godlessness and dissent that was intensified in the larger towns and especially in industrial towns with considerable working-class populations. Contemporaries were galvanized by these findings; historians continue to ponder them; ecclesiastical strategies have yet to escape from their presumed implications.[1]

Those two censuses, their results released in the course of a decade topped by the Great Exhibition and tailed by *The Origin of Species*, encapsulated a world of change. The change was economic, social, and political. The United Kingdom's Established and Dissenting Churches were vulnerable to it in varying degrees. The Dissenting Churches were manifestly in crisis. Administrative and doctrinal tensions interlocked; schism was endemic. The Dissenting Churches, however, 'Old' or 'New', were institutionally young. Although spread nationwide, they were most prosperously rooted in towns and most flexibly rooted in rapidly expanded towns: exactly where the census struck home. Membership, a registered commitment going beyond mere attendance, was at the heart of Dissenting ecclesiology; and the members of Dissenting churches were at risk socially and economically. Should circumstances work against them, they were at risk of sinking into that vast and anonymous fact of modern industrial life, the proletariat; should circumstances favour them, they were no less at risk from prosperity. Their place in the political nation was as precarious as their place in the divine economy was assured.

Institutional Dissent took many forms, congregational, or connexional, independent, or Presbyterian, but it certainly involved mutually committed responsibility, with a consequent understanding of authority. It followed that membership of a religious society was an apprenticeship in politics, whatever the member's place in the secular body politic. The political accent varied from one Dissenting polity to the next. Much depended on the role of a minister or of a leading lay person and on their relationships to each other across and within the differently constituted councils of their churches. There could be no doubt, however, of the political and social formation encouraged by membership of a Dissenting society.

It also followed that such a formation, set in the context of the new industrial towns, shaping their own institutions in an unpredictable economic climate, not to mention a changing, indeed expanding, political climate, gave scope for the exercise of leadership beyond the bounds of any religious society. With adventurous explorers to lead the way, sure-footed and suitably equipped, the ideal society, practically realized to the moral and physical benefit of all, became almost achievable. It promised to be a fact.

No decade of the nineteenth century was free from such idealism, but from the 1850s a remarkable sequence of such experiments punctuated the industrial and suburban landscape. They were essays in community, model villages, sometimes almost towns, with a large industrial enterprise as their motor. They were shaped by masterful, often authoritarian individuals, people of powerful personality, considerable imagination, comparable executive ability, and with an equal flair for marketing and manufacturing, whose prime skills were promotional, although they also had a genius for borrowing. Thus these communities were at the mercy of personal whim and they were wholly dependent on commercial success. They might be exemplary; they could never be normal nor wholly ideal. Nonetheless, their realization shaped attitudes to land use and land reform, to urban planning and aesthetics, to recreation and education, to the legislation proper and possible for improvement in all these areas, to the representative government most appropriate to an evolving community and to fostering the most natural relationships of class and gender within it. What began as the model industrial village led to the Garden Suburb and the Garden City and eventually to the New Town, transforming landscape and townscape and the understanding of community.

There is, however, a further dimension to these experiments in community: the religious impulse which drove many of the pioneers. There is no inherent reason why the promoter of an industrial community should be a Christian but, given the particular stage of society and the role of Christians within it, many in fact were. Baptists, Congregationalists, Methodists, Quakers, and Unitarians, for example, are to be found among the pioneers of nineteenth-century industrial communities. Although many of the characteristics of these egregious individualists were shared by all of them, regardless of denominational label, nonetheless denominational affiliation has its bearing. It is relevant, for example, that Saltaire and Port Sunlight were shaped by Congregationalists, or that Bournville and New Earswick were shaped by Quakers.

This chapter explores this religious impulse, the paradoxes and contradictions which contributed to their achievements and which explain their shortcomings, and suggests some consequences. Although the prime focus is the second half of the nineteenth century, their wider context stretches from the last quarter of the eighteenth century to the first quarter of the twentieth, from the evolution of what might be called philanthropic paternalism to its dissolution. Particular attention is paid to Titus Salt and W. H. Lever, but also to the Crossleys, an industrial dynasty whose contribution, though more diffuse, was perhaps more representative of a type of Nonconformity.

In 2005, Chris Mullin, a Labour MP,

> drove to see Robert Owen's mills at New Lanark, beautifully restored and displayed and so moving to think what that great man inspired. How would he wish to be remembered? As a socialist, an enlightened capitalist or a mixture of both? Whatever, his message is as relevant today as it was 200 years ago. Namely, that it is possible to make a healthy profit without grinding the noses of your workers into the dirt. Globalisers, please note.[2]

Robert Owen (1771–1858), whose legacy Mullin explored on that wet June day, stands secure in the socialist pantheon; his rationalist deism slipped with old age into spiritualism. New Lanark remains Owen's enduring claim to fame, the sublime effrontery of his aspirations caught in the New Institution for the Formation of Character which he provided for it in 1816. It had, however, been founded 33 years before that by Owen's father-in-law, David Dale (1739–1806), a humanely progressive Glasgow merchant, banker, and manufacturer whose intention was to turn New Lanark into Scotland's New Manchester. Neither Dale nor Owen (who in fact came from Manchester) succeeded in that, but their creation was for decades a magnet for visitors, most of whom deprecated Owen's wilder fancies as much as they were fascinated by his character and impressed by the general success of his enterprise. Owen's was a rigorously autocratic idealism. This mill town's buildings were distinguished by what has been called their 'robust and militaristic appearance',[3] but then these barracks were Glasgow tenements, naturally reflecting their Glasgow founder, for Robert Owen's Anglo-Welsh paternalism had been preceded by David Dale's rather less rigorous Scottish version, which should be seen as a natural reflection of his Christian development. For Dale had left the Church of Scotland to form 'Dale's Kirk', the 'Old Independents'; he acted as their unpaid minister. Dale's Kirk was a strand in the ragged evolution of Scottish Congregationalists and Baptists; it was equally part of the pre-history of the spirit of New Lanark.[4]

In 1905 Budgett Meakin (1866–1906), an enterprising journalist, 'writer and lecturer on industrial betterment ... and on Oriental life and customs', published *Model Factories and Villages: Ideal Conditions of Labour and Housing*.[5] It comprised

> practical examples of what successful business men have found it worth while doing to promote the moral and social welfare of their employees, in the hope of provoking others to like good works. The various industrial betterment schemes described are not advanced as theoretical recommendations, or as the creations of the philanthropist, but as the actual experience of money-making men.[6]

It included two Indexes, one of 'Firms, Etc.', the other of 'Model Villages, Etc.'. The latter listed 61 such places, 11 of them in the British Isles, 22 in North America, and 28 on the Continent, chiefly in France and Germany, but also in the Low Countries, Italy, and Bohemia. The firms, like the villages, were concentrated in the Continent, the British Isles, and North America.[7]

Model Factories and Villages could almost be presented as evidence for a missionary movement. Its Christian bias was quiet rather than insistent, and denominations played no part. Its thesis, however, was understatedly persuasive: industrial enterprise reaped the best dividends when it was exercised in a spirit of philanthropic paternalism, especially when exercised close to the source of wealth, and accompanied by model communities, where the dividends were moral rather than financial. Not all model communities, however, need be tied to industrial paternalism, however philanthropic; not all essays in co-operation or co-partnership need be kick-started by progressive capitalists. No conclusions were firmly drawn but an array of possibilities was suggested. *Model Factories* made no reference to

New Lanark but Dale's enlightened concern and Owen's romantic imagination were embodied in Meakin's catalogue of examples.

Moreover, Meakin himself was part of a wider if loose network. The book was published by T. Fisher Unwin (1848–1935), of the celebrated publishing Unwins.[8] In his day most Unwins were active Congregationalists; Fisher Unwin's own Dissent was more ancestral than confessional. His imprint attracted all that was advanced in literature, philosophy, and political economy, and his marriage confirmed the attraction. As a son-in-law of Richard Cobden, the Free Trade statesman, he took much of Cobden's spirit into a new age. The book was printed by Unwin Brothers, of the Gresham Press. The printing Unwins, too, were active Congregationalists; they were listed, moreover, in the first of Meakin's two Indexes.[9] There was more. Budgett Meakin lived in Hampstead, and he took as epigraph a quotation from a fellow resident, R. F. Horton (1855–1934). In 1905 few London Congregational ministers were better known than Horton and his words were strikingly to the point. They were a clarion call for the new century:

> Why should we not frankly say: The housing question is our question; healthy conditions in workshops and factories are our concern; a living wage, reasonable hours of labour, provision of work for the unemployed, harmonious relations between landlord and tenant, between capital and labour, between master and employee, are our interest?
> These things touch us because they touch Christ.[10]

Horton and Meakin are thus firmly on the Progressive Liberal wing of the Nonconformist Conscience. This is confirmed by Meakin's statement that he had presented documentary evidence gathered during his research to a promising new body, the British Institute of Social Service, of which he had been a founder.[11] For some years the Institute's Secretary was Percy Alden (1865–1944), in 1905 the Organising Secretary of the Friends Social Service Union. Alden continued and enlarged upon Meakin's work as social explorer and publicist. He had trained for the Baptist ministry, had been enrolled in the Congregational ministry, and had served as the first warden of Mansfield House, in Canning Town. He was soon to become a radical Liberal MP and eventually, although briefly, a Labour MP.[12]

A socially radical apostolic succession is thus in formation, and Meakin belongs to it. His own background was Wesleyan Methodist and there were few prominent Methodist families with whom he was not connected. His maternal grandfather, the Bristol retail and wholesale grocer, Samuel Budgett (1794–1851), was the archetypal Christian philanthropist, whose biography was called *The Successful Merchant*.[13] This background informs Meakin's evidence. Of his 11 British model villages 7 had been founded by Nonconformists: 4 by Quakers, 2 by Congregationalists, and 1 by a Primitive Methodist. Of his exemplary British firms, the jam-making Chiverses and the sewing-thread Coatses were Baptists; John Brunner (chemicals) and Henry Tate (sugar) were Unitarians; William Pretty (corset manufacturer and retail draper), J. G. Graves (mail-order) and, of course, Samuel Budgett, were Wesleyan Methodists; and William Hartley, the jam-maker, was a Primitive Methodist. For the Quakers there were Cadbury of Birmingham, Clark of Street, Crosfield of Warrington, Fry of Bristol, Palmer of Reading, Richardson of Bessbrook, and Rowntree of York. For the Congregationalists there were the Colmans (originally Baptists), the Levers, Titus Salt, and also Selincourt (mantle manufacturers), Pascall (confectioners), Hazell, Watson, and Viney (printers), and the Unwin brothers. All aimed at quality for a mass market; all owed much to inspired advertisement and constant promotion; and all were significant employers of women. They were the capitalist standard bearers of industrial society. They were also Christian standard bearers.

II. Salt of Saltaire

Their prototype was Titus Salt (1803–1876), called 'The Great Paternalist'.[14] The family was in trade, upwardly mobile but not self-made. There can be no doubt, however, about the Congregational background, its relevance, and its continuity.

Salt was baptized at Rehoboth, Morley, founded in 1763 as a secession from Morley's historic Old Chapel.[15] His father was a Sheffielder who had married into a Rehoboth family. When they moved to Bradford in 1822 they were quickly associated with the Horton Lane Chapel, already a Nonconformist stronghold, and in 1835–36 they helped build a second chapel, Salem, which was also to be a Nonconformist power house.[16] Salem's trustees comprised seven woolstaplers, five worsted spinners, three drapers, a dyer, a book-keeper, a bookseller, two joiners, and a grocer. Among them was Titus Salt.[17] If the Congregationalists of Horton Lane and Salem were faithfully represented by such men, they stood for what was moulding a new great industrial city. It made sense for newcomers to become associated with such chapels.

Salt seems not to have joined a Congregational church until late in life. This sheds an interesting light on his temperament and beliefs and on the tensions between Congregationalism and successful industry. It poses questions about how church membership was seen in nineteenth-century Congregationalism and, given Salt's chapel-building record, it sheds an instructive light on the chapel as a machine for worship and community symbol and on the Congregational church as a motor of community in what should be a free (and therefore competitive) society. The church-related schemes with which Salt was associated ran in parallel with community-related schemes, political commitments, and industrial enterprise. They interacted, the entrepreneur in tension with the citizen and both in tension with the independently minded Congregationalist.

Salt's finest Congregational enterprise was the church in his works village, Saltaire.[18] Its building, opened in 1859, was to all appearances the parish church, an architectural focal point, sophisticated, better suited indeed to a smart metropolitan suburb yet practically adapted to the needs of Congregational worship.

Saltaire's church was neither Salt's sole nor his chief Congregational concern. He gave liberally to the denomination's headquarters in London, to its northern school for ministers' sons and its school for ministers' daughters, and he provided a new site for its Bradford theological college. He also concerned himself with Congregational worship and ministry wherever he holidayed or lived. Harrogate and Scarborough benefited accordingly. So did Castleford and Lightcliffe, which might be seen as squire's churches. Salt's interest in the former arose when he leased the ancestral seat of the Earls of Mexborough, and in the latter when he lived at Crow Nest, his cherished Palladian villa. Salt was a member at Lightcliffe by 1871, the year of that chapel's rebuilding, a rich man's church, serving an eclectically prosperous community, a countrified Horton Lane for West Riding families enriched by worsted and wool. Here the Salts were at home.[19]

Their Congregationalism survived into the next generation, actively so with Salt's youngest son and his wife, and with his three surviving daughters and the husbands of two of them. Salt's eldest daughter, indeed, married one of London's leading Congregational laymen. His eldest son also married appropriately, into a family of Baptist hosiers, whose role in Leicester paralleled that of the Salts in Bradford; but these Salts slipped effortlessly into Anglicanism.[20]

In Jack Reynolds's words, Salt 'was one of the foremost employers of labour in England; perhaps the most outstanding representative in Bradford of that class whose activities transformed the economy, the social structure, the politics and the administration of this country between about 1830 and 1860'.[21]

He was a woolstapler turned worsted spinner, whose manufacturing success owed much to his mercantile sense. By 1850 he was Bradford's largest employer, internationally known, soon to be gratifyingly displayed at the Great Exhibition. It was at this point that he decided to leave Bradford for Shipley, combining the work of five Bradford factories under one roof. The 2,000 employed in five mills in 1850 became the 3,500 employed in one mill in 1876, strategically placed for transport by rail, road and canal.[22] In its day the mill had no parallel in Europe.

Propelled by his prosperity, Salt's citizenship marched with his Congregationalism. He was Bradford's second mayor (1848–49), a borough and county JP, a Deputy Lieutenant for the West Riding, still relatively rare offices for Nonconformists. He was a Bradford MP from 1859 to 1861.

Since he was a poor speaker – his imposing frame masked a speech impediment and corresponding diffidence[23] – these public honours reflected a
backstage and backbench usefulness, acknowledged in 1869 by a baronetcy,
at once the highest hereditary honour likely to come a Nonconformist's way
in Gladstone's Britain and the lowest that the establishment could decently
confer on a prominent citizen who was not yet top drawer.

In 1853, the year of Saltaire's opening, he explained to a Tory aristocrat
why he had not retired as he had originally intended. It boiled down to
influence: '...outside of my business I am nothing. In it, I have considerable influence. By the opening of Saltaire, I also hope to do good to my
fellow men.'[24] He was announcing an alternative tradition. It was dynastic,
founded on business and exploitation of property, and capable of a benevolent gloss. It was traditional, and it celebrated its environment. He had
remained an industrialist, and the result was Saltaire:

> Far be it from me to do anything to pollute the air and water of the
> place... I hope to draw around me a population that will enjoy the
> beauties of the neighbourhood, and who will be well-fed, contented and
> happy. I have given instructions to my architect...that nothing should be
> spared to render the dwellings of the operatives a pattern to the country.
> If my life should be spared by providence, I hope to see satisfaction,
> happiness and comfort around me.[25]

Successive visitors found Saltaire impressive. Lady Frederick Cavendish,
whose husband was a local Liberal MP, was amazed by the scale of
Saltaire's schools and the 'freedom of action and control' allowed to their
women teachers (each school had its 'Admirable Crichton of a Head
Mistress').[26]

In 1871 Saltaire housed 4,384 people in 775 houses (and 45 almshouses),
and a 14–acre park was about to be opened.[27] The houses were solidly built,
adequate to the best needs of the day as required by industrious operatives.
There was nothing new in the idea of a works village. Salt's woolstapling
years had taken him to the sheep-rearing estates of enlightened landowners,
with their picturesquely model villages. Larger, more recent, and more
efficient, if less picturesque, were the railway villages, Wolverton, Crewe,
and Swindon; and then there was the impact of Disraeli's *Sybil* (1845), with
its depiction of England's two nations, and Mr Trafford's model factory
village. Whether Salt had read *Sybil*, Disraeli knew of Bradford through his
Bingley friends, the Ferrands, and his novel was widely read by northern
radicals, keen to provide an ordered alternative to the chaos, immorality
and inefficiency of such places as Bradford.[28]

Order was the key. Order encouraged the sort of discipline which allowed
for the exercise of responsibility. Saltaire's park, for example, had rules: no
unaccompanied children under eight years old, no gambling, swearing,
or smoking in alcoves, no games save where specifically designated, no

political meetings without permission, but its riverside was widened for boating and swimming, and stocked for fishing.[29] Recreation was to be allowed its moral due. This was where Saltaire struck new ground. It clarified (and encouraged) the link between cleanliness and godliness. It exemplified, decades before the phrase came into use, the Nonconformist Conscience. It seemed to justify the belief that if such a community could willingly be regulated into morality, then a nation might be consensually moralized by legislation.

In 1966 the American, W. L. Creese, savoured Saltaire's mix of Italy-in-Yorkshire, its broodingly introspective *quattrocento*.[30] It celebrated the working relationship between Salt, his engineer William Fairbairn, and his architects Henry Lockwood and William Mawson.[31] These were expert provincial practitioners, enlightened without being radical. To the casual visitor all the gradations of industrial society were reflected in the hierarchy of semi-villas and terraces. In reality the residents were more socially mixed, their occupancy of particular houses depending more on the gross incomes of the families living in them than on their social status.[32] A household with several independently minded, style-conscious, mill girls lived relatively well, their ambitions encouraged at Salt's schools and furthered by classes at the Institute. An understanding of this community contributes to an appreciation of its Congregational church. This Graeco-Italian edifice, Saltaire's first public building, had a peal of bells, a drawing-room interior, and a fine mausoleum for dead Salts. The works partner most associated with the church was William Evans Glyde (1814–1884), lay preacher, Sunday-School teacher and superintendent, who had risen from an apprenticeship to a partnership in 1859.

With Glyde, ever 'as respectful towards his brother officers and the minister as any humblest member of the society',[33] we return to an updating of the Dissenting tradition. He descended from generations of Devon Nonconformists, some of them ministers ejected in 1662, but he had grown into Bradford alongside the Salts; his father-in-law and brother ministered at Horton Lane. When he died some verses were published in his memory. Their author, P. T. Forsyth, was a close friend of Saltaire's Congregational minister, and had himself ministered to a small church nearby, regarded by many as a hotbed of theological liberalism.

When social men shall make the social hour
    At last not trivial but imperial;
When personal concerns at last shall fall
    In modest tribute to the general power

When once again our civic life shall be
    A liturgy; and altars smoke unseen
To no unknown god, where hot hearts have been
    In streets and lanes, to cleanse, and heal, and free

Thou hadst the earnest in thy savéd soul
  Of the salvation of the social whole.[34]

Salt's Saltaire did not long survive its founder's death. In 1892 the business, a public company since 1881, was wound up.[35] When Budgett Meakin considered it in 1905 the glory had largely departed. It seemed so 'dismal and cramped' in comparison to what was by then seen as ideal, and the life had drained from so many of Salt's initiatives (Meakin blamed this on the failure to ensure the continued cooperation of employees in the village's management and maintenance) that it was hard to appreciate its pioneering quality.[36] However, at the turn of the twenty-first century Saltaire was given World Heritage Status as an outstanding and well-preserved example of a mid-nineteenth-century industrial town, reflecting contemporary 'philanthropic paternalism' and the role played by the textile industry. It failed to meet a further criterion: that it provided 'a unique or at least exceptional testimony to a cultural tradition ... which is living, or ... has disappeared'.[37] Yet it is that which is most truly distinctive about Saltaire.

III. The Crossleys of Halifax

On 15 March 1866 Titus Salt Jr. married Catherine Crossley.[38] The Crossleys were to Halifax and carpets what the Salts were to Bradford and worsteds. They, too, set their mark on Yorkshire's Liberalism, environment and economy. They too were Congregationalists. Their background too was socially middling, upwardly mobile but not self-made. The Crossleys were another urban dynasty, dominated in the middle of the nineteenth century by three brothers, John (1812–1879), Joseph (1813–1868) and Francis (1817–1872).

Four previous generations of Crossleys had been associated with Halifax's Square Congregational Chapel and the direct connection continued for a generation after them. John Crossley (1772–1837), the father of John, Joseph and Francis, was a weaver.[39] By 1801 he had become a foreman. Marriage was his first breakthrough. Martha Turner (1775–1854) was a farmer's daughter in service at a house whose mistress ran a good school. John Crossley was an artisan, with kinsmen who stood on their own feet, well placed to help him stand on his own feet too. He was poised either to slip into the anonymity of the lower orders (not yet quite the working classes) or to find a niche on the edge of the political nation. His religion was as independent as his social status: the Crossleys were Dissenters. He married a manager. Martha Crossley bore him eight children and played an active part in her husband's business.

In 1802 John Crossley leased a mill at Dean Clough on the edge of Halifax. Thus began 180 years of Crossley industry on that site. By the time of his death he was independent, well-to-do (he left £13,000). The story goes that back in the days when she had gone to work at 4am, Martha had vowed: 'If the Lord does bless us at this place, the poor shall taste of it.'[40] By 1837, 300 hands were blessing Crossley's place and the working day began at a more reasonable 5.30am (it continued to 8pm). Old Mrs Crossley refused to leave her home at the mill. She stayed on, so placing her parlour mirror that she could study the faces of her son's workmen as the hundreds turned into thousands, streaming past her window.[41]

It was the Crossleys who brought carpets into middle-class homes at the point at which the middle-class market became a mass market. The breakthrough came in 1851,[42] the year of the Great Exhibition, at which the Crossleys, like Salt, exhibited and for which they carpeted the Queen's retiring room.

The Crossleys branched out to the Continent, and to the United States. Their rivals had either to give up or pay up for the right to use the patent and install the steam-powered loom that George Collier had developed from an earlier American model. By 1869 Dean Clough embraced eight mills in 27 acres, and employed 4,400 hands.[43]

Of John senior's children, John was denominationally the most prodigal brother. He taught in Square's Sunday School, was a church member, and a deacon.[44] He was treasurer of the Yorkshire Congregational Union and chaired the English Congregational Chapel Building Society. Buildings gripped him and he responded to appeals with money and advice which wise committees did well to heed. His trusteeships and stonelayings extended from Yorkshire to Newmarket and Llandudno. His patronage advanced the careers of several architects, most notably Joseph James (1828–1875), whose rebuilding of Square Chapel (1857) grandly reconciled good Gothic with sound Congregationalism.[45]

Congregational education came close second to Congregational chapels. That meant Silcoates, the school for Northern ministers' sons, where John was a chairman and treasurer, and the new proprietary schools at Bishops Stortford and Tettenhall, as well as ministerial colleges in Rotherham, Bradford, Manchester, Plymouth, and Cheshunt. His younger brothers echoed John's enthusiasm. In Francis's case it embraced a Baptist cause which came with his country estate in Suffolk. There he encouraged a Congregational dimension; the chapel and its ministry were 'wholly sustained by the proprietor of the Hall'.[46] In the case of Joseph's widow (a minister's daughter who had been governess to Joseph's children by his first wife) the concern extended to Milton Mount, the school near Gravesend for ministers' daughters.[47]

John Crossley was four times Mayor of Halifax and active in its politics from the 1840s, a founder of its famous Building Society and of its Liberal newspaper, the *Halifax Courier*, and he was its MP from 1874 to 1877. A few months before his election he had a carriage accident, after which his business and philanthropic speculations became increasingly eccentric. He left the Commons and died in relatively straitened circumstances. Like

Titus Salt he had burnt his fingers in American projects promoted by Alfred Allott, a highly respected Sheffield Congregationalist and one of the founders of accountancy as a regulated profession.[48]

John was the most truly municipal Crossley. He imposed on the town centre two fine streets,[49] the Corinthian-pillared Marlborough Hall (later to become the YMCA) and the White Swan Hotel, dignified by the Crossley arms. Where the two streets met he secured a site for the Town Hall. Here England's grandest architect, Sir Charles Barry, proposed a civic palace. The Prince of Wales opened it during Crossley's last mayoralty.

Around the People's Park John and brother Francis developed some handsome villas. Behind them, good of their kind but pure speculation, were back-to-back houses; then, from 1863 to 1868, John laid out an estate of houses aimed at artisans and clerks: West Hill Park.[50] Crossley expected a return but mortgages at five per cent rather than the more normal seven to ten per cent, taken out with the Building Society, would be redeemed in thirteen years. John Crossley was that Victorian phenomenon, a five-per-cent philanthropist.[51]

The most remarkable of the Crossley family's philanthropies, bearing all the marks of John Crossley's directive intelligence, is what evolved as the Crossley Orphanage and Schools, built in the 1860s on Skircoat Moor, not far from some of the family villas.[52] The Orphanage's grandeur bears out the tradition that John Crossley had intended the site for a theological college. As it was, 400 children were housed in 'large and well-ventilated dormitories' and used workshops, gymnasia, and two swimming baths. 'As regards warming, ventilation, water supply, and drainage, the arrangements are as perfect as modern improvements can make them'.

The Crossleys envisaged an education 'to secure accuracy and thoroughness, and to avoid that which is superficial and incomplete'. That included languages, science, and mathematics for boys and needlework and household service 'adapted to their strength' for girls. Thus were contemporary gender roles enforced; but it should not be underestimated. It was to fit Crossleys' orphans 'for fighting the battle of life courageously and with that kind of self-reliance which is consistent with intelligent dependence on divine help'. There is a strategy there, aimed neither at confirming nor overturning society but at changing it for the better. An orphan needed to be aged two or over. A boy would be lodged until he was 15 or 16; a girl until she was 16 or 17. Relatives could visit them on the first Tuesday afternoon of each month. They needed to 'have been born in wedlock and deprived by death' of their father and with no other relatives capable of assisting them. It helped if they had been born in Yorkshire, of Nonconformist or Anglican parentage, in reduced circumstances, and if both parents were dead. It did not help if they were blind, deaf, dumb, had fits, were lame, paralysed, infectiously, contagiously, or incurably ill, were Roman Catholics, or workhouse paupers. If that seems to exclude the neediest, it might be recalled that there were already orphanages for the insane, incurable, or incapacitated, some of them pioneered by the Congregational minister Andrew Reed (1787–1862) whose family were closely connected to that of Mrs Edward Crossley[53] and that Roman Catholics looked after their own. It was the apparently less vulnerable who were in fact most vulnerable.

Joseph was probably the richest and certainly the least known of the brothers. At Dean Clough he was in charge of dyeing. At large he was a dynastic philanthropist. His children married into the Liberal (and Congregational) provincial press, Quaker banking, Baptist building and railway speculation, Anglican wool, and Congregational alpaca. Such connections confirmed and consolidated the Dissenting interest, and facilitated its slippage into the Anglican establishment. His son Arnold, named after Thomas Arnold, was the first of his family and one of the first of his sort to go to Rugby School.[54]

Joseph Crossley's great memorial lies on Arden Road, 48 almshouses begun in 1863, completed by his son Edward and costing over £26,000.[55] To qualify you had to be a trinitarian Protestant, recommended by a minister of religion. You were to worship in the chapel where Joseph's bust still commands an otherwise simple interior. You could not be absent overnight without permission. In return you received free medical attention, a weekly allowance, and two rooms, in buildings so commanding and spacious that they were for all the world like an old Grammar School or an Oxford College or a great medieval charity. Here tradition was turned confidently as well as comfortingly to the new age. The motives may have been mixed but mixed motives need not always be a mixed blessing.

Frank, the youngest brother, was the public Crossley. He was Mayor of Halifax in 1849, an MP from 1852, a baronet from 1863. As an MP he was one of the new breed of Nonconformist industrialists, representing great northern constituencies, unevenly yet genuinely radical, never achieving office, yet influential.

Bellevue was his Halifax house. In 1855 he built to one side of it a row of almshouses, with conditions and benefits similar to those set soon after by Joseph at Arden Road.[56] In 1856 he rebuilt Bellevue, achieving on a surprisingly small site and to a surprisingly modest scale, a well planned, grandly staircased, suggestive setting for the cream of its contents, T. H. Maguire's painting of 'Cromwell Refusing the Crown of England',[57] while a spire rose above the trees of the Congregational Park Chapel.[58] In addition the People's Park was laid out where Bellevue's pleasure grounds might otherwise have been.[59]

The park was opened on 14 August 1857. Lord Shaftesbury was there:

Went… to Halifax to attend opening of "People's Park", the munificent donation of Frank Crossley, a manufacturer with a princely, and what is better, a Christian heart. He was kind enough to insist on my attendance as "the best friend of the working classes". Speeches of course, without end.

Lord Shaftesbury proposed a toast to 'the Well-being of the People'.[60] At luncheon Frank Crossley, now in his fortieth year, spoke from the heart. He described 10 September 1855, when his party had left Quebec and entered the United States:

> I remember passing through some of the most glorious scenery on that day which I ever saw in my life. I remember that, when we arrived at the hotel at White Mountain, the ladies sat down for a cup of tea, but I preferred to take a walk alone. It was a beautiful spot. The sun was just then reclining his head behind Mt. Washington, with all the glorious drapery of an American sunset, which we know nothing of in this country. I felt that I should like to be walking with my God on the earth. I said, 'What shall I render to my Lord for all his benefits to me?' I was led further to repeat that question which Paul asked under other circumstances – 'Lord, what wilt thou have me do?' The answer came immediately. It was this: 'It is true thou canst not bring many thousands thou hast left in thy native country to see this beautiful scenery, but thou canst take this to them; it is possible so to arrange art and nature that they shall be within the walk of every working man in Halifax; that he shall go take his stroll there after he has done his hard day's toil, and be able to get home again without being tired'.[61]

Frank Crossley, the Romantic, was able to experience the 'intense', the 'intimate' movement. Frank Crossley, the Victorian, must tell others of that moment and convert them to it; he must moralize it and improve it. That explains the park's rules: open from dawn to sunset, no cricket, no bowls, no hockey, no refreshment, no music on Sundays.[62] It sounds narrowly Puritan but in a town that was so visibly and audibly polluted, it was perhaps not so narrow. Six years later came the baronetcy and Frank now purchased Somerleyton. Somerleyton's previous owner, Sir Samuel Morton Peto, was a Baptist builder, baronet and fellow MP.[63]

On the day of John Crossley's funeral, work ceased in Halifax and shutters closed along the funeral route.[64] The eldest of the three brothers was the last to die. In their faith, flair and imaginative radicalism they nonetheless remained men of their time. In the early 1870s a prominent Sheffield MP, A. J. Mundella, a large employer in Nottingham, promoted a bill to protect women and children in small textile workshops. Its opponents, who tended to be small employers supported by some big men, John Crossley among them, argued that it would interfere with the collective incomes of working-class families (such households, perhaps, as were represented by Salt's mill girls). To fight it, they formed the Association of Employers of Factory Labour. *The Times* wrote of how old alliances of capital and labour were moving into hostile camps. The employers referred to 'the organised aggression that threatens the national prosperity', by which they meant trade unions. Mundella persevered and in June 1874 wrote to a Sheffield newspaperman (and Congregationalist): 'Everyone is much pleased with the debate on the Factories Bill... I resisted Crossley...and other *millionaires*'.[65]

Yet the Crossleys had a good reputation as employers and that reputation was accompanied by a remarkable business flair. This might be encapsulated in the career of Giulio Marchetti (1843–1931), in Crossleys from 1872, a director from 1879, managing director in 1902, and chairman from 1919.[66] An Italian born in Rome, though educated in Zurich, Marchetti was Congregationally well-connected. His second wife's father had been Secretary of the Congregational Union (1852–70), and a daughter married J. H. Whitley (1866–1935), Halifax cotton-spinner, Congregationalist, and Speaker of the Commons (1921–1928).[67] The linking factor had been Marchetti's first wife, Ann Crossley, John's daughter, after whom 'Annie', the firm's big-beamed, horizontal tandem compound engine, was named.[68]

In the next generation, Joseph's son Edward (1841–1905) and John's son Louis John (1842–1891) continued the commitment. They were inventive men. Louis John's Crossley Transmitter set the pace in the telephone's earliest days. In 1879 it allowed listeners in Bradford 'one Sunday evening' to hear 'the sonorous tones' of Square's minister, Enoch Mellor, 'announcing the hymns and preaching in his own church, eight miles away; ...the singing of the congregation could be heard with equal distinctness'.[69] Four years later, Edward White was the focus for a similar experience. His Square sermon, 'by telephone...reached eight people at Bradford, Leeds, and Edward's own house'.[70]

Edward Crossley, however, was as opinionated as he was public-spirited. He decided that his views were at variance with those of Dr Mellor's successor at Square, so in 1888 Edward left for a new Congregational church. In the Isle of Wight, where he had a holiday home, he built an independent Evangelical Protestant chapel; this was increasingly his spiritual home. It was a classic case of Congregational Independency.[71]

On Frank's death, his widow shut Bellevue in favour of Somerleyton. The new baronet, Savile, did his stint in the family firm, succeeding his cousin Edward as chairman in 1905; he was Halifax's MP for six years, sitting as an increasingly conservative Liberal Unionist, but his heart was in East Anglia. He was Eton and Balliol, Master of the Waveney Harriers, and Lt. Colonel in the Norfolk Militia, and mentioned in despatches during the South African War.[72] When his peerage came (1916) he took the title of Baron Somerleyton. It was a far cry from Dean Clough and the mills at dawn. It was an even further cry when the Victorian first baronet's admiration for Oliver Cromwell was balanced by the appointment of his great-grandson as Master of the Horse, the third great officer in the Royal Household.[73]

Theirs is as classic a story as Salt's: hard work, an eye for opportunity, and the means to capitalize on the breakthrough when it came. Then, rapid riches, impressive but responsible public display, and consequent public recognition: first a baronetcy and then a peerage. The Liberalism turned

into Liberal Unionism and then Toryism, the Congregationalism became
Anglicanism. It calls to mind the comment made by the philosopher T. H.
Green:

> The English aristocracy, we are told, is not an exclusive aristocracy.
> In one sense that is true... A great capitalist generally ends by buying
> a great estate. When the recollections of the counter have sufficiently
> passed away, he or his son is made a baronet. Perhaps in the next
> generation the family mounts a step higher still. Thus the oligarchy has
> a constant means of bribing the capitalists to its support. This corruption
> is eating the heart out of the upper commercial classes, and it is but the
> highest outcome of a flunkeyism which pervades English society from
> the top to the bottom and is incompatible with any healthy, political life.
> The English gentleman, we are sometimes told, is the noblest work of
> God, but one gentleman makes many snobs.[74]

So it might have seemed with Joseph's boy, Arnold, at Rugby and Frank's
boy, Savile, at Eton but it was not quite like that with John Crossley: his
boy, Louis John, went to London's University College School.

IV. The Ultimate Paternalist: Lever of Port Sunlight

If the Crossleys exhibit every public aspect of Nonconformist life in the
nineteenth century, W. H. Lever (1851–1925) combined their achievement
with that of Titus Salt, and pushed it beyond the limit of Congregational
credibility to the point of caricature.[75] His too was the classic story of hard
work, an eye for opportunity and then the riches, the public display, and
their secular consequence – a baronetcy (1911), a barony (1917), and a
viscountcy (1922). By the third generation political Liberalism had been
tamed into Conservatism and a barely residual Congregationalism had
been retained as an inherited responsibility. His grandson was Senior
Stewardship of the Jockey Club (1973–1976) and Knight of the Garter
(1988).[76]

Lever's Congregationalism was traditionary, domestic and familial, with
corresponding social, commercial and political dimensions. He was born
into it and he married into it. On his wife's side it went back several generations.[77] His father, however, had come new to it. In November 1831, James
Lever (1809–1897) moved from Bolton to Manchester to make his way as
a grocer. James was a Churchman but his principals were Grosvenor Street
Congregationalists and their example told on him.

At Grosvenor Street James was gripped by a sequence of sermons and
by John Angell James's devotional best-seller, *Anxious Inquirer* (1834). In

the Sunday School he met his future wife, a cotton mill manager's daughter. So here too was middle management, retail this time, rising to the spiritual occasion in a dramatically shaping northern town. Those were momentous years for commercial and political England and James Lever felt that he was taking a momentous step. He wrote formally 'To the Church of Christ assembling at Grosvenor Street Chapel...' to seek membership, submitting, in a tone of proudly humble independence, a detailed narrative of what God had done for his soul, a 'Declaration of Faith' which was printed *in piam memoriam* after his death. [78]

He returned to Bolton. Thanks largely to him, St. George's Road Congregational Church had been built in 1863, as well as a daughter church in his honour and memory in Blackburn Road in 1897. Three generations of his descendants were in their memberships and leadership. This was the spiritual climate which fostered the growth of his elder son and a surprising number of that son's business associates and senior managers. That son never repudiated it. Indeed, much that was distinctive in his religious observance was consistent with the confidently modernizing Congregationalism of St. George's Road. This was due to the minister, Charles Berry (1852–1899), who liked to call himself a 'Broad Evangelical'.[79] 'The great theme of his preaching was the Fatherhood of God which he conceived to be the central and essential attribute of deity.'[80] Fatherhood bred brotherhood and brotherhood had implications for church relations. Yet he declared: 'I am a Churchman, I am a High Churchman, I am a Catholic Churchman',[81] and his Chairman's address to the Congregational Union in May 1896 stated: 'Congregationalists are churchmen, as opposed to individualists. We are living members of an organism, not loose atoms wandering in eternal isolation... Churchmanship is the natural, the protective, the educational, concomitant of discipleship.'[82]

Such language left its mark on W. H. Lever. In his son's words, the church of Lever's dreams 'was Congregational in government, Anglican in architecture, liturgical in its form of service, pastoral and not sacerdotal in its ministry'.[83] In later life he was frequently to be found worshipping in two dream churches in London, at St. Peter's, Vere Street, an Anglican proprietary chapel, where F. D. Maurice (one of Charles Berry's early heroes) had ministered, and where Canon Page Robert now preached the purest milk of the Broad Church gospel;[84] and at the King's Weigh House, a historic Congregational transplant from the City, where John Hunter (1901–1904) and W. E. Orchard (1914–1932), men who were *sui generis* in Congregationalism, ministered.[85]

Lever was a church builder. Blackburn Road was the first of his schemes, an exercise in filial piety, as its church-opening rhetoric made clear. John Watson preached extempore on the family, an institution whose absence would bring anarchy to Church and State and whose presence revealed God's Fatherhood and man's brotherhood.[86] Langford Burrows, the new church's minister wanted to feel sure that the working men, for whom especially that Church had been built, would come in their hundreds to worship there and to join in a service which he promised them, as long as he remained minister of that people, should ever be marked with brotherly feeling and tender sympathy and Christian love.[87]

Similar sentiments informed the church co-operative scheme, initiated in 1919, for which Lever provided the financial foundation. Not all Bolton Congregationalists liked the scheme, for the concept of endowment ran counter to their treasured voluntaryism, but H. A. Hamilton recalled it with gratitude: 'The Ministers had regular fortnightly meetings. Deacons had quarterly conferences and Church Members an Annual Festival. As a young fledgling minister, I found this fellowship a great strength.'[88] Fifty years ahead of its time, the Bolton Group anticipated key aspects of the United Reformed Church.

It was his Wirral trio of churches where he most clearly exercised his influence. Christ Church, Port Sunlight, epitomized Lever's ideal. It was a prominent focal point in the village. Lever set the tone for this at the stonelaying:

They decided to build a church in which worshippers would learn that the way was clear and open between their souls and their God. They had selected Gothic as the most suitable form of architecture and they had called the church Christ Church because it was their wish that nothing should be stressed that tended to divide. They wanted a church that would be a visible expression of Christian unity, a church in whose worship all Christian people except those of extreme views could share.[89]

Lever provided room and ministry, he facilitated the fellowship's legal establishment and he influenced the style of what evolved. Given that Christ Church was primarily a works church in a works village and that works and village were the creation of one man, it was inevitable that the fellowship would display a wide spectrum of tensions as it developed into a Congregational church. The minute books illustrate this;[90] the relationship in Christian fellowship of managers and workers whose church office did not necessarily reflect the works hierarchy, the expectations of newcomers from a wide range of denominations, the explosion of temperament in choir and Sunday school, the constant awareness which everybody had of Lever and, in due course, his son, and the corresponding determination of the Levers to stand at arm's length from church decisions whatever the temptation to intervene. All Congregational churches with successful businessmen in their memberships or on their diaconates had to contain such tensions and many did so more fruitfully than is realized; this was their largely unsung contribution to the accommodation of democracy in the secular body politic.

Christ Church was a thriving church listed in the *Congregational Year Book*; it was not, however, affiliated to the Cheshire Congregational Union. A great-nephew of Lever's, a life-long Congregationalist, declined to transfer to Christ Church as not being a true Congregational church.[91] Christ Church was Lever's personal gift to the village and he steadily dignified his gift. The choir, for example, was paid, gowned, and surpliced at his expense. The Hulme Levers wished to commemorate the birth of an heir by giving a silver cross for the communion table, but a cross in church, other perhaps than in stained glass, was a contentious matter for many Nonconformists. It was three months before this cross was 'gratefully accepted'.[92]

This was industrial squirearchy, however Congregational the accent. Each wish of the Levers was communicated to the Church Committee though not always acted on at once. The careful but uneasy relationship continued after W. H. Lever's death under his son. In 1929 those tensions were focused on the search for a new minister. Although not a member of the Cheshire Congregational Union, Christ Church had recourse to the Provincial Moderator, a relatively new figure in Congregationalism, as well as to the new Lord Leverhulme. Delicate negotiations followed which included a discreetly high-powered meeting in London. At a church meeting in Port Sunlight the Moderator and Lord Leverhulme spoke, and a Vacancy Committee was set up.[93] The minutes hint at underlying difficulties, some of them the small change of Congregational life, but more of them showing the difficulty of being a truly Congregational 'parish' church, representative of a community at once wider and yet more geographically defined than a gathered church.

The difficulties were overcome. A minister was found. Lever Brothers arranged his Public Welcome, the women of Christ Church presented him with a silk gown and cassock, and his induction was a model of its kind:

> All the ministers attending were gowned; they met with a surpliced choir in the choir vestry; and walked in ordered procession to the door of the church, where the new minister was received by them and taken with them up the central aisle, preceded by choir boys and other choristers singing a processional hymn. Officiating ministers took up their position in the choir stalls; the other clergy sat in the further seats of the chancel. The Moderator, Minister and Church Secretary made their statements standing at the front of the chancel; the concluding part was taken within the Communion rails, where the new minister remained until the Benediction. The whole was dignified and impressive.[94]

Later the new minister carefully explained to the committee the terms of Christ Church's newest endowment, of 7,500 Preference Shares in what was now Unilever subject to the proviso that no pew rents were charged; he reminded the committee that 'the appointment of a new minister must receive the approval of the holder of the Viscountcy of Leverhulme'; and he intimated his wish to hold early morning communion on Easter Day.[95] This remained Congregationalism with a difference.

The Wirral's other two Lever churches, St. George's Thornton Hough and Neston, were studies in endowed contrast. Neston was short lived. Lever converted a failing Liberal Club into a church, and gave it ecclesiastical shape, including three stained-glass windows to commemorate the seventeenth century. A manse was built, the minister's stipend was endowed and an institute, playing field, tennis courts and bowling green, emphasized the cause's role in the social and recreational as well as the spiritual life of the village. It lasted for thirty years (1908–1938), but with a Presbyterian congregation already attracting prosperous newcomers there was less opportunity for village Congregationalism to take root.[96]

Thornton Hough lies midway between Port Sunlight and Neston. Thornton was a squire's village and St. George's was his church. It need not have been that way. Its architect was convinced that Lever would not have built St. George's had there been a proper parson at the parish church; relations between them were 'like a knife'.[97] Lever went about it with a mixture of high-handedness, bonhomie, genuine principle, and an eye for opportunity. In 1903 Thornton's Nonconformists were Wesleyans: 'Then, by negotiations with Conference, their chapel came into the possession of Mr. Lever, who, at a meeting held on Tuesday evening, 27 September, 1903, explained that in future the chapel would be known as the Congregational Chapel'.[98]

The transfer seems to have been painless: day schools were opened and when a permanent church replaced an iron one, its name, St. George's, recalled Bolton's St. George's Road as much as England's patron saint; its roll of members included Lever's son, four of Lever's sisters, and a Lever brother-in-law was church secretary.[99] St. George's was the Levers' church. Photographs of three viscounts were displayed in the vestry into the 1970s, as if they were patrons of the living. Well into the 1960s flowers were provided monthly from the Manor and house parties came for the Christmas services.

Through the London and Colonial Missionary Societies, Congregationalists had been among the more creative pioneers of overseas mission. No Congregationalist of Lever's prominence and generation could have been unaware of the claims of overseas mission but missionaries too were keen advocates of their wares and their achievements and their perspectives could be searchingly different from those of secular entrepreneurs, however enlightened. Lever's missionary perspectives were too shrewdly calculating to be insightful, however sensibly he justified them. He admired what he regarded as truly practical missions (the Jesuits of the Belgian Congo scored highly there) but his sense of practicality had its limits. The medical side of the Baptists' Bolobo Mission was 'as near perfect as possible'; the self-improvement side aroused his scorn,[100] and his snap judgements suggest his vulnerability to the accusations of forced labour which dogged his Congolese operations in the last decade of his life and diminished if not destroyed his reputation.[101]

Perhaps the key to all this lies in the nature of his belief, or lack of belief. Angus Watson (1874–1961), a fish processor, and like Lever a lifelong Congregationalist, pin-pointed the contradictions in Lever's character and beliefs.[102] He recognized 'the living power of his spiritual faith', and the 'background in his life that was definitely Christian' but Lever:

> Had no faith in immortality, and said more than once to me that he believed that death ended all. This was one of the keys to his complex character. Material things meant much to him, because the preparation for the spiritual life was, after all, secondary.

He also noted that Lever 'was not a creator...but he had a genius for adaptation'.[103] That has a bearing on Lever's understanding and presentation of community. It also bears on his attitude to church membership, which he never took up, and his brief attraction – common to many of his generation – to Christian Science and Spiritualism; and it explains his Freemasonry.[104]

With this we turn to Lever's obsequies. They began quietly at the London house in which he died. The funeral itself was at Christ Church.[105] Almost simultaneously there were services in Bolton, Boston (Mass.), Bristol, Kinshasa, London, and Stornoway. First, however, he lay in state in his Art Gallery, amidst rivers of flowers, between busts of his late wife and himself, and in front of Lord Leighton's *Daphnephoria*, a Roman romp of plump young men scampering and ripe young girls simpering.[106] This pagan grandeur was for a Congregationalist, although the only body to which he could commit himself in membership was a Masonic Lodge; Freemasons expected no belief, just the ritual of comradeship and the comfort of service in brotherhood. By birth and sympathy he belonged to the oldest, most democratic, of the English Free Churches but, by temperament an autocrat, he could not surrender. He remained an Evangelical Free Churchman for whom there was no Evangelical experience. That is the most suggestive clue to the magic of Sunlight.

Sunlight owed everything to soap, a staple of the grocery businesses, and W. H. Lever was the son of an increasingly prosperous retail and wholesale grocer. In 1872 Lever became a partner in his father's firm.[107] In 1874 he married a bride from a family in St. George's Road Congregational Church.[108] Lever's commercial training had been grounded in the mutuality of a family business and honed by the commercial travelling at which he excelled. Since 1874 the firm had marketed Lever's Pure Honey Soap. Honey, of course, had nothing to do with it. Lever determined to market a perfect popular soap under a perfect brand name, as facilitated by the 1875 Trademarks Act.[109] By the 1890s Sunlight Soap was the United Kingdom's best-selling soap, with the stage set for Lever, after years of takeovers, lawsuits, and relentless publicity, to become the head of a multinational combine, in which he was Sole Ordinary Shareholder.[110] This Free Trade Liberal had built up one of the biggest commercial and industrial combines yet seen.[111]

When asked his secret, Lever, the Englishman whom the *Toronto Globe* bracketed with Carnegie, Rockefeller and Ford, replied: 'I organize, deputize, and criticize'.[112] The authoritarian side of Lever's character grew with success, age and deafness, yet this Liberal Free-trader naturally promoted mutuality and self-improvement in mutuality, those secular expressions of Congregational Independency. He had a genuine horror of monopoly. Yet his personality, methods and buccaneering success ensured that he was the ultimate monopolist. This was played out in his business empire from accumulation to near disintegration. Disaster was averted by a structured de-personalizing which began even before his unexpected death.

His upbringing and his business formation encouraged what W. J. Reader called his 'lifelong passion for planning, for building, and for regulating people's lives for their own good as he saw it' and what W. P. Jolly called his 'continuing interest in the social microcosm, especially one conceived, constructed and furnished with inhabitants by himself'.[113] From the turn of the twentieth century he expressed it in prosperity sharing (the welfare and benefits schemes), out of which grew co-partnership (the sharing of profits). As he told Birkenhead's Literary and Scientific Society: 'Labour of itself can never produce wealth... But if Labour is well directed, if the fairy of good management appears on the scene, all is changed, and Labour can and does produce wealth beyond the dreams of avarice.'[114] And as he told his employees: 'If you leave this money with me, I shall use it to provide for you everything which makes life pleasant – viz. nice houses, comfortable homes, and healthy recreation. Besides, I am disposed to allow profit sharing under no other than that form.'[115]

Sharing was a function of paternalism. While philanthropy allowed for imagination and might even be prodigal, sharing implied mutuality and opened the door to equality. In the early twentieth century it appealed to many Nonconformist employers. It was a responsible businessman's alternative to the Co-operative Movement. It had a moral flavour which Charles Wilson described as 'a curious mixture of the ethical principles of the Band of Hope and the precepts of Samuel Smiles'. It was bound to fail. Full co-partnership was impossible in so complex an enterprise, and Wilson noted that a co-partner's average annual dividend never exceeded £20. Lever, 'individualist though he was...failed to grasp the delicacy or the importance of these problems of social obligation which he had set himself'.[116]

He was the first Wirral employer to introduce the eight-hour day and ten years later he advocated a six-hour day[117] but Lever failed to implement a working day of two six-hour shifts because of what it would mean for the established patterns of his employees' lives and because of trade union opposition.[118] He supported the payment of MPs in 1906 and the introduction of Old Age Pensions in 1907 and he favoured women's suffrage. In such cases he was ahead of many seasoned men of affairs.[119] His argument for pensions was a characteristically blunt mix of contemporary pragmatism and classical Liberalism. He was

> not sure that thrift was the highest form of citizenship... the State should do for the individual citizen what it was out of his power to do for himself, and when it was for the advantage of the State and the well-being of the citizen to have it done.[120]

The ambivalence of Lever's stance was unintentionally highlighted by *Progress*, the firm's magazine, when it quoted, in its memorial issue, the assessments of three leading journals. For the *Morning Post*, Lever's life was 'a standing refutation of the Socialist doctrines; for no social effort could have created what the world owes to his individuality'. For *The Times*, 'Lever had the ideal of socializing and Christianizing the machinery of industry and adapting to modern requirements the old spirit of brotherhood which characterized at their best the days of hand labour'. And the *Spectator* suggested that it would 'pay Labour to encourage, even very carefully to cultivate, men like Leverhulme'.[121]

The Levers, like the Crossleys and Salts, took education seriously. W. H. Lever took an interest in the Cambridge rebuilding of Cheshunt College; he warmed to its nondenominational foundation as a college for evangelical ministry.[122] Hulme Lever gave to Caterham School, although it was felt that he could have been more generous.[123] The real impact, however, was to be seen in the schools at Port Sunlight and Thornton Hough and in the reconstitution of Bolton School. His endowments in his lifetime to the University of Liverpool gave a bracing edge to Red-Brick University scholarship,[124] and his will established a trust for education and research. His trustees shaped the Leverhulme Trust into 'the chief non-governmental funder of individual research in the second half of the twentieth century'.[125] Here, perhaps, was the most imaginative consequence of Congregational Independency and its encouragement of self-improvement in mutuality.

Where, however, should we place Port Sunlight, which was for many Lever's best advertisement? In 1916 A. G. Gardiner found Port Sunlight, 'a garden city which is one of the first and still one of the best object-lessons in the science and art of industrial housing...'[126]

In 1887 Lever, with an architect friend, William Owen, feeling that the Warrington soaperies were unfit for purpose, looked for, found, and bought an apparently unpromising site: fifty-two Merseyside acres of creek and marsh. In fact the unpromising site promised excellent land and water transport, it tapped on to a plentiful labour supply, and its marshiness had been greatly overstated. Twenty-four acres would do for the soaperies, the rest for the village.[127]

Building began in 1888. By 1907 there were 720 houses, rising to nearly 900 on well over 200 acres and housing 4,000 people.[128] So developed a striking union of art and nature. The creeks were first used, then drained and transformed into gardens and dells. Houses and trees were placed to give an artfully leafy informality to the streetscape. The density was low and the spaciousness was accentuated by building the houses in blocks, enclosing allotments on the inside but fronted outside by gardens which the firm maintained lest individual householders turn them into chicken runs. By 1910 the village was said to have cost £350,000 and its upkeep took twenty per cent of the rent roll; there was no profiteering here.[129] So joyously traditional (even the inn, which at first was run on temperance lines, looked like a manor house), the houses were fresh, sensible, and well planned with piped hot and cold water, an inside bathroom, and no attics.[130]

Then an interesting thing happened. The University of Liverpool's architectural school developed concepts of the City Beautiful realized in the American Beaux Arts style. Lever was impressed. In 1909 he offered prizes to Liverpool students for the development of Port Sunlight.[131] The winning scheme imposed a formal axis of avenues on the existing informality, two great boulevards, one leading to Christ Church and the other, at right angles, to an Art Gallery. Thomas Mawson (1861–1933), the Congregationalist whose firm implemented the scheme, was an entrepreneurial landscape architect with considerable civic consciousness, wide international contacts, and influence to match.[132]

Not all shared these enthusiasms. A Bolton trade union official told Lever in 1919 that 'No man of an independent turn of mind can breathe for long the atmosphere of Port Sunlight. That might be news to your Lordship, but we have tried it. The profit-sharing system not only enslaves and degrades the workers, it tends to make them servile and sycophant.'[133] A Congregational minister who had been 'quartered' there told Angus Watson that at times he felt 'intended to be an advertisement for "Sunlight Soap" more than for the Kingdom of God'.[134]

This was, however, a rare achievement. Port Sunlight was not simply a rich man's whim. From the late 1890s he had been exercised by questions of land ownership, advocating the municipal ownership of land and new methods of communal regulation to cater for city living.[135] Despite appearances Port Sunlight did not reflect a flight from the city and Lever, although never an easy associate for civic idealists, supported the Garden City Association and kindred bodies.[136]

Lever was a world-class capitalist. Commentators referred loosely to Black Port Sunlights, but the Congo's Leverville was a parody of Sunlight and the company's justification of its increasingly criticized policies reads as uncomfortably with a contemporary as with a twenty-first-century gloss.[137] Leverburgh, in the Western Isles, was never given the opportunity to develop but Lever's failure to grasp the complexities of Scottish attitudes in Lewis and Harris remains inexcusable in a Nonconformist Liberal of his generation.[138]

In 1921, Lever Brothers transferred their headquarters from Port Sunlight to London.[139] Lever saw a building opportunity although it was not until 1930–32, after Lever Brothers had merged with the Dutch Margarine Unie and Lever House had become Unilever House, that his palace was built.

V. The End of Paternalism

The Salts, Crossleys and Levers were at once exceptional and representative. As Congregational captains of industry they were the victims of their own success. The engagement of manufacturers with housing and co-partnership schemes for their workforces and with lifestyles in general continued into the first half of the twentieth century. Sir Halley Stewart (1838–1937), the brickmaker and founder of Stewartby, in Bedfordshire, provides a parallel rather than a contrast.[140] F. H. Crittall (1860–1935), the metal window frame manufacturer and founder of Silver End, in Essex, though latterly 'indifferent to all organized religion', was reared in Congregationalism, and Silver End had its Congregational church.[141] J. S. Ruston (1869–1939), whose engineering firm industrialized Lincoln and whose family had been Lincoln's leading Congregationalists, envisaged a 'Ruston Garden Village' in the immediate aftermath of the Great War; it was to be called Swanpool.[142]

That was a sign of the coming age. The economics and politics of model villages were changing. The future of the Quaker Cadburys' Bournville and the Quaker Rowntrees' New Earswick had been assured by making them over to trustees. Budgett Meakin called this 'propaganda by deed'.[143] The propagation of the ideals of community and co-partnership, of industrial mutuality, now lay less with industrial and commercial entrepreneurs than with a new breed of expert. They were organized busybodies, practical visionaries, entrepreneurial networkers, experts in social exploration, pioneers of a new politics, men like Percy Alden and, most representative of them all, W. H. Lever's contemporary, Ebenezer Howard (1850–1928), the Congregationally formed pioneer of the Garden City.[144] From the first, Letchworth and Welwyn, Howard's prototypes, had flourishing Free Churches with strong Congregational components, and Hampstead Garden Suburb's Free Church must have seemed like the future at prayer, with its radical sprinkling of Labour MPs, discriminating journalists, and well-placed civil servants.

The Second World War induced the birth of the Welfare State. The post-war New Towns were social necessities, not philanthropic luxuries. Health and education were as necessary to national security as profit and the armed forces. The state was the nation and the nation was a confederation of communities. The ideal was possible. Or so it seemed. The Free Churches, with Congregationalists to the fore, had to a remarkable degree staked out the ground and those embarrassingly tall poppies, the great paternalists, had played their part, at once fleeting and determinative. Their successors were less and less likely to be Free Churchmen, less and less likely to be locally based and locally credible.

These tendencies had long histories. In 1921, the year that Lever's headquarters moved to Blackfriars, Francis D'Arcy Cooper (1882–1941) joined the unofficial 'inner cabinet' which Lever belatedly instituted.[145] From 1923 Cooper was formally a director, and indeed Vice-Chairman. From 1925 he was Chairman. Cooper belonged to a new breed. He was neither a Lancastrian nor a Congregationalist and he was not an industrialist although he proved to be an outstanding industrial manager. He was a chartered accountant. It was Cooper whose advice extricated Lever Brothers from the mess into which the purchase of the Niger Company had threatened to precipitate it; it was Cooper who rationalized, modernized and depersonalized what had turned into a perplexing dictatorship, and who engineered the merger with Margarine Unie which made Unilever one of the largest companies in Europe. The accountant was replacing the paternalist as the face of large-scale industry, and the responsibilities were different.

The legislative constraints were also different. In 1939, William Blackshaw's *The Community and Social Service* appeared,[146] one of an occasional series published by Pitmans dealing with social administration, public assistance and local government. Blackshaw (1866–1953), a recently retired Congregational minister, was a model of contemporary ministry.[147] He was well-educated (Oxford, Dublin, St. Andrews, Marburg, and Berlin), with contrasting but demanding pastorates in the centre of Sheffield and the London suburbs, including the worlds of Free Church philanthropy and paternalism. The heart of his experience, however, lay in the Settlement movement. In Sheffield he was founder and warden of the determinedly unconventional Croft House Settlement (1901–1913) and in London he was co-warden of the Mansfield House University Settlement, Canning Town (1926–1938). He was felt to be 'an intellectual man' brimming over with 'enthusiasm for the poor'[148] and on the theologically and politically liberal wing of Congregationalism. Blackshaw had, in 1905, delivered a paper to the Leeds Autumnal Meetings on 'Institutional Churches'. His message was straightforward: 'The Congregational Church must be the Church of the poor as well as of the rich if it is to continue to be the Church of Christ'. It must, therefore, be 'the home of the people of the slum, and, taking them as it finds them, it must endeavour, from the basis of their common and felt needs, to lift them to a higher level of manhood and womanhood'; and those ministering to it, preaching 'in the main, outside in the streets and courts', should be 'educated, cultured men, who have philosophical tastes and broad human and social sympathies'.[149] Fifteen years later Blackshaw addressed the fourth International Congregational Council at Boston (Mass.) on 'The Church and the Social Order', and five years after that he was in Stockholm for the seminal Conference on Life and Work.[150]

The Community and Social Service had originated in lectures delivered in the Training Department of Mansfield House University Settlement, intended as historical and contextual introductions for groups of Free Church and Anglican ordinands meeting professionals in the statutory and voluntary sectors of social service. The result was a manual summarizing where matters stood with regard to health, environment, housing, insurance, the poor law, juvenile delinquency, education, administration, local government and London government, and the relation of statutory and voluntary social service.[151] His surveys included a brisk reference to Saltaire and those later products 'of individual action', New Earswick, Bournville and Port Sunlight, but for Blackshaw they were already the admirable legacies of a world that had moved on; and Blackshaw's manual, so up-to-date for 1939, was itself rapidly to be superseded by the world of William Beveridge and a post-war determination in which socialization was at last poised on the edge of socialism.

6

Slums and Salvation

Peter Catterall

I. Introduction

Until the mid-eighteenth century the tightly-packed streets of London constituted the only significant British city. Rapid urbanization thereafter created new mission fields, and new challenges, for the churches. The resulting distinction between the countryside and the newly urban was noted by Elizabeth Gaskell, the wife of a Manchester Unitarian minister, in her novel *North and South* (1854–85). Solid Nonconformist citizens, conscious of their weight in British society following the 1851 religious census, took pride in their contribution to urban dynamism. At the same time, however, there was also consciousness of those excluded from that dynamism. The same census drew attention to the chapels' failure to reach these groups, and the visibility of these social and material as well as spiritual needs of the urban poor steadily grew. Thus, in his Congregational Union chairman's address in 1929, T. Rhondda Williams reflected on his early ministry in Bradford:

> I went on preaching the old Gospel to the individual, urging him to get his own soul saved, and I assured him that, if he did, there would be a mansion awaiting him in heaven... It was only when I went back to the place after being some years away that I realised how perfectly dreadful the conditions of the houses were. And then I felt amazed at my previous blindness.[1]

He was by no means alone in this epiphany, or in discerning in the urban slums of late Victorian Britain peculiar challenges. As the Wesleyan Methodist George Jackson commented: 'religion has no more chance to flourish in the slums of our large cities than wheat in a coal-mine'.[2]

Alongside the emerging idea of the industrial city there was thus a growing sense of an urban setting as a distinctive and difficult mission field.

II. The Early Nineteenth Century: Domestic Mission and District Providence

Cities did not immediately acquire this reputation. Indeed, Gilbert argues that the social changes unleashed by the industrialization accompanying urbanization were conducive to the growth that evangelical Nonconformity – primarily Methodists, Congregationalists and Baptists – enjoyed around 1800.[3] Appealing differentially to skilled artisans, it complemented their sense of craft pride and workplace discipline through emphasizing industry and self-improvement. In stressing conversion and salvation it spoke to the self-worth of workers expressing their status in settings where the Anglican-flavoured hierarchies and disciplines of the countryside were attenuated, whilst providing them with networks of social, financial and spiritual support. The mechanisms used, such as itinerant preaching, also helped to appeal to such groups. Lay leadership affirmed status and facilitated rapid diffusion in settings such as Methodist class or camp meetings where artisan leaders were expressing experiential religion amongst their peers.

Arguably politics, rather than urbanization, was more of a challenge for evangelical Nonconformity. Wesleyan Methodist leaders were particularly apt to draw a dichotomy between religion and irreligious radicalism during the crackdown following the reform protests of the years between Waterloo and Peterloo (1815–19).[4] They thus sought to discipline, not least through a wave of expulsions, a laity equipped with a biblically-inspired symbolic language and becoming politically restive through economic hardship and changes in production processes. Although many individual lay Methodists like William Lovett were prominent in the protests against the punitive labour market disciplines of the New Poor Law of 1834 and the subsequent development of Chartism, official Wesleyanism was unsympathetic to both.

Nonconformity instead could be portrayed, and could portray itself, as being primarily concerned with the spiritual wellbeing of the middle classes. As a leading London Congregationalist, Thomas Binney, put it in his address to the Congregational Union in 1848:

> Our special mission is neither to the very rich nor to the very poor. We have a work to do upon the thinking active, influential classes…which, gathering into cities, and consisting of several gradations there, are the modern movers and moulders of the world.[5]

Congregationalism was rather better represented amongst the urban lower classes than Binney suggested,[6] though some observers noted that the very poor could not afford to attend Dissenting chapels.[7] This was a matter of church finance. With a lack of endowments there was a corresponding reliance on congregations composed of the middle classes or the regularly employed working classes. Given their overwhelming preponderance in the general population it was nevertheless highly probable that working-class folk formed a majority both of the congregations and of the unchurched, although Nonconformists increasingly reproached themselves for neglecting the latter.

The consequences of this neglect seemed more apparent in light of the 1851 religious census. By establishing a contrast in the minds of contemporaries between rural piety and urban irreligion,[8] especially amongst the lower orders, it helped define the urban mission field as distinctive. However, many contemporaries were already predisposed to accept its findings about the unconscious secularism of the urban poor. The Anglican evangelical, Baptist Noel, had warned in 1835 of half a million Londoners 'living without a public acknowledgement of God, and in contempt of all the means of grace'.[9] Noel was accordingly a moving spirit in the cross-denominational (though Anglican-led) London City Mission (LCM) established that year to take the Gospel to those urban denizens who would not come to hear it. A City Mission had already been founded in Bristol in 1826[10] and it was joined in the 1830s by analogues in other major cities such as Manchester.

In 1833 a similar cross-Protestant alliance founded the Manchester and Salford District Provident Society (DPS). Such bodies were established in various major towns and cities in the 1820s and 1830s by people like William Felkin, a leading Baptist layman who played a key role in creating the mechanics institute and DPS in his native Nottingham.[11] The aim was to improve the financial management and moral conditions of the poor in the interests of social harmony.[12] The Liverpool DPS, which served as a model for many others, described its mission as being 'to rescue the lower orders from the miseries of poverty and vice, and to make them the authors of their own independence and virtue by encouraging them to form prudent and useful habits'. Through inculcating prudence, not least in encouraging the urban poor to eschew early marriage, they made a quasi-Malthusian contribution to tackling overcrowded and insanitary conditions.[13]

Charitable visiting was well-established, if often Anglican,[14] before 1800. For instance, the Methodist John Gardner founded the Strangers Friend Society in London in 1785 'to relief the destitute sick poor, without distinction of sect or country', an innovation rapidly extended to other cities such as Bristol.[15] With the city missions and provident societies that emerged in the 1820s and 1830s this work became more extensive and systematic. Nor was it just provided by evangelicals. The work Joseph Tuckerman started in Boston in 1826 inspired a series of Unitarian imitations in Britain, beginning with the Domestic Mission founded in London in 1832.[16] These were, in the words of the Liverpool Domestic Mission established in 1836, 'to carry the light and hope of our Divine Religion into the moral heathendom by which we are surrounded'.[17]

The LCM adopted a very statistical means of assessing such work: for instance, its 1855 Annual Report noted 967 cases of 'decided reformation of life' over the previous year.[18] The work was largely carried out by visitation and tract distribution by paid lay evangelists, of whom many were Nonconformists, whilst to provide free rudimentary education and religious instruction ragged schools were developed. These originated earlier in the century, but the term and the Ragged School Union founded in 1844 seem very much to be initiatives of the LCM.[19]

The Unitarian missions also established ragged schools, as well as other services such as libraries and provident societies to encourage savings. Their Liverpool North End Mission additionally spawned what became the Liverpool Co-operative Society and a Nurse Society, to teach the rudiments of cleanliness, ventilation and nursing.[20] These were agencies to help the clients of the Mission to help themselves. Indiscriminate charity was deprecated as likely to compound the improvident habits or intemperance seen as the prime causes of want. Visiting and personal enquiry were not the least means to screen out imposters and ensure that aid went to those least likely to waste it.[21]

III. Temperance and Preventative Intervention

Following the spate of drunkenness stimulated by the ill-conceived 1830 Beerhouse Act, which led two years later to the founding of the teetotal movement in Preston, Nonconformists were increasingly inclined to associate that waste with alcohol abuse. Indeed, the evils of drink – including an oppressive industry befuddling the soul, the pubs competing with the chapels and the poverty resulting from the misallocation of meagre household resources – were widely agreed amongst Nonconformity by the end of the nineteenth century. The combination, which the nineteenth-century temperence movement offered, of resistance to State-sanctioned oppression and liberation of the individual soul both reflected, and appealed to, Nonconformist sensibilities. Bands of Hope became characteristic of chapel organizations and Nonconformity became the backbone of the disparate temperance movement. It was, however, not particular to Nonconformity. Furthermore, whilst the redemption of the drunkard was not unlike the conversion experience sought by the chapels, it was not the same. An emphasis on temperance, however, reinforced too readily the view that poverty and social problems largely reflected individual failings.

There was nothing distinctively urban about these diagnoses. Indeed, the social problems of Victorian cities were neither novel nor unique: some of the worst slums were found in rural counties like Norfolk.[22] It was more a matter of scale, such as the hundreds of homeless boys Thomas Barnardo found in London's East End in 1866, prompting him to establish his orphanages. Part of the context was the deaths resulting from the periodic cholera outbreaks after 1830, the last of which hit London in 1866. Although the scourge of water-borne diseases was effectively tackled by the work of Sir John Snow on water quality and Sir Joseph Bazalgette on sewerage, other communicable diseases such as tuberculosis remained virulent. Victorian cities thus made manifest for the first time the social and spiritual needs resulting from unprecedented concentrations of disease, vice, poverty, criminality and poor housing amongst populations vulnerable no longer to the rhythms of the harvests but instead the vagaries of the trade cycle. By the 1860s the poorest parts were attracting a steady stream of middle-class 'slum tourists'.[23] The very rise of such a pastime was redolent of the growing social, cultural, economic and geographic gulf separating slum denizens from their visitors.

Some significant Free Church attempts to bridge that gulf nevertheless occurred in the 1860s. Following Barnardo's initiative, in 1869 the Wesleyan Methodist Thomas Bowman Stephenson was taken to meet some London orphans. It struck Stephenson that what they needed was the security of a family-like environment: accordingly the National Children's Homes (NCH) which he then established were organized into small units significantly staffed by trained women workers. This reflected German influences: the family units derived from the *Rauhe Haus* of Dr Wichern of Hamburg,[24] whilst the workers were modelled on the deaconesses of Pastor Theodore Fliedner of Kaiserwerth, whose tending of the wounded so impressed Stephenson when he subsequently visited the battlefields of the Franco-Prussian War.[25]

Women's roles in the City and Domestic Missions had been largely confined to managing tract depots and fund-raising.[26] The LCM, in particular, had paid male missionaries. Women were, however, prominent in the visiting work of the District Provident and similar societies.[27] The shift into domiciliary care by Barnardo and Stephenson now expanded women's opportunities for service. Additionally, the advent of substantial Nonconformist charities provided outlets for the philanthropic talents of wealthy female chapel-goers who otherwise had limited opportunities within the constrained labour market of the time. Women began to appear on the boards of hitherto male-dominated charities. They became increasingly active in founding orphanages or aiding outcast women. In 1856 the Reformatory and Refuge Union was established as an umbrella organization for this burgeoning charitable sector. Such developments – alongside Victorian technological achievements such as the spread of press, post and railways – contributed to a greater momentum which aided the growth of national rather than local charities.

Initiatives such as Barnardo's and the NCH also marked a shift in Nonconformist views of the nature and causes of social need from an emphasis on moral rescue. They were now trying to protect the young from falling victim to social evils in the first place, for instance through the employment Barnardo's found for 50,000 street children in its first forty years.[28] Aiding prisoners' children had already been initiated by some ragged school pioneers, such as the Unitarian Mary Carpenter in Bristol. Following the 1870 Education Act the ragged schools disappeared (although in some cases the name remained) and attention shifted instead towards prevention. Three years later the Congregational minister Benjamin Waugh urged the creation of juvenile courts and detention centres to prevent the Poor Law and criminal justice system institutionalizing children, trapping them in criminality.[29] It was thus no longer enough simply to encourage provident behaviour amongst the respectable poor to save them from the exigencies of the Poor Law. Instead there was a shift towards what would later be called preventative intervention.

IV. Salvationists and Sinners

Another significant innovation was the creation in 1865 of what became in 1878 the Salvation Army. This arose when William Booth, an erstwhile Chartist and minister with the Methodist New Connexion, was asked to lead the undenominational East London Special Services Committee in attempts to evangelize the poor districts around Whitechapel. Booth, like Stephenson, was to make innovative use of the ministry of women. His partnership with his wife Catherine served as a model for spousal ministry. He encouraged an activist form of ministry amongst his followers, both men and women, using the latter as sympathetic interlocutors with the unsaved. For, instead of the traditional gathered church of Nonconformity, Salvationists were sent out to save sinners in public houses or alleyways.

The methods may have been distinctive. The primary focus, however, was much the same: the winning of souls. Conversion had to be genuine: Booth initially deprecated cheap eating-houses for the poor because 'by relieving their physical necessities I should be helping to create...religious hypocrisy and pretence'.[30] Nonconformists could certainly feel that the superior resources of the Established Church were too often deployed to encourage a culture of cadging covered by a superficial religiosity.[31] Unsurprisingly, Salvationist opposition to this culture was frequently unwelcome amongst slum-dwellers. Hostility to their invasive attempt to impose alien values in impoverished areas, sometimes including derisively imitative 'Skeleton Armies', was thus social as well as religious in origin. Contemporaries detected in the 'pretension of the Army to superior piety' a provocative spiritual arrogance.[32] This opposition brought a shift in tactics. Booth later observed 'I have been a soul-saver all my life, but I find that many souls cannot be reached unless you deal with their circumstances'.[33] Therefore in the 1880s he initiated hostels for the homeless, support for families of prisoners and, in common with other local churches, the feeding of strikers' families during the 1889 great strike in the London docks.

One particular set of souls Booth sought to reach was that of prostitutes. They had long been a target for evangelism. In the early nineteenth century there were various asylums where they could receive food and shelter, read Bibles and consider repentance.[34] Yet attitudes towards them were shifting. As depicted in Mrs Gaskell's novel *Mary Barton* (1848), the fallen woman might once have been respectable, then abandoned and left to sink into the abyss. Concern about their plight was clearly reflected in the way Mrs Gaskell's fellow Unitarian, Mrs Edmund Kell of Southampton, promoted brothel visiting and in the dramatic growth of Magdalen homes from sixty in 1856 to 300 by 1906.[35] Medical opinion in the 1850s meanwhile expressed growing concern at the risk of prostitutes infecting wider society. The Contagious Diseases Acts 1864 and 1866 resulted, allowing medical inspection of women in naval and garrison towns on their suspicion of being prostitutes. The subsequent campaign against legislation seen as official sanctioning of prostitution, invasive of women's liberty and hypocritically redolent of oppressive sexual double-standards was led by Josephine Butler, the wife of an evangelical Anglican clergyman. Her efforts were widely supported, particularly by Congregationalists, Wesleyans and Quakers.[36]

Historically Nonconformists had felt excluded from and suspicious of the State. Yet the idea of state action to protect the weak from their own weaknesses was already familiar to temperance campaigners. The paradox that campaigning to alter state policy drew attention to what the State might do more widely for society can be illustrated by the effect on one of those most galvanized by Mrs Butler's activities, the ardent temperance advocate and Wesleyan, Hugh Price Hughes. At the launch demonstration of the National Vigilance Association (NVA) on 22 August 1885 he proclaimed:

> It is an awful fact that at this moment the only way by which a woman can secure bread is by the sale of her body; and we ought to cause such a change in the social condition of this country and every other, that it may no longer be possible to make statements of this kind.[37]

By the time of the successful conclusion of Mrs Butler's efforts in 1886 Hughes was supporting the related campaigning journalism of W. T. Stead. This editor of a London evening newspaper, the *Pall Mall Gazette*, was a son and brother of the Congregationalist manse. On 6 July 1885 Stead began publishing a series of articles known collectively as 'The Maiden Tribute of Modern Babylon'. In these he called for raising the age of consent from 13 to 16, drawing attention to the incidence of child prostitution.

A House of Lords committee in 1881 had already reported on such young girls being recruited and trafficked.[38] This prepared the ground for the findings of the London Congregational Union's pamphlet, *The Bitter Cry of Outcast London* (1883) – ably publicized by Stead in which squalid overcrowding was depicted as leading to illicit sexual relations. Incest was presented as common. The surprise for the author[39] was not that slum-dwellers took to drink and sin, but that they were not more depraved.[40] As with the Contagious Diseases Acts, the situation was worsened by misguided state action. The Artisans' Dwellings Act 1875 replaced poor housing with properties at higher rents unaffordable to those crowding ever more into the remaining slums. This legislation again had the paradoxical effect of softening Nonconformity's traditional wariness of the State. Growing awareness of its role in and responsibility to wider society after 1851 no doubt played a part. No less important, however, was the awareness that if the State could make things worse by ill-conceived interventions, it might also ameliorate them, with far more resources to do so than the churches.[41]

V. Changing Attitudes in the 1880s

The Bitter Cry, the positive response it received, and accompanying developments of the 1880s marked a significant shift in Nonconformist thinking about social need. In 1847 the leading Congregationalist, Edward Baines Jr, had proclaimed: 'It is *not* the duty of the Government to feed the people, to clothe them, to build houses for them, to direct their industry or their commerce, to superintend their families, to cultivate their minds…'[42] State provision would in Baines' view undermine individual moral responsibility. However, rather than simply inculcating faith and provident habits, some form of preventative intervention had already been sanctioned for children. This was both to help orphans who could not help themselves and, more radically, to break cycles of deprivation.

As Mary Carpenter observed to the Newcastle Commission on education in 1861, 'the low moral, intellectual and often physical condition' of the working class ensured these were likely continually to recur, 'unless a helping hand is held out to the children to aid them to rise to a higher and better life'.[43]

That helping hand was increasingly moving beyond simply visiting the working-class home to intervening directly in childcare. That moral suasion was no longer deemed sufficient was exemplified by two developments of the 1880s. First the work of health-visiting, which was the outgrowth of home-visiting concerned with the care of infants, became increasingly prescriptive. Secondly, to tackle the demoralizing circumstances producing these cycles of deprivation, there was growing willingness to undermine parental responsibility in the name of child protection. Hitherto the response to familial neglect or child abuse focused on reclaiming the malefactor from sin (and often drunkenness as well). The case of Mary Ellen Wilson in New York, and the consequent founding there of a Society for the Prevention of Cruelty to Children in 1875, validated the idea of completely removing a child from an abusive setting. Similar societies were established in Liverpool and by BenjaminWaugh in London in 1883–84 which five years later became the National Society for the Prevention of Cruelty to Children (NSPCC), the same year that an Act for the first time provided powers to punish parental abuse, including the removal of their children. The NSPCC set up an inspectorate to uncover abuses, supported by statute and the local magistracy. The necessity of protecting the vulnerable thus prompted changing Nonconformist attitudes to both society and State with remarkably little comment or dissent.

This shift from a voluntaristic approach to social problems should not, however, be exaggerated. The Wesleyan Forster Crozier's response to *The Bitter Cry* that 'The Gospel must be first. Better houses would do little unless the people were made better'[44] represented the views of large numbers of his fellow Nonconformist ministers down to 1914. *The Bitter Cry* and its advocates nevertheless contended that unless social circumstances were addressed the Gospel had no chance. The leading Birmingham Congregationalist, R. W. Dale, pointed out 'if the drainage is bad and the water, praying will never save…from typhoid'.[45] Therefore, *The Bitter Cry* argued, the state must 'secure for the poorest the rights of citizenship': this was necessary 'before the Christian missionary can have much chance with them'.[46] Mission also needed to be reconceived: 'Deeper, broader and simpler must this work be than any which can be carried on upon denominational lines. In such a forlorn hope there is no room for sectarianism.'[47]

This cross-denominational clarion call chimed with Hugh Price Hughes' thinking. A deeply committed and successful evangelist, Hughes now coined the term 'Forward Movement' to express aspirations to – as he put it the previous year at an inter-denominational conference about *The Bitter Cry* – 'bring back the alienated masses to the social brotherhood of Christ'.[48] Accordingly they had to follow the Salvation Army to where those masses were.

VI. Re-establishing an Inner City Presence

For years the movement had instead been in the opposite direction. By 1858 the Wesleyan A. C. Whitby was noting that 'The tendency of dissent is to deal with the middle classes, and when the middle classes forsake a given neighbourhood the Chapel is removed as the seat-holders are gone'.[49] The Nonconformist presence in Victorian cities became increasingly marked by the contrast between thriving suburban temples and the struggling causes left in impoverished inner-city areas, deprived of their main financial supporters. In 1884 the Wesleyan conference established committees to consider spiritual destitution in London and the related problem of 'Old Chapels in Large Towns', many of which were failing to reach their surrounding 'dense populations living in vice and indifference'.[50] In consequence, as the Wesleyan J. Scott Lidgett warned in 1891, where social problems are acutest, there are fewest to solve them; where Christian worship, teaching and philanthropy should be most beautiful, they are weak and unattractive; where a united and persistent effort should be made to give healthy and happy colour to the monotony of life, and to open to toiling men and women the resources and enjoyments of God's world of Truth, Beauty and Goodness all around them, there is a total absence of those who can organise and lead it...[51]

Reflecting on the willingness of Nonconformity to abandon 'difficult causes', the Liverpool Free Church Council ruefully commented some years later, 'It seems as though Evangelical Christendom has adopted an attitude towards the slum districts that can only be called a counsel of despair.'[52] Those outposts remaining, Lidgett felt, were either too weak or 'officered and attended almost entirely by classes between which and the labouring population there is an almost total absence of sympathy'.[53] As W. J. Rowland reported subsequently on how chapel respectability could obstruct mission work: 'a set of men are got hold of and devoted, and they become so respectable that they get into almost a different social grade. The difficulty then is to serve the class originally sought.'[54]

His report (1908), commissioned by Liverpool Free Church Council, pointed out various barriers to effective mission, not least competitive chapel-building. The evidence furnished by the religious census of 1851 had been misread as indicating a need for urban church extension. Even in a city growing as fast as nineteenth-century Liverpool the result was increasing chapels per head of population: from one to 4,860 in 1800 to one to 2,203 in 1900.[55] As Robin Gill has pointed out,[56] unless these chapels were steadily recruiting a higher proportion of the population, and from 1850 they were ceasing to do so, they would accordingly appear to be emptier. Their coffers certainly were as a result of the debt this building spree involved. Subsequent increases in tax and inflation, particularly during the First World War, exacerbated these financial difficulties.

To tackle the resulting wasteful overlapping of resources W. J. Rowland suggested establishing a Free Church parish system across Liverpool.[57] The Bitter Cry's idea of co-operation for spiritual and social work had already been taken up in Southwark after the 1889 Dock Strike.[58] Nowhere, however, did such initiatives achieve sustained success. Their only fruit were the national and local Free Church Councils established in the 1890s. Arthur Black concluded from his survey of the Free Churches in London in 1927 that such developments remained expedient, but the necessary local co-operation had disappeared because of 'the elaborate development and steady pressure of denominational machines upon ministers and churches'.[59] It was certainly these denominational machines – strengthened to promote the Forward Movements of the late nineteenth century and to tackle the financial pressures unleashed by the First World War – that in the inter-war years took on the painful responsibility of rationalizing the resources over-committed during the late nineteenth century.

If the Free Church parish idea made little headway, in other recommendations Rowland lauded two innovations already successful elsewhere: the Brotherhood movement and the institutional church. Primarily introduced to overcome working men's aversion to the dullness of church services, what were originally called Pleasant Sunday Afternoon meetings were launched in 1875 by the Congregationalist John Blackham in West Bromwich. They offered a combination of idealistic addresses, often on social issues, and brief, bright and thoroughly unecclesiastical gatherings, addressing a constituency – men – seen as particularly hard to reach. Changing its name to Brotherhood and spreading out across the denominations and country, by 1911 membership was over half a million. That year its former president, William Ward, claimed that 'Here at any rate has come into being a movement that is bridging the gulf that for so many years has existed between the churches and the working classes.'[60]

VII. Institutional Churches and Central Missions

The Brotherhood was an example of the broadening range of activities associated with chapels. By the 1890s some were referred to as 'institutional churches'. Reflecting current shifts in theology from an emphasis on salvation to one of fellowship under the Fatherhood of God, through various societies they organized the steadily increasing leisure time of their adherents. In areas with poor homes they competed with the pubs and music halls to offer comfort and entertainment, not least to attract the menfolk always comparatively absent from their congregations. By the Edwardian period some chapels even featured purpose-built billiards rooms.

Creating an institutional church was a response to outward movement that had left former Nonconformist citadels surrounded either by slums or, as at Oldham Street, Manchester, by shops and warehouses. The result in the latter case, in 1885, was the inauguration of Manchester Central Hall to serve local workers,[61] as part of Wesleyanism's wider Forward Movement. T. Bowen Stephenson suggested that these Central Halls should have a large (hired) auditorium, supported by philanthropic activities. As in Hughes' West London Mission (WLM), launched in 1887, they could thus feature carefully tailored evangelical and social work for various target audiences. Free sittings would, it was hoped, tackle the barrier most cited by contemporaries to church attendance by the poor, though it is dubious whether pew rents really made much difference,[62] any more than their rapid disappearance did over the next few decades. In their absence financial support had to come from elsewhere within the Connexion, wealthy local benefactors or even from outside the country. It was nevertheless forth-coming. By 1900 the Wesleyans had four Central Halls in London alone. Other denominations followed. Some were patterned on the institutional church/central hall model. Thus Congregationalists and Baptists both launched their own Forward Movements in the 1890s, resulting in develop-ments such as the Claremont (Congregationalist) and West Ham (Baptist) central missions in London's East End. New foundations in provincial cities, particularly by Methodists, continued to the 1940s.

The other model was that of Toynbee Hall, founded by the Anglican Canon Samuel Barnett[63] in Whitechapel in 1885. This brought middle-class well-educated young men to serve amongst the urban poor, inspiring many imitators from both universities and public schools. These included East End institutions such as the Congregationalists' Mansfield House Settlement, the Wesleyans' Leysian Mission or the university extension work central to Lidgett's Bermondsey Settlement. By 1934 there were 29 residential settlements in the capital and 15 elsewhere.[64]

The aims, especially of the latter model, alongside evangelism, were social harmony and aesthetic improvement. Thus Mansfield saw itself as 'a centre for all classes' – including as a meeting point with the often Nonconformist leaders of the growing Labour movement[65] – an oasis within a defiled environment where local entertainment was a fight and for 'their architecture and their music they have strings of houses or returning drunks'.[66] Alternative attractive social institutions were needed: as the Baptist J. H. Shakespeare put it, 'Why should the gin palace be the most comfortable and the finest building in the street?'[67]

Institutional churches were not just about fellowship, education and personal improvement. The Congregationalists' Whitefields Tabernacle under C. Silvester Horne, which with John Clifford's Westbourne Park Baptists could compete for the claim to be the original institutional church, introduced a poor man's lawyer service.[68] This, particularly in London, became a common feature of the innovative welfare services offered. Care homes were introduced for groups ranging from unmarried mothers and their children in Manchester, through the Baptist West Ham Central Mission's convalescence and old people's homes, to the WLM's hospice for the dying (respectable) poor. The WLM also instituted a crèche on lines pioneered in London by the Quaker Marie Hilton in 1871 following her observation of similar facilities during the Franco-Prussian War. This provided support for working mothers and medical checks on their offspring. In West Ham, reflecting awareness that open-air schooling alleviated air-borne diseases, the nursery was in a garden. Some acquired children's holiday homes. Bermondsey opened a child welfare clinic in 1931.

Such initiatives reflected widespread contemporary anxieties about the physical deterioration of the urban poor. Insalubrious slums harboured communicable diseases like typhoid and tuberculosis that preyed on people weakened by malnourishment. Hughes' brother-in-law, Howard Barrett, who founded the WLM's medical service and dispensary, noted 'that the malady from which a very large number of the poor applicants for my advice and medicine were suffering was Hunger'. Amongst the medical supplies distributed by his extensive health-visiting service was liberal quantities of beef tea.[69]

For such work Hughes and his wife Katherine followed the Salvation Army's extensive use of women's services. The interdenominational Sisters of the People which Katherine instituted tapped into the idealism of middle-class women, using their skills in nursing, education and social work. They visited the sick, the imprisoned and the indigent, taught domestic skills, collected and distributed secondhand clothing, ran shelters for abused wives and prostitutes and schools for disabled children. Women's talents for charity and sympathy were perceived as becoming central to mission. Reflecting this, Stephenson created the Wesleyan Deaconess Order in 1890. Deaconesses also came to be widely used in the urban institutional churches and missions of the Baptists and Congregationalists from the 1890s.

VIII. Unemployment and Political Challenges

The work of T. Bowen Stephenson, Hugh Price Hughes and his wife appeared in a society increasingly afflicted by unemployment. There was growing working-class insecurity in the labour market. Unemployment, which periodically plagued industrial districts, could no longer be attributed to the improvident fecundity of the poor with the same sort of casual Malthusianism that the DPS had assumed in the 1830s. Nor could it be remedied by the creation of savings clubs. Unemployment also eroded the view 'that the universe was so ordered that the man who best pursued his own interest was best advancing the interests of all', as the Methodist economist Sir Josiah Stamp later explained.[70] Experience in the 1880s suggested more structural difficulties: Stamp's Unitarian counterparts Philip Wicksteed and J. S. Jevons were already drawing attention to trade cycles and unemployment resulting from lack of demand. By the end of the decade the new socialist organization, the Social Democratic Federation, was organizing large unemployment demonstrations. These prompted the social investigations of the wealthy Unitarian shipowner Charles Booth. Whilst some of the socially-concerned middle classes attempted to reconnect with the urban poor by living amongst them, Booth's work marked another way of trying to bridge that social gulf. His monumental surveys provided a detailed map of the plight of the London poor. Booth was followed by other social explorers, notably the Quaker chocolate manufacturer, B. Seebohm Rowntree, whose study of York in 1901 provided the first attempt to establish a poverty line. There were other examples before the outbreak of the First World War such as the Baptist Dorothy Jewson's work in Norwich, which continued to 1914.

Rowntree's distinction between primary and secondary poverty drew attention to the poor worsening their plight through drink and improvidence. A rising concern about gambling prompted, in the 1920s, by such activities as greyhound racing and football pools, ensured Free Church social anxieties remained focused upon secondary poverty. After all, secondary poverty is more tractable to the life-changing effect of conversion. Primary poverty, which Rowntree put at some 35 per cent of York's population, poses different challenges. The need to tackle a principal source of this, unemployment, had been recognized in the 1840s by the Domestic Missions.[71] It was not until the work schemes and job registries of the late nineteenth-century Central Halls and Settlements, however, that this problem was directly addressed, paving the way for the labour exchanges established by the Liberal government in 1909. Even then, as C. Ensor Walters – who succeeded as Superintendent of WLM on Hughes' death in 1902 – put it, 'Soup kitchens, wood-chopping and cheap lodging houses will not of themselves solve the social problem.'[72]

He was not alone in this view. In 1922, two years after the Communist Party was founded, one of its organizers complained to the *Methodist Times* that 'ministers and missioners not only preach acceptance of things as they are, but actually minimise the normal effect of bad conditions by providing temporary work and meals for the unemployed'.[73]

Communists were particularly active in places like South Wales. Their critique prompted R. J. Barker of the Wesleyan Central Hall, Tonypandy to seek to demonstrate the rival merit of a Christian social order founded upon fellowship. To Communism's classless society he responded with the Comradeship of the Common Table and the mutuality of the Community House he established in 1928.[74] Barker's attempts to engage with and adapt the messages of the Left for evangelical purposes, combined with his preaching talent, were reasonably successful. Others were less so, as the inter-war demise of radical chapels like Congregationalist Greenfield, Bradford or the Baptist Pembroke Chapel, Liverpool bears witness.

IX. Redesigning the City

An alternative approach to the problem of the urban unemployed was to move them elsewhere. For Barnardo this involved imperial emigration schemes. William Booth's 1890 *In Darkest England and the Way Out*, however, proposed farm colonies in England. There was nothing particularly new about this 'back to the land' concept, but it inspired the Salvation Army to establish a colony at Hadleigh in Essex to provide sustainable work. The concept remained attractive: farm colonies featured amongst the schemes to tackle unemployment put forward by Lloyd George's heavily Nonconformist-influenced Council of Action at the 1935 general election.

Subsequently they became the means of addressing particular client groups: for instance, in the 1930s Whitechapel Methodist Mission used one of these farms to remove young men on probation from the pressure of local peer groups to re-offend,[75] whilst by the early twentieth century, Hadleigh was serving adults with special needs.

Booth's farm colonies also reflected long-standing concerns about the state of Britain's unplanned, overcrowded and insalubrious cities. Robert Owen's model factory village of New Lanark in Scotland was among the most celebrated early attempts to plan a spatially-organized community away from the chaos of the new urban environment. Various Nonconformist businessmen followed, ranging from the Unitarian Gregs at Styal to the Quaker chocolate manufacturers, the Cadburys and the Rowntrees who created model villages at Bournville and New Earswick respectively. The Congregationalist Titus Salt located his new mill overlooking the countryside outside Bradford in the 1850s accompanied by the Italianate village of Saltaire.[76] His soapmaking counterpart, Lord Leverhulme, later built Port Sunlight for his workers.

In such instances the Nonconformist wealthy, instead of deserting the poor, took them with them. These were expressions in bricks and mortar of the coincidence of interest between masters and men generally assumed by mid-Victorian political economy. They provided for the wellbeing of their workers through the quality of the housing and the built environment and, in cases like Saltaire, the exclusion of public houses. They were in planning and concept the products of paternalism. Being dominated by one firm made them economically viable.

The alternative was to plan such communities as the Congregationalist Ebenezer Howard attempted in his 1898 *Garden Cities of Tomorrow*. These were to be small-scale reconnecting, like Booth's farm colonies, an increasingly urban population with the countryside. At Letchworth (1904) and Welwyn Garden City (1920) in Hertfordshire Howard's ideas were put into practice. Amongst his inter-war followers was the Bermondsey Settlement graduate, Quaker doctor and Labour MP, Alfred Salter: his enthusiasm for replacing slums with vernacular-style cottages, space, light and gardens earned Bermondsey Council the accolade of having done 'more slum-clearance than the whole of the rest of London put together'.[77] Inter-war church housing trusts did similar work in Birmingham and inner London.

Slum clearance promised the eradication of conditions in which '[b] ad health, vice, physical and moral deterioration' and intemperance flourished.[78] Nevertheless housing policy continued to replicate earlier errors: the Baptist Geoffrey Shakespeare complained that the rents on houses built with subsidies introduced in the early 1920s were prohibitive to all but 'the aristocracy of the working classes'. Extensive slum clearance only followed when the national government, in which he served as housing minister after 1933, replaced these with subsidies under Labour's 1930 Slum Clearance Act linked to the actual clearance of insanitary districts and the numbers rehoused. Special associated services, Slum Clearance Sundays, were part of a carefully orchestrated public opinion campaign accompanying these efforts by the Ministry of Health in the 1930s.[79]

X. Inter-War Challenges: Associational Culture and Unemployment

Some four million new dwellings were built during the inter-war years. By 1937 twelve million people lived on estates built since 1918 often devoid of much except housing. As W. H. Lax of the Methodist Poplar Mission lamented, 'Too often a large estate is built upon and the houses occupied before we have a church ready for the new residents'.[80] Community associations arose in the 1930s to fill the void. The community centres these provided often featured aspects of the chapel community, including religious activities, but usually within a secular context.

Secular entertainments could be used for evangelical purposes, as the institutional churches had demonstrated. The inter-war years saw the adaptation of new technologies, such as the cinema, to such purposes. Realizing that films often contained wholesome messages infused with Christian values, Thomas Tiplady established the Ideal cinema service at his Lambeth Methodist Mission. The growing popularity of the new medium enabled him to reach people who might otherwise be put off by 'the language of Zion'.[81] Screens were used, through pictures and text, to mediate the experience of corporate worship. At its peak, weekly attendance was around 8,000. Such successes prompted the Methodist bread manufacturer, J. Arthur Rank, to enter filmmaking in the 1930s as a means of feeding people's spirits as well as their bodies.[82]

Nevertheless, there was the risk that the result of such schemes was merely entertainment, not the cultivation of Christian commitment. S. J. D. Green argues that the churches became dangerously dependent upon the former and its associational culture by 1914.[83] The community associations of the 1930s housing estates and the post-war New Towns demonstrated that, if the chapels had come to need that associational culture, that culture did not need them. This complicated the chapel's task of establishing itself in what could prove unpropitiously soulless territory.

The problem of unemployment meanwhile became more acute, long-term and structural. In 1923 the National Free Church Council passed a resolution urging 'Churches to throw open Halls and Schoolrooms for shelter and by music and in other ways to brighten this time of monotonous anxiety'.[84] The Congregational Social Service Committee listed suggestions such as: provision of reading rooms; alleviation of special distress; help with claim forms and finding employment; facilities for craft work, such as boot repair; and the arrangement of concerts, games and amusements.[85] Hope

Street Unitarians in Liverpool in the early 1920s provided free medical aid to the unemployed.[86] Such efforts were, however, largely confined to larger causes or, as with the shirtmaking established in 1930s Wealdstone, inter-denominational groups of churches.[87]

Some of the worst distress was experienced not in urban areas but in the coalfields. The decline of what was often easily the main source of jobs in the area and the financial hardship which followed the miners' lockout in 1926 left whole communities economically devastated. Led by the Quakers at Maes-yr-Haf, educational settlements began to appear. Industrial re-training centres and land settlement schemes were introduced, mainly in the South Wales coalfield. Large numbers of allotments were created and at their peak some 120,000 men were being supported on Quaker schemes.[88] This was, however, only achieved through government assistance.

XI. The Rise of the Welfare State

State intervention in housing, education and social security had steadily been growing. The welfare provided by the churches was increasingly seen as the moral duty of the State. Such developments were welcomed by the great pulpit policy entrepreneurs of the late nineteenth century like Clifford, Dale, Horne or Hughes. However, with the emergence of Social Service Unions the distinctive articulation of the religious values underpinning welfare provision evaporated. Much the same occurred to voluntary social work. That staple of charitable activities, the domestic visitor, all but disappeared, replaced by local social services. As a Unitarian enquiry put it in 1969, 'Where the church led the Welfare State followed and went further, catering for the social needs not merely of the poor but of almost all classes'.[89]

This did not necessarily lead to a disappearance of church social work in inner cities. Indeed, the circumstances of the Second World War led to innovations such as the introduction of factory chaplains and the Pacifist Service Units (PSUs) which were often Quaker led, set up in Liverpool, Manchester and Stepney to assist bombed-out families, and in Methodism, to William Gowland's Christian Commando Campaigns, an adaptation of the open-air evangelical meetings long conducted by Gowland and his predecessors outside factories and docks. At the point at which domestic mission was diminishing, this drew attention to a new field of activity, the workplace. By 1945 a number of ecumenical industrial missions and chaplaincies were emerging, to be focused in the Industrial Mission Association. From the 1960s this concept was also applied to shopping centres. These industrial chaplaincies were increasingly full-time appointments, demonstrating a shift in thinking from mission based on where people lived to where they foregathered.[90]

Industrial mission was an important wartime innovation. Older forms of mission, meanwhile, adapted. The West Ham Central Mission, for instance, opened a new care home for boys in Essex in 1948. However, an opinion poll in the same year found 90 per cent felt there was no longer a need for such charitable activity.[91] That which continued often became dependent upon State funding, with corresponding diminution of autonomy. For instance, the Family Service Units (as the PSUs had become by 1948) started as 'willing amateurs....[with] a particular sympathy for the outcast'.[92] Their resulting special calling to assist 'the problem family', however, became hedged with regulation and professionalization.[93] Willing amateurs were no more and a crisis in the pensions fund required for the professionals who replaced them led the charity into liquidation in 2006.

Similar processes affected the Free Churches' medical work after 1945. This had steadily expanded during the inter-war years. W. H. Lax, for instance, established dental, chiropody, physiotherapy, optical and cancer clinics in Poplar. After the advent of the National Health Service in 1948 only chiropody and a new psychotherapy service, added as a means with dealing the consequences of the Blitz, survived.[94]

State action also impacted on how inner-city social work was carried out. One example is the Salvation Army's night patrols to befriend prostitutes and, if possible, bring them to salvation. These were suspended because of the wartime blackout in 1939. They were not revived in London until 1954, when anxieties about the growth of vice rings had already led to the setting up of the Wolfenden enquiry. The resulting 1959 Street Offences Act, however, removed the girls from the streets and thus made the Salvation Army's work more difficult.[95]

Remaining church social work frequently became ancillary to the State. Work and training schemes, for instance, established to respond to the high unemployment of the 1980s were often heavily dependent upon local or central government funding. By 2005, the WLM had an annual budget of £2.5m for work with the homeless and alcohol or drug dependency. The religious element had become even more subsumed in the healthy living centre Andrew Mawson[96] established in a rundown Tower Hamlets church in 1984. Staff in such large organizations were increasingly professionalized (particularly after the 1993 Charities Act), regulated and secularized. Links between their founding churches and organizations such as NCH became attenuated.[97]

The problem was how 'to recover the image of a church engaged in corporate social action'?[98] Some forms of outreach developed in the late nineteenth century no longer worked. The Brotherhood, which had become increasingly non-denominational in the inter-war years, never recovered its pre-1914 strength, and disappeared after the 1960s. Before the First World War the children of the slums surrounding Bradford's Wesleyan Mission welcomed the various treats, outings and Christmas parties but in the 1960s and 1970s local children often tried to smash the place up instead.[99] Meanwhile, Manchester Methodist Mission gave up the lodging-house visiting so long a staple of their inner-city work because they could no longer get the men to listen.[100] Some large institutional churches proved difficult to adapt and were sold. The churches' over-reliance since the late nineteenth century, on a combination of social work and associated culture, had, it seemed, marginalized their relevance.

XII. The Theology of Loitering

The solution the Unitarians suggested in 1969 was placing the church at the heart of communities disrupted by changing social behaviours and post-war housing policies. Amongst the new challenges was the settlement of large numbers of immigrants, initially from the West Indies, then from the Indian sub-continent, in the 1950s and 1960s. The Methodist Geoffrey Ainger sought to apply lessons gleaned in New York's Harlem in building cross-community links between the local West Indian and white populations following the 1958 riots in Notting Hill.[101] A similar, more sustained initiative was the ecumenical Newham Community Renewal Programme established by the Congregationalist Clifford Hill in 1971. This was an early attempt to build what the Cantle Report (2001) would call community cohesion. Such efforts, however, were not common. Instead, black-led churches emerged and, by 1976, had established their own umbrella organization.

Innovation lay in how churches interacted with communities. There was a shift away from formal programmes towards building informal relationships. Bill Kyle, the Methodist minister who founded Highgate Counselling Centre in 1960, put it thus: 'What we have to give is love, warmth, persistence...a quality of counselling that is different. Otherwise we should be just a pale shadow of the social services.'[102] In the late 1980s Central Methodist Church, Birmingham accordingly 'moved from being a primarily activities based organization to one which is founded primarily on a one to one contact',[103] ministering to individual needs. Graham Routley, a Baptist minister in Newham, argued:

> There is a real ministry for a church in making its premises available to people...open all week and staffed as a drop-in centre, a Good as New shop which becomes regularly used by folk on low incomes, a Parent and Toddler group. Around all of these initiatives cluster small communities of people.[104]

Inner-city churches now had to minister to more diverse communities with fewer social relationships. Family breakdown and an increasingly elderly population led to some 36 per cent of the population living in sole occupancy by the 1990s. From the 1970s there was also a growing problem of drug misuse, addressed by the importation of rehabilitation centres for addicts as pioneered by David Wilkinson in New York in the 1950s.

The Welfare State offered a complex web of social security programmes, but not mechanisms to tackle the increasing problem of social isolation. Churches could position themselves at the juncture between need and social welfare, dispensing not social services but (often state-funded) advice, fellowship and, in places where there was none, a sense of community. Advice covered everything from housing and consumer matters to CV preparation and job training. The social isolation of the elderly, meanwhile, was addressed by lunch clubs, supermarket runs and day trips. Rather than formal means of community engagement, encounters were more spontaneous, through coffee lounges, crèches and even laundrettes.

Some churches sought to facilitate these by seeking virtue in small groups and therefore getting closer to the community. This was the lesson drawn by John Vincent in his ministry in Sheffield from 1970, not least to ensure a more equitable division of labour between rich suburban and poor inner-city causes. The founder of the Urban Theology Unit and of a ecumenical grouping of small congregations in his adopted city, Vincent advocated, in his President's address to the Methodist Conference on 24 June 1989, the break up of

> our great congregations into small dynamic mission-and-worship units, making Christianity present in an accessible form in housing estates, tower blocks, suburban old folk's homes and community association halls, and creating British 'basic Christian community' churches.[105]

Successfully establishing such a church in rundown Penrhys, South Wales in the late 1980s helped John Morgans 'transform a housing estate into a village'.[106] The approaches Vincent suggested did not just have an urban application. The Methodists' Mission Alongside the Poor Programme had already, since 1983, been applied generally across the country. Similarly, the Anglican inspired Fresh Expressions initiative,[107] taken up in the first decade of the twenty-first century by the Methodist and United Reformed Churches, listed various new initiatives to locate churches within communities in both rural and urban areas. As Morgans' wife Norah put it, many of these are exercises in 'carefully being alongside...the theology of loitering'.[108]

This loitering was in response to the more complex society apparent from the 1980s, shaped by values and interests as well as class. It featured more communities for the churches to get alongside. They, in turn, required a flexible range of programmes, as some initiatives seem to have been easier to sustain than others. For instance, despite the growing numbers of children from broken homes, the ecumenical but Pentecostal led Access

Centre established in Derby in 1990 to provide a supportive and neutral space in which such children could meet their familes was not to last.

Indeed, one facet of the 1990s onwards was the Pentecostalists' growing involvement in social mission, facilitated by a shift in emphasis from social programmes towards meeting personal need. Restorationist churches of the type which spread rapidly from the 1970s onwards were characterized by stress upon strong, mutually supportive local churches actively seeking converts. But it was not until the debt crisis and recession of the early 1990s that they began to build new charitable organizations, such as Christians Against Poverty, founded by John Kirkby in Bradford in 1996. The motive was to rescue people from impending mortgage foreclosures and evictions for non-payment of rent through debt-counselling and rescheduling. To do that, Kirkby observed, 'Because we are looking for sustainable poverty relief we have to empower clients to trust us and to change how they live'. The clients had to be ready to embrace that change themselves. The approach was therefore different from that of the District Provident Socitieties' taking prudence to the poor: for Kirkby, 'We need to have the confidence in God's ability to to bring people back to us if they don't respond first time around.'[109]

In some cases Pentecostalists established this presence and social outreach in the inner city through a very different approach from the small-scale initiatives advocated by Vincent. An example is Abundant Life Ministries (ALM), set up by the amalgamation of three small Bradford churches in 1976. Alongside its two-thousand-seater auditorium and youth centre it also services emergency housing, an outreach programme called 'Love Your City' offering food, clothing and friendly faces, particularly to prostitutes, and a weekly breakfast club for the poor and homeless. These are developments of programmes originating in the nineteenth century. Yet there is also outreach using new technology. ALM has its own record label. Meanwhile, in the 1990s Andy Hawthorne of The Message Trust developed hip-hop bands and the theatre company 'In Yer Face' for youth evangelism in Manchester. He followed this in 1997 with the Eden Project. Buses had been used as cheap and mobile replacements for village chapels from the 1950s. However, using buses kitted out with musical, sports and IT equipment as mobile youth and outreach centres, initially on the run-down Manchester estate of Wythenshawe, was novel and has since been widely imitated. Other organizations have established Jobs Buses.

Hawthorne is an example of a new breed of late twentieth-century social entrepreneurs. Whereas their late nineteenth-century forebears established institutional churches, Hawthorne and Steve Chalke[110] of the Oasis Trust have created social enterprises; the latter, starting in 1985 to work with local homeless people in London, has become a global endeavour. They have been joined by black church leaders such as Nims Obunge, who created the crime reduction charity The Peace Alliance, and Les Isaac, the founder of the Ascension Trust. Drawing on efforts in Jamaica to tackle street gang culture, Ascension introduced street pastors in Brixton in 2003 to patrol the high streets of towns and cities offering help, sympathy and, where receptivity seems likely, the Gospel, to the revellers and binge-drinkers they find there.

XIII. Conclusions

The street pastors are a markedly different form of engagement from the City Missions of their early nineteenth-century forebears. Then attention was focused on domestic visiting, taking religion to the working-class home. By the 1930s such techniques were increasingly ineffective.[111] Campaigns against drink and the Contagious Diseases Acts shaped awareness of the ways in which environmental circumstances blocked receptivity to the Gospel as well as undermining traditional Nonconformist suspicion of the State. In the final decades of the nineteenth century institutional churches accordingly developed a range of programmes to bridge the social gulf felt to separate them from the urban poor. The advent of the Welfare State may have disrupted this model, but innovations nevertheless continued to occur in the 1940s. Social need became more complex from the 1960s and cities more ethnically and religiously mixed. Informal means of outreach therefore replaced organizational structures inherited from the 1880s. By the 1970s John Vincent was arguing that often depopulated inner cities required smaller, more flexible church organizations. But at the same time the institutional church model was being reinvented, albeit with a more youth-oriented focus.

Such large organizations are only sustainable in urban settings. Nevertheless, problems such as binge-drinking, drug culture, poverty, alienation from God and from society can be found in market towns as well as Manchester. Outreach devices such as street pastors are as applicable in both locations. Urban mission has become less distinctive. The way it is delivered has also changed. There was a shift of emphasis from winning souls to caring for the vulnerable and, through increasingly informal means, providing them with a sense of community. In the process, many of the mechanisms pioneered by the churches to achieve this were taken on by the State, but often in ways that only addressed the material needs of the suffering poor. Tackling social and spiritual needs as well remains the mission for the churches in the cities.

7

Campaigners and Co-operative Societies
David M. Thompson

One enduring image of the contribution of the Free Churches to society is that of campaigning for social justice. But it was not always so, and at the height of the most closely fought campaign of all – over elementary education at the turn of the nineteenth and twentieth centuries – there were voices pointing out the danger of identifying Nonconformity too closely with a political programme.[1] Even when due account is taken of the Levellers in the Civil War and Commonwealth period, it remains the case that eighteenth-century Nonconformity was overwhelmingly respectable; and Methodist revivalism soon sought the same degree of respectability. So where does the campaigning image come from?

I. The Quaker Contribution

Without doubt the answer must be the Society of Friends. However, the Quakers were actually unusual by comparison with other Dissenters from the Church of England in several important respects. First and foremost, they undertook responsibility for their own poor as far as they could, rather than leaving them to the parochial system of poor relief established under the Act of 1601. The pioneer in this respect was John Bellers (described by Karl Marx as 'a veritable phenomenon in the history of political economy'[2]), who published in 1695 *Proposals for Raising a Colledge of Industry*, designed to provide a means of investment for the rich and employment for the poor in order to increase the national wealth rather than diminish it. Both Bristol and London Meetings established workhouses on his model, and it was only after parliamentary efforts to establish a Friends' joint stock company had failed, that Counsel's opinion was sought to establish that such schemes would be legal if confined to Friends only.[3] Bellers also published pamphlets on the care of the sick and the improvement of medicine, as well as the reform of criminal law. Quaker provision for their poor, in turn, entailed a detailed system of record-keeping, including the accurate enumeration of members, and a corresponding organization, which could handle and report the details to the powers that be. It is possible that the organizational structure of the Society influenced John Wesley in setting up his own societies: he was certainly the first Nonconformist, apart from the Quakers, to collect regular information about class membership in various places.

The most important respect in which the Quakers set a trend was in their persistent rejection of certain otherwise accepted social norms, for example, the taking of oaths – the exemption of Quakers from which was recognized by an Act of Parliament of 1722 – and the fight against tithes, which took more than a century to make any impression and resulted in some penalties for Quakers, who refused to pay. This greater readiness to defy social conventions and even the law of the land was not found among the Presbyterians, Independents and Baptists, who constituted the larger part of the 'Old Dissent'.

The eighteenth-century parliamentary context was also different. It was, and still is, the case that any properly drafted petition to parliament would be noted. But, whereas today the normal practice is to refer petitions to the relevant government department for a response, in the eighteenth (and even the nineteenth) century, there was a good chance that such a petition would be debated; indeed, in principle, it might become the basis for remedial legislation, since the government of the day used significantly less parliamentary time for its own business. This was, for example, the way in which the anti-slavery issue was brought to parliamentary attention.

Furthermore one feature of the general political context, which has probably been under-estimated in previous political history, is the significance of the great multiplication of societies, both in London and the growing provincial towns in the period after the Revolution of 1688. Historians of particular movements have noted this for their own purposes, for example, the foundation of the Society for the Propagation of the Gospel and the Society for Promoting Christian Knowledge for the Church of England at the end of the 1690s, or the various societies to support education, particularly of the poor. But any student of local history will be aware of the way in which the growing towns spawned societies of all kinds. Apart from those already mentioned, these included hospitals (town infirmaries), poor relief (within defined occupational groups) as a substitute for the Poor Law, moral reformation, and mutual benefit societies for insurance against sickness and old age. Most of these did not discriminate on a religious basis.[4] The important thing about such societies, however, is that they operated within a defined legal framework (that of the unincorporated association) and had a defined membership. This structure may well have influenced the ways in which lawyers sought to make sense of the existence of Dissenting congregations, which were clearly outside the established Church of England, but were able to hold property and receive contributions from members, with a variety of functions, expressed in greater or lesser detail in their trust deeds.

II. Prison Reform

Although the society was destined to become the instrument for achieving social changes in the nineteenth century, individual initiative was still the most important element in the eighteenth. Whereas John Bellers' writings on prison reform are almost completely forgotten, John Howard's name is preserved in the name of the main campaigning body for penal reform to this day. Howard's father was a merchant who did not indulge in conspicuous consumption, and apprenticed his son to a commercial career. By contrast John modified the family house in Hackney to make it more fitting for a gentleman, and also spent an increasing amount of time on the family estate at Cardington in Bedfordshire. He was a Congregationalist, not a Quaker, having been educated at Moorfields Dissenting Academy in London, where he met Richard Price. After his father's death in 1742 he went on a Grand Tour and on his return in 1748 joined the Stoke Newington Congregational Chapel. He followed a life of leisure and married his landlady; but after her death he moved to Cardington, and with the help of his second wife and his relation, Samuel Whitbread, set about developing it as a model village, rebuilding cottages, establishing schools for the children, banning public houses, cockpits, prize-fighting and gambling. Whereas his father had paid a fine of £500 for refusing to be Sheriff of London under the Test Act, the son became High Sheriff of Bedford in 1772. As Sheriff he was responsible for the county's gaols; but his experience of seeing both those who were found not guilty and those not committed for trial by a grand jury unable to escape from gaol until they had paid fees to the gaoler, the clerk of assize and others, led him to tour the country when his year of office was over to investigate conditions in other counties. By mobilizing his friends in parliament to press for a Select Committee, Howard was able to present evidence to it; and in 1774 he was examined before the whole House. He was not only publicly thanked for his evidence by being summoned to the bar of the chamber, but also was gratified by the passing of two bills – the first to release without payment of any fee all those whom a grand jury had failed to find guilty, and the second to preserve the health of prisoners and literally 'clean up the prisons' by regular maintenance of the buildings and provision of medical advice and infirmaries. His book on *The State of the Prisons in England and Wales* (1777) was dedicated to the House of Commons. Subsequently he toured the prisons of Europe (at his own expense) from St Petersburg to Naples, and as far east as Venice, publishing the results of his researches and creating a European, as well as an English, reputation for himself.

Yet Howard's overall achievement was mixed. He resigned as one of the Prison Commissioners set up under the Act of 1778 because of minor personal disagreements with his colleagues; and there was no institution established to sustain his personal observations until the Prison Commission of 1877. When Elizabeth Fry first entered a prison in 1813 very little had actually changed since Howard's day. Even the inspectorate established in 1835 had only minimal duties. An Act of 1823 facilitated the establishment of local Discharged Prisoners' Aid Societies, usually at a county level; these came together in a central Society in 1924. The Howard Association was formed in 1866 to continue Howard's campaigning work and united, in 1921, with the Penal Reform League to form the Howard League for Penal Reform. Furthermore Howard's emphasis on prisons rather than prisoners meant that, although his proposals were taken into account in the construction of the new prisons of late nineteenth-century England, nothing was done to tackle the question of whether prison was for rehabilitation or retribution. Howard's work had shown the evil of making prisons dependent on the profits of those who ran them, but even that point has been rejected in recent years. Finally, like many who are consumed by an enduring passion, he unfortunately neglected his son, who, after a dissipated life at Edinburgh University and then at Cambridge, eventually ended his days in a lunatic asylum. Howard therefore stands out as the example of a philanthropist who was essentially an individualist. Despite his achievement as possibly the first person thoroughly to research a social problem he was unable to ensure that his research was embodied in a concrete programme of reform.[5]

III. Anti-slavery

In contrast to the partial success of prison reform, the Anti-Slavery Movement is usually cited as a striking example of campaigning success, with significant Nonconformist involvement, in that Quakers consistently provided most of the financial support required. The pattern of this movement is significant in embodying the principle of a national committee, with a high proportion of MPs in its membership, and a large number of local auxiliary societies to collect funds and provide information. The earliest anti-slavery societies were products of the Meeting for Sufferings (the Quakers' national executive) after 1783, but the Society for the Abolition of the Slave Trade was founded in 1787, which significantly involved leading Anglican evangelicals as well, notably William Wilberforce. This group launched the mass petition campaigns of 1789 and 1792; and they were indeed mass petitions – that from Manchester contained 20,000 signatures (compared with 9,000 on the largest petition from the Yorkshire Association for parliamentary reform a decade earlier) – and there were 519 petitions altogether.[6] Those from smaller provincial towns contained the signature of almost every literate inhabitant, often recruited through local Literary and Philosophical Societies. Whilst most of these signatories were middle-class professionals, there were also many shopkeepers and artisans. The details of viable legislation were, however, left to MPs and the political elites who were expected to manage such matters. Thus Wilberforce's personal influence with Pitt had secured his support for anti-slavery by the beginning of the 1790s, but the influence and size of the West India lobby delayed action for more than a decade. The length of time between 1787 and 1807 illustrates the long lead-time that such campaigning required, notwithstanding the impact on domestic politics of the French Revolution and the subsequent wars.

It was still another 26 years before slavery itself was abolished in 1833. That was not just a consequence of the Reform Act of 1832 and the extension of the franchise which resulted: it was the result of another concerted campaign, which had begun again in earnest in the 1820s with the Anti-Slavery Society of 1823 and the Agency Society of 1831. Both of these employed lecturers and published periodicals to advance the cause. There was a significantly different emphasis: now slavery was depicted as a 'sin' (notwithstanding the problems of the biblical evidence for this) and therefore it needed to be abolished immediately; ideas of gradual change were marginalized. The religious element was not new: evangelicals had been drawn to support the movement because of the primacy they attached to the doctrine of redemption and their understanding, based on the Old Testament, that Britain was suffering God's judgement because of holding people in bondage. Furthermore the public campaign inaugurated by the Baptist missionary, William Knibb, on his return to England after the brutal suppression of the Jamaican slave revolt at the end of 1831, was undoubtedly influential in rousing opposition on religious liberty grounds among Dissenters and led to 200 anti-slavery pledges from candidates in the December 1832 general election.[7] This contrasted with the more traditional emphasis of the Quakers – a uniquely trans-Atlantic community in their internal relations – that the support of measures to enforce slavery entailed contradiction of the peace testimony. The new element that 'immediatism' brought was that, because of the religious status of the cause, parliament might legitimately be compelled to act, if it would not act willingly – which was a much more radical emphasis in politics than had been experienced before.

Nevertheless the speed with which slavery was abolished in 1833 may have given a misleading impression of the success of such campaigning, since the importance of the West Indies to the British economy was declining, and there had been evidence that the Caribbean colonies were continuing to import slaves despite the Act of 1807. Arguably therefore slavery might have been abolished anyway – and the Act of 1833 also provided a seven-year transitional period, in which conditions for the indentured labourers actually deteriorated. More significantly, the Anti-Slavery movement there-after was split – with one part feeling that their work was done, and the other that the next task was to abolish slavery throughout the world. The latter was doubtless a noble ideal, but the means to achieve it were never thoroughly thought through. The British and Foreign Anti-Slavery Society, founded in 1839, and supported by such prominent Quaker radicals as Joseph Sturge, became a typical Nonconformist pressure group, which cheered itself up over the failure to achieve its primary objective by empha-sizing little advances here and there.[8]

IV. Poverty and the Poor Law

One theme that recurred in the anti-slavery arguments was the question of whether labouring artisans in Britain were better or worse off than African slaves in the Caribbean. Abolitionists took it for granted that they were better off; those who defended slavery were inclined to highlight what they regarded as the humane treatment slaves received from plantation owners by comparison with the carelessness with which artisans were left to sink or swim in the domestic labour market. Serious analysis of the problem of poverty had to wait until the end of the nineteenth century; but the question of the poor was there from the beginning. By 1800 with the increase in population (itself not finally demonstrated until the Census of 1801) and the beginning of the growth of industrial towns, the Elizabethan Poor Law was starting to creak. The developing science of political economy sought a solution to the problem of poverty that recognized the 'laws' of supply and demand. In such a system indiscriminate poor relief was regarded as a cause of low wages for labourers and a drag on the industrious because of the burden of the poor rates. The biblical doctrine of Providence had been extended by eighteenth-century theologians to justify the political and economic *status quo*, and Philip Doddridge's *Rise and Progress of Religion in the Soul* (1745) influenced many Anglican evangelicals to follow suit.

Thus the pessimistic conclusions of Thomas Malthus about the conse-quences of uninhibited population growth led to the development of the distinction between the 'deserving' and the 'undeserving' poor, and the policy conclusion that poor relief should be confined to those who entered the parish workhouse – the principle of 'less eligibility'. This policy was eventually enacted by the Poor Law Amendment Act of 1834, one of the first reforms of the new Whig government. (This illustrates the tendency, which has since become universal, to call any change of policy, regardless of its consequences for good or ill, a 'reform'.) The opposition to the new Poor Law did not include many Nonconformists – at least not among those who were liable to pay poor rates. On the other hand, when it came down to more specific problems, a Congregationalist whig like Edward Baines, Jr, editor of the *Leeds Mercury*, supported factory legislation to protect children (though not adults) and did not think it practical to refuse outdoor relief (i.e. not in the workhouse) to those who were rendered temporarily unemployed in industrial districts.

Baines had made his own way by self-help, rather like John Howard nearly a century before. In 1843 he offered a vigorous defence of the social, educational and religious state of the manufacturing districts in two letters to the Prime Minister, Sir Robert Peel, in which he took particular exception to the description of the areas given by Lord Ashley when introducing his Factories Bill in the House of Commons earlier in the year. Pointing out that official statistics showed that the situation was worse in Westminster than in Leeds, Baines argued that Ashley had deliberately and misleadingly collected the worst examples of degradation, at one point even confusing evidence from Sheffield and Leeds. The essence of his argument was that the factory system improved the lot of the workers by comparison with the position of those in agriculture, and that the voluntary system of providing schools had given sufficient accommodation for the population. In other words, industrialization was beneficial to the labouring poor. From some points of view this was all shadow-boxing. Ashley had originally been motivated by hatred of manufacturers, before he became convinced that there was a genuine problem, to which he devoted the rest of his life; and Baines' antipathy to the landed interest led to mutual recriminations rather than any effective attempt to understand or tackle the problems of poverty.[9] In fact, the idea that outdoor relief disappeared after 1834 is a myth propagated by those historians who never bothered to examine the local evidence but naïvely believed that Acts of Parliament achieve their objectives.

There were Christians who supported the People's Charter (the 'Chartists' as they were called). The Charter was outwardly a manifesto for political reform, but gained support in the economic depression at the end of the 1830s and the beginning of the 1840s. The 'acceptable face' of Chartism was the Complete Suffrage Union, which gained the support of many non-Wesleyan Nonconformist ministers. Edward Miall's *The Nonconformist*, founded in 1841 to promote disestablishment of the Church of England, became the official organ of the Union (Miall was a former Congregational minister in Leicester), and the Quaker, Joseph Sturge, was another prominent supporter. Some two hundred Dissenting ministers signed the Memorial in favour of manhood suffrage in 1841. Joseph Rayner Stephens, a radical Wesleyan Methodist minister, who was eventually expelled from the Connexion, was also a keen supporter, just as he had been a prominent opponent of the New Poor Law and a supporter of Factory Reform.[10]

Edward Baines, Jr, perhaps not surprisingly, was a keen supporter of free trade, as epitomized by the Anti-Corn Law League, and used the *Leeds Mercury* to canvass the League's ideas throughout Yorkshire. The significance of this in the discussion of working-class poverty is that it was believed that the increase in economic activity, which would result from free trade, would improve the living standards of poor and rich alike. The repeal of the Corn Laws (which had protected British agriculture since the Napoleonic Wars) in 1846 split the Conservative Party for a generation, and did not seem immediately to damage agriculture. That had to wait for the development of railways across the North American prairies and the invention of refrigeration for meat imports from Australia, New Zealand and Argentina. At that point agriculture went into a depression from the 1870s until the temporary respite offered by the First World War. Many of the rural poor disappeared through emigration.

There was no uniform feeling among Dissenters about the question of poverty in the early nineteenth century. The traditional organized groups in the Old Dissent – the Dissenting Deputies and the Dissenting Ministers – were based in London to secure easy access to parliament, and not really in touch with provincial opinion at all. Their principal concern in the early nineteenth century was to secure basic civil rights for Nonconformists, in which they had partial success by the 1830s. But attitudes towards the New Poor Law were divided, as the discussion of Baines illustrates, with manufacturers generally in favour regardless of denominational allegiance. Some Nonconformist MPs tried on several occasions unsuccessfully to secure legislation for minimum wages in various industries, but other Nonconformists were opposed to this. Similarly attitudes towards trades unionism in the first half of the century were very much divided, with several leading Quaker and Congregationalist manufacturers taking a strong line against any workers found belonging to a trade union. The 'Tolpuddle Martyrs' – six agricultural labourers, who were sentenced to transportation in 1834 for belonging to a union – attracted no support from the Wesleyan Conference, even though four of them were Wesleyan members, including two local preachers. Nor did the Conference take any part in trying to secure their return, which was eventually achieved. Although Michael Watts has demonstrated that there were more working-class Nonconformists than has often been supposed, even among Congregationalists and Wesleyans, the dominant Nonconformist voice on social policy was in favour of *laissez faire*.[11]

This did not inhibit charitable work among the poor, led by the Unitarian Domestic Missions in large towns, such as Liverpool and Leicester. They were called 'domestic' missions because the missioner concentrated on house-to-house visitation, not so much to evangelize as to investigate the social circumstances of the families concerned and to provide monetary relief as needed. Dorcas Societies were well established in many urban congregations, providing sheets, blankets and other assistance for pregnant mothers. Such activities fitted the underlying idea of the voluntary benevolence of the individual, but did not usually lead to any changes in local policy. What they did do, however, was to provide a developing bank of information about domestic conditions, which at least had the potential to bring social policy down to earth from the abstractions of economic theory to the realities of urban poverty. Edward Baines was a great supporter of such urban activities, because he believed that voluntary societies provided a bond of association in urban areas, which was unnecessary in the countryside because of the traditional landlord and tenant relationship – an idealized view of rural England. There were, in fact, few comparable movements in rural areas, where the traditional seasonal unemployment experienced in agriculture was actually intensified by the decline of rural textile industry through the development of machine-based textile work in urban factories, even before the long agricultural depression after 1870. There were few parts of the country where rural Nonconformity was not to be found, but it always lacked the 'glamour' of its urban counterparts.

V. The Co-operative Movement and Building Societies

Local areas were also the place where the early co-operative societies were established. Normally these are seen as principally associated with the 'Christian Socialism' of F. D. Maurice and his friends from 1848 to 1854. In fact, the Industrial and Provident Societies Acts of 1852 and 1855 were the greatest legislative achievements of that movement, and Maurice's colleague, John Malcolm Ludlow, became the first Registrar of Friendly Societies. The Acts provided a legal framework in which people could contribute to simple savings schemes, with the opportunity for the proceeds to be invested in productive activities. Co-operative trading, as exemplified in the Rochdale Pioneers of 1844, was a different activity, with the intention of ensuring that members obtained good prices for their shopping and a dividend on their purchases. The Rochdale group were more influenced by Owenite ideas than Christian, and there is no evidence to suggest that any of them were Nonconformists. But there were examples of co-operative trading outside the Co-operative Wholesale Society. John Spedan Lewis, son of the John Lewis who set up his draper's shop in Oxford Street in 1864, began to share profits with his employees in 1920, and later set up a formal partnership structure, which in 2011 had over 76,000 partners.[12] His model was followed by Ernest Bader, a Baptist from Switzerland, who became a Quaker in Britain: he corresponded with Lewis, and transformed his own chemical company, not without difficulty, into the Scott Bader Commonwealth. Another example is the Daily Bread company, the first of which was founded in Northampton in 1980 and the second in Cambridge in 1990, which has a specifically evangelical Christian origin and specializes in the distribution of Fair Trade products. This is also true of Traidcraft plc (1984), founded by Richard Adams, who also advised Mark Hayes, the founder of Shared Interest, a co-operative and loan society, designed to support investment in Africa and Asia. Both Traidcraft and Shared Interest have Christian origins, the former involving many local churches in selling its goods and the latter attracting support from those who want to make a direct financial contribution to the support of small farmers and traders in the 'third world'.

The ideas of co-operation appealed greatly to ordinary members of Nonconformist churches, and many of them became involved in the Co-operative movement. In Leicester, for example, the CWS boot and shoe factory employed many Nonconformists, notwithstanding the availability of Nonconformist-run factories of a more traditional kind. There was also a natural development into building societies. The Leicester Manufacturing Boot and Shoe Society, known locally as 'Equity', began production in 1887 and was employing 170 workers within three years. This came close to realizing the ideal of a 'brotherhood of workers', with all the workers holding shares, and outside investors were only allowed one-third of the seats on the management committee. J. T. Taylor, a Church of Christ member and a founder of the Independent Labour Party, who worked at Equity, also encouraged the formation of the Anchor Boot and Shoe Productive Society, also led by a Church of Christ member, Amos Mann. Both groups led to the foundation of building societies, and the Anchor group developed plans for a garden suburb on 28 acres of land at Humberstone, a village on the edge of the city.[13] The Leicester Temperance Building Society (which amalgamated with the Leicester Permanent in 1974, and subsequently with the Alliance Building Society, when they were allowed to go into banking) was run by local Churches of Christ businessmen.

In fact, Nonconformists were to the fore in many of the building societies of the nineteenth century. Beginning in 1775 in Birmingham, such societies spread through the Midlands and into Yorkshire and Lancashire in the early nineteenth century. Initially these were envisaged as terminating societies, that is, when the initial subscribers had paid off their loans on their houses, the society was wound up. The first permanent society was established in 1845. By 1854 they had become a savings vehicle for many people and by 1880 their assets were £54m, having more than doubled in the previous decade. The Planet Building Society was established by Wesleyan Methodists at Wesley's Chapel, City Road, London in 1848. Its assets grew significantly in the 1860s, topping the million-pound mark by 1870. But in the 1870s it ran into financial difficulties, because of its failure to make sufficient provision for reserves. Although it avoided complete collapse, its assets fell sharply and steadily through the rest of the century, only recovering in the inter-war period. In 1939 its assets were £2.4m.

The Liberator Building Society, founded by Jabez Balfour, a Congregational lay preacher, in 1868 had a Board which included many prominent Baptists and Congregationalists. By 1891 it had assets of nearly £3.5m and was the largest society in the country, supporting the building of chapels as well as houses. Its collapse in 1892 following the failure of Balfour's London and General Bank led to losses of £1.6m by its members, ninety per cent of whom were church members and ten per cent widows or single women. The result was more government regulation and a steady process of consolidation whereby small societies were merged with larger ones. It took twenty years for the total assets to reach the 1890 level.

Neither the Planet nor the Liberator were ever household names. One that remained so was the Abbey National, which was the result of a merger in 1944 between the National Permanent Mutual Benefit Building Society of 1849 and the Abbey Road and St John's Wood Permanent Benefit Building Society, which began in a Baptist church in 1874 and met there until 1891. The Primitive Methodist, Sir Robert Bruce Wycherley, and the Wesleyan, Sir Charles Harold Bellman, were significant figures in managing the Abbey. It was second in size only to the Halifax, again a merger in 1928 of two earlier Halifax Building Societies, the second of which had strong links with Wesleyan, Methodist New Connexion and United Methodist figures.

Only with the relative decline of Nonconformity in the later twentieth century did the proportion of Nonconformist personnel in leading positions in such societies become apparent. It may seem a long way from campaigning to building societies; but such institutions were one important means whereby Nonconformists could express their ethos of self-improvement. Often too they were associated with Temperance Societies, which explains why 'Temperance' appears in the title of some of them. Only in the third quarter of the twentieth century did the proportion of houses in owner-occupation pass fifty per cent. With the opening up of the mortgage market from the 1980s and the progressive demutualization of building societies following the Building Societies Act of 1986, that original ethos disappeared, together with the world that had created it.[14]

VI. Temperance and Sexual Immorality

Clear Nonconformist thinking on questions of poverty was probably distracted by two other campaigns – one against drink and the other against sexual immorality – which dominated the later part of the nineteenth century. Both campaigns fitted easily into the standard model of human beings as sinners to be saved, and both had a sufficient degree of truth behind them to make them plausible. In particular, they drew attention to the significance of human agency rather than social structures – a concept much easier to handle theologically than the latter. Similarly the concerns for what became known as the 'civic gospel' and education were examples of improving material conditions rather than tackling the basic question of wages; and the education question came to assume a disproportionate dominance in Free Church politics in the last quarter of the century, important as the principles concerned were.

The campaign against drink was not in its origins religious at all. In early nineteenth-century England beer and spirits were safer to drink than water or even milk: only tea was a competitor, but tea consumption did not reach far enough down the social scale to be relevant. The drink interest was, of course, linked to the landed interest more generally, and public houses were the main places for the social recreation of the poor, and sometimes the only ones. The Beer Act of 1830 freed the sale of beer from the control of the magistrates, and initially advocates of temperance (literally understood) saw this as advantageous on the ground that free actions are more morally virtuous than forced ones. Moreover initially beer was the 'temperance drink' because spirits were regarded as the real enemy. In the 1820s temperance was simply one aspect of a middle-class lifestyle that campaigners wished working people to adopt. The philosophic radicals, such as Bentham, Place, Lovett and Owen, were all temperance advocates.

Evangelical Nonconformists were slow to form temperance societies, and teetotalism was even slower to catch on. In 1841 the Primitive Methodist Conference declared its approval of teetotalism and the Wesleyan Methodist Conference declared its opposition to it. The anti-spirits movement emerged first among the textile manufacturing areas in Ulster, Glasgow, Lancashire and Yorkshire, possibly because of its impact on factory hours. Indeed one dimension of it was that if less money were spent on drink, more would be available to spend on consumer goods, with benefits to the economy. As with anti-slavery, Quaker money was available to finance temperance activity, notwithstanding the Quaker involvement in brewing beer. American temperance influence was also at work on Presbyterian ministers in Ireland and Scotland, and on those Scots who moved south. The first temperance society was founded by a Scottish worsted manufacturer in Bradford, Henry Forbes, in 1830 and the London Temperance Society (which quickly changed its name to the British and Foreign Temperance Society, with a panoply of bishops, Quakers, Congregationalists, Baptists and Methodists on its regional auxiliaries) held its first meeting in 1831. But Nonconformists became suspicious of the establishment bias of this London-based organization, and the more radical teetotalers had a stronger base in the north. Joseph Livesey in Preston, a Scotch Baptist, became one of the keenest critics of the established church.

The move from attempting to influence legislation to attempting to reform drunkards required a significant shift of emphasis. In this context teetotal meetings almost assumed the character of religious revivals with testimonies, temperance songs and lectures on the evil of drink, all leading to the climax of 'signing the pledge'. There were clashes not only with mobs got up by local publicans, but also with more moderate temperance societies. For several working-class men, employment as a temperance lecturer was a means of social mobility. Brian Harrison's analysis of the

leadership of the teetotal movement between 1833 and 1874 also demon-
strates overwhelming (but not complete) allegiance to the Liberal Party.
From the late 1840s Bands of Hope were organized, aiming at children, but
some leaders were uncertain as to whether this was a diversion from the
more serious task of changing adults or an enlightened attempt to secure
the allegiance of the next generation.

   The focus of the movement switched back to political change, however,
with the formation of the United Kingdom Alliance in 1853, with
headquarters in Manchester rather than London until after the First World
War. The aim now became the prohibition of the sale of alcoholic drink
following the example of the law introduced in Maine, USA, in 1851.
The Alliance also admitted non-abstainers as members, and their political
influence was helpful. Ironically, however, when the Liberal Government
succeeded in passing a Licensing Act in 1872, to restrict the opening hours
of public houses, the Alliance was indifferent because it did not go far
enough, and the level of working-class hostility to its implementation was
considerable. Nor is there evidence that it significantly reduced the level of
drunkenness. In fact, throughout the temperance campaign no research was
done into the causes of drunkenness at all. The assumption was that good
could be achieved by moral suasion, in effect, justification by works.[15]

VII. A Civic Gospel

One of the side-effects of the temperance movement, however, was a
greater concern with morally purer forms of working-class recreation. Thus
the concern to develop public parks, libraries and concerts – the cultural
dimension of the 'civic gospel' – was one aspect of temperance concern for
an improved local environment. Alongside this went the concern for appropriate infrastructure – clean water supplied to every house, mains sewerage,
the provision of gas for light and cooking: all of these were part of the
'civic gospel' which is particularly associated with the work of Joseph
Chamberlain, George Dawson and R. W. Dale in Birmingham in the 1860s.
The leading figures in Birmingham were Unitarians and Congregationalists,
and the programme was achieved through political dominance of the
town council. It was indeed a key element in this programme that it was
municipal socialism, rather than anything controlled by the state. This
not only meant that it was much easier to secure the necessary majority
for action; it also affirmed the significant distinction between what could,
and should, be achieved locally, and what had to be the task of central
government. In this respect the suspicion of a large state was of a piece with
traditional *laissez-faire* economic doctrine: the difference, by comparison
with today, is that there was no cap on the amount of local income which
could be raised to support such policies, because the idea that 'the State'
embodied both the national and the local had not yet been invented, nor

the associated ideas that national expenditure includes local expenditure, whereby much income for the support of local activities comes from Whitehall. The 'civic gospel' was not confined to Birmingham, though in places where the denominational balance lay more in the Anglican than the Nonconformist direction, it was not so obviously a Nonconformist movement.

One issue, which did affect the viability of a civic gospel, was the quality of housing. The initial expansion of the towns had been more or less completely unplanned. The back-to-back houses of the industrial north, given a certain charm by Lowry's paintings of Salford, meant that the front door was the only way in and out. In the Midlands terraces with small gardens and an external WC were more common, whereas in London the six-storey buildings of the Peabody Trust in their day represented a considerable advance on the slums which existed before. In fact, London dominated the stories about poor housing from Gustave Doré's engravings and Henry Mayhew's six-volume *London Labour and the London Poor* of 1851. A series of Housing Acts was passed in the 1870s, following the pioneering work in slum clearance and the provision of working-class housing in Birmingham and Liverpool.

In 1883 a report written by the Secretary of the London Congregational Union, Andrew Mearns, appeared, entitled *The Bitter Cry of Outcast London*.[16] It was a penny pamphlet which, although it said little that was new, had an immediate effect, not least through the publicity given to it by W. T. Stead's *Pall Mall Gazette*. Mearns had been a Congregational minister in Chelsea, and part of the novelty of the tract, apart from the catchy title, lay in the fact that a minister of religion, rather than a journalist, was writing about the subject. What was originally a tract on the need for Christian missionary work among the poor was presented as a tract on the need for improved housing. When Mearns was called before the Royal Commission on the Housing of the Working Classes in 1884, he was questioned particularly about his statement that 'incest is common', and his comments on sexual morality in general. But what was perhaps most damning in his pamphlet was his description of how crime and prostitution paid so much better than hard work, enabling the immoral to have the better rooms. Here there are the beginnings of a systemic analysis of the problem of poverty. In the short term, however, the emphasis lay more on the need to eliminate sin than poverty.

Throughout the nineteenth century there had been examples of individual Nonconformist entrepreneurs making sure that their workforce was well housed. This was so in Titus Salt's Saltaire in Yorkshire, for example. Another example was Cadbury's 'model village' at Bournville in Birmingham towards the end of the century. This moved into the 'Garden City' movement of the early twentieth century, with developments at Hampstead Garden Suburb in London, and Welwyn and Letchworth Garden Cities after the First World War. There were also many smaller suburban developments in other towns, often related to a Nonconformist-inspired building society, such as that in Humberstone, Leicester, referred to above.

The emphasis on sin is well-illustrated by one very public response to Mearns – General William Booth's *In Darkest England and The Way Out* (1890). Much of it was ghost-written by W. T. Stead. The Salvation Army, which was the new name devised by Booth in 1883 for his Christian Mission in Whitechapel, was already well-known, certainly in London, by the end of the decade. Again the title echoed themes more familiar elsewhere, notably Stanley's *In Darkest Africa*, published that same summer. Part of the shock value of the book, therefore, was to turn the spotlight away from popular concern to civilize the Africans by missionary endeavour and on to the need to civilize those living in the heart of the Empire. In his Preface Booth referred to the impact made on him as a child by the sight of the poor stockingers 'wandering gaunt and hunger-stricken' through the streets of his native town (Nottingham). His chapter headings also captured in a series of memorable phrases the elements of his argument: 'The Submerged Tenth', 'The Homeless', 'The Out-of-Works', 'On the Verge of the Abyss', 'The Vicious', 'The Criminals', 'The Children of the Lost'. In the second part he set out a less often remembered scheme of Deliverance, illustrated by a memorable frontispiece. Booth envisaged three main stages: the City Colony,[17] the Farm Colony and the Colony across the Sea. Most work went into establishing the various institutions associated with the City Colony; there was a Farm Colony at Hadleigh in Essex for a number of years, but the ideals of co-operative farms and smallholdings ('three acres and a cow', to adopt a popular political slogan of the time) did not prove so easy to implement in practice with the kind of people Booth was seeking to rescue. The overseas colony did not really materialize in the way envisaged, though the spread of the Salvation Army throughout the Empire was in one sense a manifestation of this. The key to all the programmes was the willingness to work; without any clear sense of what the work would contribute to the economic output of the country. In this sense there was no advance on, and even a retreat from, John Bellers' 'Colledge of Industry' of nearly two hundred years before. Perhaps even more interesting as a reflection of the operation of the New Poor Law, some sixty years later, is Booth's statement that there were 190,000 in the workhouse, 968,000 in receipt of outdoor relief, and 20,000 out of work.

In fact, many of the programmes the Salvation Army set in train were not unique to them, though they were probably organized on a larger scale. By the 1890s many urban Nonconformist churches were what were known as 'institutional churches'; in other words, they had a range of social activities for those in the neighbourhood, which went far beyond traditional Sunday Schools, women's meetings, Bands of Hope and Bible Classes. Even a modest Nonconformist church might have a gymnasium, a coffee shop, sports clubs (some modern professional football clubs had their origins in Nonconformist churches), a women's sewing class, where the emphasis was on teaching the necessary skills, boys' and girls' clubs – eventually Christian Endeavour and Scouts and Guides. Some of these activities might be integrated with Local Authority provision after the First World War.

VIII. Poverty Again

By the end of the 1880s Charles Booth (not to be confused with William) had begun his study of the *Life and Labour of the People of London*, which was eventually published in three series of volumes. In this gigantic undertaking he was assisted by a number of researchers, who processed the information for him. Although the Third Series was devoted to religious influences, the project was in no way inspired by religion or religious beliefs. But with it the model of social research into working-class life was well and truly launched. The slightly irritating thing for the historian confronted with so much information gathered about London is that it was not an industrial town in the sense in which the newly grown towns of the midlands and north were; and there are few comparable surveys for them. The only thing we do have is another Quaker-inspired project: the study of York (not an obviously industrial city) by Seebohm Rowntree, *Poverty: A Study of Town Life* (1902).

Rowntree quickly rejected an approach based essentially on government statistics, reports of Medical Officers of Health, local reports of the Charity Organization Society etc. Instead he decided to undertake a detailed investigation into the social and economic conditions of the wage-earning classes of his city. The kind of questions he wanted to answer were as follows:

> What was the true measure of the poverty in the city, both in extent and depth? How much of it was due to insufficiency of income and how much to improvidence? How many families were sunk in a poverty so acute that their members suffered from a chronic insufficiency of food and clothing? If physical deterioration combined with a high death-rate ensued, was it possible to estimate such results with approximate accuracy?[18]

He decided that the only way to answer these questions was to make a house-to-house survey, which comprised 11,560 families living in 388 streets, giving a population of 46,754. A crucial distinction Rowntree made was between 'primary poverty' and 'secondary poverty' – the former being a state in which there was insufficient income for the minimum necessities, and the latter being one where wasteful expenditure takes the family below the line. The concept of the 'poverty line' as the distinction between these two types of poverty has subsequently become standard. To understand the latter, he had to investigate the diet of sampled families over periods of at least three weeks and sometimes up to two years.

Rowntree demonstrated that the payment of universal old-age pensions would only reduce poverty by one per cent and that the age groups most exposed to poverty were children who were not yet earning. It is an open question how far Rowntree's work influenced the campaign for old-age pensions, which Lloyd George introduced in 1908. But it certainly exposed the paradox that the raising of the school-leaving age, advocated on educational grounds, would actually increase the poverty of the poorest – something not recognized in social policy until 1998 when maintenance allowances were introduced for those staying on at school after 16.

IX. The Social Gospel and Social Thought

One shift, which began before the First World War but continued after-wards, was the rather loose collection of ideas summed up in the phrase 'social gospel'. The term seems to have been coined by the Anglican, Brooke Foss Westcott, preaching at Lightfoot's consecration as Bishop of Durham in 1877. He used it again in his Westminster Abbey sermons, gathered as *Social Aspects of Christianity* (1887).[19] In the United States it was developed as an aspect of the work of the American Evangelical Alliance, but it was also picked up in English and Welsh nonconformity. Here it is most often associated with the minister of the Congregationalist City Temple, R. J. Campbell, who used it in passing in his *Christianity and the Social Order* (1907) – a sequel to *The New Theology* of 1906 – essentially arguing in his advocacy of socialism that the original Gospel preached by Jesus had more to do with social change than salvation from sin.[20] In fact, the term had been used as the title of a book in 1902 by T. Rhondda Williams, a friend of Campbell, who was also an advocate of the New Theology. Williams had worked in a coal mine from the age of nine to thirteen, but he then studied at a grammar school in Cardiff and trained for the Congregational ministry at Carmarthen College. After initially serving a Welsh-speaking congregation in Dowlais, he moved to Neath and then to Greenfield church, Bradford (1888–1909) and later to Queen Square church, Brighton (1909–31). Williams became a Christian socialist in Bradford to the dismay of some members of his congregation.

The addresses given by Williams were essentially a development of Dale's 'civic gospel' in Birmingham with a socialist tinge, in that his principal examples were of public services that could have the profit element taken out of them by being put in the hands of local councils. There was nothing that would strike a reader nowadays as having anything to do with nation-alization. Interestingly his penultimate address was concerned with how to 'manufacture' good local councillors. Later in his Bradford ministry he made friends with Keir Hardie, the leader of the Independent Labour Party, and in the 1918 General Election he contested the Cambridge Borough seat for Labour (on principle, rather than with any hope of being elected).[21]

Similar ideas had been articulated by the Baptist, John Clifford, and the Congregationalist, J. B. Paton, who was particularly anxious that the Free Churches should unite on social questions.[22] In 1906 the Social Questions Committee of the National Council of Evangelical Free Churches commissioned a book on *The Social Mission of the Church*. It was edited by C. Ensor Walters of the West London Mission, with 16 essays by leading Free Churchmen; Paton wrote the Foreword and emphasized that alongside the preaching of the Gospel of the grace of God, the Church had its manifold ministries of healing and help to the world, which were the necessary testimony to the Gospel it preached.[23] The essays, though well-intentioned, were short on practical suggestions – a point aptly illustrated by a confession on the part of Rhondda Williams that, after a sermon urging people to social service in general terms soon after moving to Bradford, he met a group of young people outside his vestry who asked him to tell them what he wanted them to do; he had been non-plussed by the question and resolved thereafter always to be clear what he was advocating in practice.[24]

The response to socialism within Nonconformity depended in part on whether it was seen as an economic question or a moral question. Employers and those identified with them tended to see it as the former, and therefore held that the Church as such had no competence in the matter; advocates of the social gospel saw it as a moral question and therefore regarded it as a necessary concern – indeed where it was understood as part of the primitive teaching of both Jesus and the early Christians, it was essential. The result was a significant division which, coupled with an increasing sense of disillusionment with the political process as a result of the failure of the Liberal Government of 1906 to resolve the education question, led to the beginning of the split between Liberal and Labour voting on the part of Nonconformists in the 1910 General Elections and the effective withdrawal of many Nonconformists from active involvement in organized political action altogether. This was particularly true in South Wales, as Robert Pope has demonstrated, but the same process has also been observed in the Durham coalfields.[25] What may be more relevant is whether this was especially marked in mining areas, both because mining unions had originally been strongly Liberal in their politics (many miners becoming eligible for the vote in 1867 rather than 1885) and because of the declining profitability of British mining, which produced chronically bad industrial relations from 1919, if not earlier. Pope cites Will Paynter's description that the South Wales Miners' Federation provided 'an all-round service of advice and assistance to the mining community on most of the problems that could arise between the cradle and the grave'.[26] Few other trade unions had either the need or the opportunity to do the same and therefore did not displace the chapel community so easily.

A different approach was reflected in the life of Malcolm Spencer (1877–1950), half a generation younger than Williams. Spencer had one of the most creative minds in twentieth-century Nonconformity, and was the brains behind several of the inter-church initiatives of the period, including the British Council of Churches. Despite being orphaned at eight, he won scholarships to Manchester Grammar School and Corpus Christi College, Oxford, gaining a First in Mathematics. When his medical condition disqualified him for missionary service he went to Mansfield College, Oxford under Andrew Martin Fairbairn[27] and became Assistant Minister at Duckworth Street Church, Darwen. It was his only pastorate, because he became a Travelling Secretary for the SCM, eventually becoming Social Service Secretary after the famous Matlock Conference of 1909. Spencer suggested the formation of the small group known as 'The Collegium', of which William Temple became President and the first publication of which was *Competition* (1917). The significance of the Collegium is twofold: first, it aimed 'to produce literature on social questions based on a definitely Christian conception of society'; but secondly, 'that all literature issued by the Collegium shall be the work of corporate thought and prayer, "and not merely the private work of individual authors"'.[28] This represented a new and distinctive style in campaigning work – a self-conscious attempt to write something, which was more than an individual point of view by methodologically embodying the social. From 1925 to 1948 Spencer was Secretary of the Social Service Committee of the Congregational Union, transforming the scope of that body and its role within the denomination. He was also one of the Secretaries of the Conference on Christian Politics, Economics and Citizenship at Birmingham in 1924 and the first Secretary of the Christian Social Council from 1928, which became part of the British Council of Churches after 1942. Spencer had a profound influence on Temple and, because of his self-effacing personality, was appropriately described by his biographer as 'a holy back-room boy'.[29]

Spencer's work illustrates the way in which the Nonconformist influence in the twentieth century was subsumed into a wider ecumenical or inter-denominational context. It also shows how the campaigning groups of the nineteenth century were institutionalized in expanded views of the role of the various Churches nationally. The various Social Service or Social Questions Committees of the national bodies became, in effect, campaigning institutions in their own right. Ironically the significance of this has only been realized as a result of the reconstruction of the Ecumenical Instruments at the end of the 1980s. There had developed a feeling among some that the Community Affairs Department of the British Council of Churches had become too detached from the grass-roots attitudes of local churches; this may have been stimulated by the new political polarization resulting from the Thatcher Government. In order to involve the Roman Catholic Church in the new Ecumenical Instruments, it became necessary to cease this work. So at the beginning of the twenty-first century there was once again a common team for social issues among the Baptists, Methodists and the United Reformed Church, reminiscent of the work of the National Council of the Evangelical Free Churches a century earlier.

X. Racial Discrimination

In the later twentieth century the Churches collectively began to face systematically issues of racial discrimination, partly as a result of the World Council of Churches Campaign to Combat Racism from 1968, and partly because of domestic legislation, such as the Race Relations Acts of 1965, 1968 and 1976, which made discrimination on grounds of race illegal. The British Council of Churches established a Community and Race Relations Unit as part of its contribution to the WCC Campaign. There was gradually an increased emphasis on securing equality of access, for example into the ministry of the Church. The most significant example of an initiative arising from a Nonconformist source is the League of Coloured Peoples, founded in 1931 by Dr Harold Moody, a Congregationalist who had been born in Kingston, Jamaica in 1882. Unlike many others who took initiatives in this area, Moody's inspiration was 'his profoundly held faith, the motor that largely drove his activities'.[30] Arriving in Bristol in 1904 he went to King's College, London, graduating in Medicine in 1912. He was refused a post at King's College Hospital because of his colour, and worked as medical superintendent of the Marylebone Medical Mission instead. After his marriage to a white woman, Olive Tranter, he began to experience personal abuse. He opened his own medical practice in Peckham, south London, and his family were members of Camberwell Green Congregational Church, where he was a deacon and Sunday School superintendent.

For the whole of his life Moody worked against discrimination. In 1921 he became Chairman of the Colonial Missionary Society, which had taken over responsibility for West Indian missions, in conjunction with the Jamaica Congregational Union, from the London Missionary Society (LMS) in 1909. He was later Chairman of the Christian Endeavour Union (1936) and the LMS (1943) – described by Norman Goodall as 'a powerful advocate in word and person of the Christian doctrine of racial equality'.

By 1936 the League had 260 members, one third of whom were white. It became more overtly political after the Italian invasion of Abyssinia, whilst not being as radical as a group such as the International African Service Bureau, which included Jomo Kenyatta in its leadership. The League did secure the setting up of a Royal Commission to investigate workers' conditions in the West Indies, and Moody secured a sympathetic hearing at the Colonial Office. Its most significant achievement was probably the Charter for Colonial Freedom, agreed in 1944, which demanded full self-government for colonial peoples at the earliest possible opportunity, and an end to all discrimination against people on grounds of colour – a Charter which foreshadowed the resolutions of the fifth Pan-African Congress in Manchester in 1945, involving Jomo Kenyatta, Kwame Nkrumah and Hastings Banda. Moody was not against the idea of Empire, and in many ways has been forgotten because of his relative conservatism. The League did not long survive his own death in 1947.[31]

Other initiatives in responding to issues of racial equality were not so much the result of campaigning societies as direct action by the Churches. After the increase of direct immigration from the West Indies in 1948 – first of men, then of their families – it was necessary to make adequate provision in local churches to respond to these largely Christian immigrants. The evidence suggests that most churches failed to do so in adequate numbers. One exception was St James' Presbyterian Church, Sheffield,[32] which began 'services for coloured people' in the early 1950s and elected its first black elder, Stewart Brown, in 1964. He was appointed MBE for services to race relations in Sheffield in the New Year's Honours List for 2000. Between 1966 and 1975, Madge Saunders from the United Church of Jamaica and Grand Cayman, who was ordained as a Deaconess for work at St James' alongside the minister, served the whole community in a truly remarkable way.[33] But there was still a long way to go.

XI. Local and Central Government Funding: Prisons and Probation

Another theme, which characterizes the twentieth century as a whole, is the way in which local or central government undertook a steadily rising proportion of the funding for various social work and welfare services. The result has been a situation in which at the beginning of the twenty-first century the state seems to be imposing its will on the actions of various church bodies engaged in the general welfare area. At first sight this may seem like interference in religious freedom, particularly if churches or groups within them disagree with the direction of government policy. However, a second look usually reveals that, although the bodies which manage the type of assistance concerned are church-related charities, the funds which they use are grants from national or local government. As Frederick Temple warned Randall Davidson in 1898 in relation to elementary education, once the National Society accepted state funding on a significant scale for its schools, it lost its freedom to run them in the way that the Church wished. The significance of this shift may be seen in three distinct areas: prisoners' aid, and the development of the Probation Service; reformatories, orphanages and children's care; and the development of case-work in social work that led eventually to social work becoming a formal part of Local Authority welfare services.

Despite the arguments of Elizabeth Fry relatively little was accomplished by way of prison reform in the next century. Most of the efforts of the Churches in this area were led by the Church of England, and the distinctive Nonconformist contribution was limited. Nevertheless various Nonconformist churches did organize Prison Visitors' Associations, if a prison was nearby. In the larger cities some congregations organized prison gate missions to meet prisoners on their release. Susanna Meredith (daughter of an Irish prison governor) began to visit women prisoners from 1865; when this was restricted by Sir Edmund Du Cane, the chairman of the directors of convict prisons, she established prison gate missions outside the London women's prisons to offer accommodation, a meal and employment. The Prisons Act of 1877 closed down two-thirds of the prisons under local control and transferred responsibility for all to the Home Office. One consequence of this was not only uniformity, which restricted the work of prison visitors, but also secrecy; Susanna Meredith complained about the prison commissioners to the Gladstone Committee in 1894, and Du Cane (who still seems to be admired by some as a reformer rather than the reactionary he was) told the same Committee that women visitors did not get on with the staff.[34] Visitors were not allowed for male prisoners until 1922. Attention therefore had to be concentrated on prisoners after their release. In most counties of England and Wales by 1880 there were Discharged Prisoners' Aid Societies. Prominent Nonconformists were often involved: thus Samuel Whitbread (grandson of the friend of Howard) was the Vice-President of the Bedfordshire Society in 1874, and Samuel Fielden, the Unitarian manufacturer, helped the Manchester Society in its early years. In 1924 the Central Discharged Prisoners' Aid Society (Incorporated) was formed, and its successor body became the National Association for the Care and Resettlement of Offenders in 1966 (simply NACRO since 1999) – the largest criminal justice-related charity in the country. The provision of full-time prison chaplains was a Church of England responsibility in the early nineteenth century, but the Prison Ministers Act of 1863 permitted the appointment of non-Anglican chaplains. For the most part, however, Free Church prison chaplains have been part-time, normally serving also as ministers of local churches. The transfer of responsibility for all prisons to the Home Office in 1877 meant that all chaplains were brought under the authority of the prison commissioners, and this has resulted in an ambiguous role for them: are they independent, are they agents of the prison, or are they agents of the Church? It has proved difficult to provide a permanently satisfactory answer to these questions.[35]

In the 1850s there was a new focus on the prison system with the end of transportation, which meant that all criminals had to be dealt with in this country. The origins of the modern Probation Service (nowadays called – with a doubtless unintended, ironic nod to Foucault's view of prisons as social surveillance – the Offender Management Service) are also to be found in this area of philanthropy. A donation given to the Church of England Temperance Society led to the foundation of the London Police Court Mission in 1876. The aim was to prevent those whose criminal behaviour was affected by drink from suffering prison sentences, and thereby falling into a criminal existence; and from 1879 magistrates had the power to hand offenders over to a specified supervisor, extended by the Probation of Offenders Act of 1887. By 1900 there were a hundred such missioners.

Wesleyan and other Nonconformist missions were established in Liverpool and other provincial cities. The Probation of Offenders Act of 1907 created the modern Probation Service, and recognized those who were already at work in the field. Between then and the Criminal Justice Act of 1948 the Probation Service was steadily professionalized, and the role of those funded by charities fell away.[36]

A different kind of preventative measure was also the work of Susanna Meredith. She established the Princess Mary Village Homes at Addlestone in Surrey in 1871 for the daughters of criminals, in order to prevent them following in the footsteps of their parents. Another woman who exercised great influence in this field was Mary Carpenter, eldest daughter of a Unitarian minister in Bristol, whose book *Reformatory Schools* (1851) was a call to action in order to prevent juvenile offenders becoming adult criminals. Her ideas were propagated at a conference in Birmingham in 1851. She founded a reformatory school at Kingswood in 1852, and another one for girls at the Red Lodge in Park Row, Bristol, in 1854. There had already been a school founded at the Stretton colony in Warwickshire as early as 1818; others were founded by Joseph Sturge, who attended the Birmingham Conference, at Stoke Prior near Bromsgrove, and Captain O'Brien in Newcastle upon Tyne. Carpenter's evidence to a parliamentary enquiry on juvenile delinquency in 1852 influenced The Youthful Offenders Act of 1854, which authorized the establishment of reformatory schools by voluntary bodies, certified by the state and partly funded by the Treasury. The primary significance of this development for the present chapter is that it initiated a pattern for statutory-voluntary relations, which was to be developed further in the twentieth century. By 1900 the number of juveniles in prison had dropped from 15,000 in the 1850s to 2,000.[37]

XII. Orphanages

Better known is the story of the development of orphanages, which multi-plied in numbers from the 1850s, partly as a consequence of the rapid growth in population. The pioneers were Andrew Reed, the Congregational minister of New Road Chapel, London, and George Müller of Bethesda Chapel, Bristol. Reed appealed for London orphans as early as 1813, but the London Orphan Asylum was not founded until 1825, with new buildings at Wanstead opened by the Prince Consort in 1841. However, his fellow governors insisted on the use of the Church of England catechism, so Reed resigned and started again at Richmond in 1844. He later pioneered work among mentally handicapped children. Müller was a Prussian who had undergone a Pietist conversion at Halle in 1826 and came to Britain to work with the London Society for Promoting Christianity among the Jews. However, he married Mary Groves, sister of one of the founders of the Open Brethren. Bethesda Chapel, Bristol was bought for him, and from there in 1836 he opened his first orphanage, modelled on Francke's orphanage in Halle, followed by a number of others.[38]

The best known group of orphanages was undoubtedly Dr Barnardo's Homes, the largest group in the country. Like Meredith, Thomas Barnardo was Irish: in 1862 he was baptized as a member of the Open Brethren and was inspired by Hudson Taylor to be a missionary. But his candidacy was delayed and while a student at the London Hospital, as well as teaching at a ragged school and preaching on the streets, he established the East End Juvenile Mission in two cottages in Hope Place. This was the first of a series of cottage homes, based on an idea originating in continental Europe. In 1876, when Lord Cairns, the Lord Chancellor, opened his first Barnardo girls' home in Barkingside, the slogan 'No destitute boy ever refused admission' was changed by substituting 'child' for 'boy'. Although his self-willed character resulted in a series of personal battles that dogged his later career, the publicity for a system that combined philanthropy and mission had a lasting positive effect.[39] Today the effectiveness of orphanages is often questioned by secular historians; but it is difficult to see what better alternatives there were in the nineteenth century.

XIII. The Charity Organization Society and Social Case-work

All these developments illustrate the close relationship between campaigning and social action, usually with an explicitly Christian missionary intention. All of them in different ways shared the system, which has become known as 'social case-work'. The essence of it is very simple: each individual has different circumstances, and effective assistance needs to be adapted to those circumstances. It was pioneered by a body, which subsequently has had a bad press in the history of social action, the Charity Organization Society, founded in 1869. The criticism is due to the fact that its founders were totally against the principle of indiscriminate charity, and for this reason were unhesitating supporters of the New Poor Law of 1834, with its emphasis on removing 'outdoor relief', a policy which we have noted as not having been thoroughly implemented in the years following. The Society was influenced by the ideas on welfare of the Church of Scotland minister, Thomas Chalmers, at the beginning of the century, and it had the support of the Liverpool Unitarian merchant, William Rathbone, who pioneered a Charity Organization Society in Liverpool in the early 1860s. Octavia Hill, grand-daughter of another Unitarian social reformer, Dr Southwood Smith, but herself a convert to the Church of England through her friendship with F. D. Maurice, was also involved. John Ruskin bought three working-class houses in Marylebone in 1865, of which she became the manager; and she may be said to have pioneered the 'case-work' approach here. A third prime mover was the former Unitarian minister, Henry Solly, who had been one of the Dissenting ministers at the Birmingham Chartist Conference of 1842, and was a strong supporter of co-operative societies and working men's clubs – he founded the Working Men's Club and Institute Union in 1862 and became its first paid secretary a year later, though he fell out with them over the sale of alcohol. He established the London Association for the Prevention of Pauperism and Crime in 1868 and from this the Charity Organization Society was formed.[40]

The Charity Organization Society was a typical product of the great and the good with the Bishop of London as President. C. S. Loch, who was Secretary of the Society from 1875 to 1913, articulated more clearly than anyone else his belief that poverty was the result of a moral failure, and indiscriminate charity contributes to and exacerbates that failure. This was the view that Rowntree sought to combat in *Poverty: A Study of Town Life*.[41] However, the lasting legacy of the Society lies not so much in its ideology, as its methodology and the contribution which this made to the idea of social work, as it developed into a profession in the twentieth century.

The final area of campaigning/social action is work with groups of adults and children. Modern social work has gained significantly from the development of the Settlement Movement in the late nineteenth century, primarily in London, but also in other cities. The initiatives here are usually associated with the Church of England, but Nonconformist theological colleges such as Mansfield College, Oxford also supported a London Settlement. The other development was in youth work, through the Boys' and Girls' Brigades, which were explicitly Christian in origin and outworking, through the Scout and Guide Movement associated with Baden Powell, himself the son of a prominent Oxford divine, and through Boys' Clubs from the 1860s.[42] From these models there emerged the idea between the Wars of youth clubs, and the Methodist Church in 1951 committed itself to such clubs as its primary method of working with young people, rather than the long-established Sunday Schools, but with mixed success as a 1961 report from the Methodist Youth Department demonstrated.[43] These voluntary developments in the early twentieth century led to their adoption by Local Education Authorities in the period after 1945. By this route youth work became an established part of social work in general. More recently the focus shifted towards the care of pre-school age children, particularly as the need for organized child care developed as more women went out to work from the 1960s onwards.

XIV. The Peace Movement

This chapter has deliberately not concentrated on 'foreign policy' campaigns after the Anti-Slavery movement. They were nevertheless a constant feature of Nonconformist life in both the nineteenth and twentieth centuries. The

Peace Movement was a concern of all Nonconformist churches, and seemed to have achieved great things by the two Hague Conferences in 1899 and 1907. However, the writing was on the wall when Britain secured an exemption in relation to South Africa in the 1899 Convention; and within the year the Second South African War had broken out, further reinforcing Nonconformist divisions between Liberal imperialists and Pro-Boers. All the achievements seemed to crumble on the Western Front in 1914–18. Nevertheless, the League of Nations Union picked up much of the same peace and arbitration enthusiasm between the wars, but suffered another series of blows in what seemed to be international weakness in Abyssinia, Spain and ultimately at Munich in 1938. Most Nonconformist churches were more concerned with overseas missions in Asia and Africa between the wars than with what was happening in the European Churches, with which (apart from the Baptists and Presbyterians) they had relatively little to do; but only the Presbyterian Church of England had an Assembly Committee specifically concerned with European Churches.

After 1945 the 'lesson' of non-interference in other countries' internal affairs, which had been the policy norm in relation to Germany in the 1930s, was learned. But the results were controversial. The Campaign for Nuclear Disarmament never gained majority support in any church other than the Quakers, despite attempts at careful leadership on the issue in general from the British Council of Churches; whereas the Anti-Apartheid movement was better supported. But the legacy of British imperialism left the British Churches generally with a sense of guilt about what view, if any, they should take when the post-colonial democratic regimes turned into dictatorships. It was easier to rally support in favour of former mission churches in the Congo (which had been Belgian) or Angola (which had been Portuguese); and the Baptist Missionary Society (BMS) was involved in both areas. In the case of Angola, where the Portuguese had suppressed any reporting of their brutal atrocities in putting down the revolt of 1961, BMS publicity secured international debate; Brian Stanley called it 'the most recent (and arguably the last) example of the power of "the nonconformist conscience" to affect political events'.[44] But it neither toppled the Salazar regime nor brought Angola independence. It gradually became clear that the most effective way of proceeding (if effectiveness is the relevant criterion in this context) was through the Commission on International Affairs of the World Council of Churches. In due course the World Evangelical Alliance came to assume a similar role for those on that side of the religious spectrum.

XV. Conclusion

The nineteenth-century story illustrates the very slow rate of progress towards what might be called an evidence-based approach to social policy; in the twentieth century the state annexed social policy as its own concern.

Economic theory on the one hand and political convictions on the other (in so far as the two are unrelated) were the main influences on social policy throughout. This may seem a rather depressing conclusion for those who have emphasized the significance of Nonconformist campaigning on various social issues. But it is important to retain a sense of hard-headed realism about what Nonconformity could achieve politically. Its great strengths were, on the one hand in the committed individual, who was prepared to follow his or her conscience, regardless of the political or social consequences, and on the other in what was organized in and through local congregations, rather than in the preparation of the detailed legislation necessary to institutionalize social change. Campaigns in foreign affairs generally had a lower priority, and their success was almost impossible to measure. Even if the churches had been united, which they were not, the decision about whether to act as a pressure group from outside or to seek the lower-key role of seeking to influence from within has always been problematic.

8

The Welfare State and Beyond: The Reshaping of Community Work

Lesley Husselbee

I. Introduction

In the aftermath of World War II it became clear that a new pattern of social responsibility was emerging in British society. Much of the involvement in education, health and welfare of the churches and Christian philanthropists in previous centuries was now the role of the State. Rather than initiating and providing their own programmes to meet major societal and community needs, the churches were either being supplanted in these tasks by government and statutory bodies or were being invited into collaborative partnerships. All this took place against an initial backdrop of post-war reconstruction, followed by the social challenges related to changing patterns of housing, employment and popular culture from the 1960s onwards.

Deprived of their previous roles, many churches responded to these events in incarnational ways and identified new ways to serve the risen Christ by caring for the individuals and communities around them. Some Christians drew explicitly on the insights offered by Liberation Theology to resource them in this ministry. Other Christian activists were unaware that the theology underpinning their late twentieth-century grassroots ministry owed much to Latin Americans such as Gustav Gutiérrez,[1] Leonardo and Clodovis Boff,[2] together with such educationalists as Paulo Freire.[3] These potential influences were added to during the 1980s by the emergence of ideas drawn from Black,[4] Feminist,[5] and Womanist theology,[6] highlighting the importance of black and ethnic minority groups as well as women in community work. There might not seem to be a great deal of similarity between life in a deprived inner-city British community and that in a South American shanty town. What these contexts could have in common, though, was the presence of a Christian community where the Bible narrative of liberation was being related to the need for transformation in the lives of poor and marginalized people, both in and beyond their immediate neighbourhood.

Alongside the influence of new theological understandings the second half of the twentieth century also saw the emergence of community development methods and training as ways of initiating change in local communities. British Churches have had a history of trying to bring about transformation in the world around them and, post-World War II, Free Church inheritors of that tradition were well placed to recognize community development as a powerful new tool through which the Church might express its ministry and mission. The resulting church-sponsored community work initiatives may have begun in small ways, with very few people, but they often proved to be influential for both church life and society.

As had often been true in church history, theological theory was slow to follow ministerial praxis. In 1975 a working group of the British Council of Churches (BCC) and the Conference of Missionary Societies in Great Britain and Ireland gave an early definition of church involvement in community. The report *Community Work and the Churches* stated:

> Community work is an area of activity which explores the means whereby citizens can be encouraged to act collectively in order to identify their own community needs and to make their contributions to the meeting of these needs.[7]

The working group identified community work as a means of social change, particularly within the voluntary sector. Examples of organizations using this approach included church-based housing associations and tenants' associations, Toc H, the YMCA and YWCA, Councils of Churches, and the Mothers' Union.[8] Many of these community initiatives had their origins in the style of community work which the churches had initiated in the nineteenth century, especially in inner-city areas. The report recognized the importance of ministers and clergy understanding community work values, noting that theological colleges did not generally teach community work theory. There was also appreciation of the significant support for community work given by the Community and Race Relations Unit of the BCC. Regional consultations noted that community work often happened at parish and congregational level, in neighbourhood centres, in area-based projects and through individual people employed by local authorities or by churches (including clergy). The need for a Christian critique of community work was identified. Churches were in the business of enabling people to be human, to live in the love of God, and to recognize the potential of every person to reflect the image of God.[9] The BCC saw its role as supporting community work by providing the churches with education, evaluation of community work training and encouragement for theological reflection.

Although the Churches had begun to embrace the insights of community work, not all Christians understood this in the same way. Some instinctively involved themselves in community work so they could speak to the condition of the people around them and share the Gospel. Others, including many of the Free Churches, served their communities without making any overt reference to the mission of the Church. Either way, people's motivation was clearly related to their ecclesiology, their understanding of church membership, their personal commitment, and their view of the relationship between belief and lived faith. This varied picture of Christian motivation for community involvement has been further elaborated more recently as partnerships with non-denominational or ethnic minority churches and with those from other faith communities have emerged. Throughout this unfolding story the Free Church presence has continued to be significant.

II. Post War (1945–1979)

Between the end of World War II and the election of Mrs Thatcher's first government in 1979, British society underwent a number of significant changes, all of which impacted on the lives of local churches. One was the altered face of urban living, due to the renewal and replacement of the nation's housing stock, after years of underinvestment followed by the destructive force of German air raids.[10] Despite being virtually bankrupt, the Labour government wanted to make good the 'homes for heroes' pledge made after World War I. In 1945 the Minister of Health, Aneurin Bevan, recognized adequate housing as a key basis for good health and the new administration encouraged local councils to provide this. Factory-built 'prefab' houses solved an initial need. Many returning service men and women now married, set up home and had families, creating the 'baby-boom' generation of the 1940s and 1950s.

The 1950s saw a new government response to the nation's housing crisis in the form of high-rise living, which created a different urban landscape from the terraced streets and back-to-back housing of the past. Embracing the modernist ideas of respected architects such as Le Corbusier, local housing authorities built tower blocks in many towns and cities. The aim was to provide airy living space, decent kitchens and bathrooms. The tower blocks presented a new challenge for councils, agencies, community groups and churches in terms of communicating with the people who came to live there. In an attempt to avoid major population shifts, apartment blocks were sometimes crammed on waste land near the centre of cities, accommodating large numbers of families in relatively small areas. Some of these 'streets in the sky', such as the Hulme Crescents estate in Manchester and the Byker estate in Newcastle, won awards. Other tower block developments were Alton Estate in Roehampton, south west London, and the thousand-flat Park Hill estate in Sheffield.

Such council housing was built to Parker Morris standards, which later in the 1960s included provision of central heating, upstairs bathrooms and downstairs toilets. Many people enjoyed the better living conditions but not the estates themselves. It was difficult to find supervised areas for children to play, people felt unsafe because of vandal damage to lifts and stairs, and the consequent retreat into individual flats destroyed any sense of community. Some of the estates which had been rapidly erected in the 1950s, often from inferior building materials, needed replacement forty years later.[11] Problems of water ingress, damp and rocketing heating bills were common.[12]

Churches initially became involved in the new council estates by building churches. Their focus then progressed to working in the failed or 'sink' estates. In one challenging estate, Blackbird Leys on the outskirts of Oxford, experienced community worker Jim Hewitt was recruited by the ecumenical Church of the Holy Family in the 1960s. Many ministers' families were not keen to live in such estates, so single ministers were required, not least as often churches in these estates could not provide housing.

Post-war housing was also swelled by the New Towns which grew as a result of a Royal Commission report in 1946. The first phase included Bracknell, Crawley, Stevenage, and Welwyn Garden City. Such developments posed a challenge to the churches, whether they responded as individual denominations or worked ecumenically to create new worship centres. Joan Miller, a Methodist deaconess, was sent to the Methodist chapel in the old part of Bracknell.[13] She met resentment and resistance from the existing congregation to the incomers from inner London. The new arrivals, she found, were often isolated, disoriented and without community facilities and structures. Her response was to begin work with the new residents, especially the women, who were often housebound with young children. Out of this came a number of community initiatives created by the people as they responded to their need and discovered allies. This built up communal identity and offered a new start.

Further generations of new towns included Runcorn in the 1960s and Milton Keynes in the 1970s. The new town centre Church of Christ the Cornerstone in Milton Keynes began in a library, before a purpose-built ecumenical 'mini St Paul's cathedral' was built on the edge of the shopping area. A detailed study of churches in the new town highlighted some of their difficulties in serving the new communities in Milton Keynes:

New congregations struggled to resource new buildings which in the early days were far too numerous to be sustained. They were often poorly sited, tight budgets meant that building materials were cheap, and designs were often inadequate, thus producing buildings with a lack of spiritual luminosity inside and external presence and visibility outside. Absence of clear management structures hampered a proper integration of community and church use in the multi- or dual-purpose buildings. Ecumenical ventures often foundered on different levels of expectation, resourcing and management by the parent denominations.[14]

Improved post-war housing and the benefits of the Welfare State did not end the reality of poverty for many, as was recognized during the 1970s. So began a search for alternative and creative ways of addressing the problem. At the same time there was a growing interest in greater public participation in decision-making at the local level.[15] One strategy was the Community Development Project, an experiment launched in 1969, whereby 12 projects in areas of social deprivation were studied.[16] The original aim of exploring the need for people's participation in community shifted to consider questions of inequality and de-industrialization.[17]

Community work, with an interest in community action and organizing, had begun emerging in the late 1950s and early 1960s from the role of community centre wardens. The profession of social work was also evolving, with some workers based in new housing estates and doing much educational work. They helped people within local communities to identify social needs and find effective ways of meeting them. The 1968 *Gulbenkian Report* urged that local people be helped to 'decide, plan and take action to meet their own needs'.[18] In England an initial emphasis on education changed to a focus on worker action.[19] Meanwhile in Scotland, following the 1975 Alexander Report and the emergence of new local government structures, community education services were established in most regions.[20]

In the post-war period the newly formed British Council of Churches expressed concern about poor work conditions and unemployment,[21] while many churches across the country responded locally. The Methodist Church in suburban Thornton Heath, south London, remodelled its premises in 1966 to accommodate a youth centre. Two years later it became a pioneer by providing a base for community work.[22] Between 1969 and 1985 a group of Congregational churches in South Leeds came together with ministers, voluntary social workers and volunteers to create two elderly persons' day centres, two meals on wheels services, a family centre, a hostel for homeless young people, a training workshop for unemployed young people and a community transport system.[23] In 1978, St Ives Free Church in Cambridgeshire altered the their large town centre premises to provide a multi-purpose church and community centre with two ground-floor shops.[24] Several projects including a volunteer bureau were accommodated in the redesigned building.

Some churches discovered their community role in response to a crisis. The disaster that struck the South Wales mining village of Aberfan in 1966, when a school and houses were engulfed by coal waste, led to community rebuilding for which the churches contributed a significant impetus.[25] The lead was taken by the Council of Churches for Wales which, with monies from the Welsh churches in Toronto, Canada, was able to set up an office, first in a caravan and later a house, and place a minister with a brief to work in the community. The Churches of Christ sent a minister to serve their vacant church and two national charities seconded social workers. These were at the heart of the slow process of rebuilding community that culminated in the Queen opening a new community centre in 1972.

Changing patterns of employment, caused by the decline of industries such as cotton weaving, engineering, mining and motor manufacturing, also affected many parts of Britain during the post-war years. Unemployment began to be a serious problem in many areas and trade union disputes increased.[26] In 1964, Harold Wilson's Labour government encouraged the development of technological and service industries by founding the Ministry of Technology to help the UK compete in the global market. However, the demise of traditional heavy manufacturing industries continued.

The Christian response concerned industrial mission. This had developed from such organizations as the Industrial Christian Fellowship, the Seaman's Mission, and the work of chaplains in wartime munitions factories. Modern industrial mission began in Sheffield in 1944 when Leslie Hunter, then Bishop of Sheffield, appointed Ted Wickham as industrial chaplain in the diocese. The aim was to take the church outside traditional buildings, and to provide ministry, particularly in Sheffield in the steel industry. This led to the Sheffield Industrial Mission which became ecumenical in the 1960s. Similar or parallel initiatives sprang up in most industrial areas, normally on an ecumenical basis.

Bill Gowland of the Industrial College in Luton encouraged evangelical Methodist churches to develop links with industry.[27] In 1949 the Methodist Conference agreed on the preparation of plans for intensive evangelical work in the South Yorkshire Coalfield, centred around Doncaster. Two decades later the Methodist Home Mission department encouraged industrial chaplains to support lay people in improving conditions of work.[28] Another approach drew on the example of the French 'worker priest' movement. Here, priests identified themselves with the world of work by taking up jobs in industry, while ministering to their colleagues. In the 1960s this helped to inspire the Bishop of Southwark, Mervyn Stockwood, to set up non-stipendiary ministry, subsequently also adopted by the United Reformed Church in the 1980s.[29]

The 1960s heralded many sociological and cultural changes in British society. New technologies developed, including the computer. New production techniques brought down the price of goods, wages were higher and people had more money to buy consumer items such as washing machines and refrigerators. Car ownership increased and by the end of the decade 75 per cent of families owned a television set, something that had previously been a rarity. Teenagers emerged as a significant social group with spending power. As Prime Minister, Harold Macmillan, famously said in 1957: 'most of our people have never had it so good'.[30]

While immigration has been a feature of British society for many centuries, it was encouraged in this period by British governments aiming to fill labour shortages. First Polish and Italian immigrants came. In 1948 the SS *Windrush*, notoriously, brought immigrants from the Caribbean. They were followed, over the years, by immigrants from the Indian sub-continent (largely Muslim) and later by arrivals from Eastern Europe, Africa and the Middle East. All have provided challenges for British society and local churches. Sadly, as mass immigration continued in the 1950s, there was also a rise in racial violence and prejudice against immigrant workers. Many areas including Birmingham, Nottingham and West London experienced rioting. By the 1970s the government had greatly restricted immigration[31] and in 1976 it set up the Commission for Racial Equality, the statutory body charged with tackling racial discrimination.

The churches' response to an increasing immigrant population, especially in major cities, also frequently reflected the suspicion of the newcomers. Many previously white churches struggled to adapt as they became multiracial. Mansfield Road Baptist Church, Nottingham, for example, received a steady stream of Jamaican new arrivals from the 1950s onwards.[32] On the surface, church members were hospitable and welcoming, but their minister detected hidden racial prejudice. Not until the 1990s did the church arrive at the point of having a mission statement that the church be inclusive.

One minister who challenged discrimination was Robert Gillespie of St James' Presbyterian Church in Sheffield. He was disturbed to discover that many West Indian immigrants were being robbed of their dignity. St James' had been one of the few white working-class congregations in the city. One day, Gillespie's daughter brought a black friend home for tea.[33] Gillespie heard what conditions were like for her and the black community in the area so he decided to do something about the situation. He began by inviting a family to live in the dining room at the manse, and for much of the time Gillespie was at the church there would be a family in residence. As time went on, Mr Gillespie set up a Housing Association and the church gave land for flats to house vulnerable adults. If Jamaicans asked Mr Gillespie for a job reference he would always give one. He also recommended people for housing. At the time there were still signs up saying, 'No coloureds' and the only way around this was to have a reference from a white person. Those who came with a personal reference, or educational qualifications, from Jamaica were made to feel inferior as the only qualifications that counted were British. One woman who received a reference from Mr Gillespie got a job as a hospital cleaner and continued in the post for forty years. Mr Gillespie also encouraged immigrants to obtain

UK qualifications. In 1965 a request was made by St James' Church for someone from Jamaica to work with immigrants in Britain. The United Church of Jamaica recommended Madge Saunders, a women's worker with 17 years' experience.[34] She said later:

> The greatest problem I had was to tackle the Church. When more than ten immigrants went into a church, the host people in the community left the church... Thank God that the immigrants listened to the advice I gave them and while I was there we had no racial problems. The churches began to take responsibility for the West Indians and the immigrants began to find their niche in the churches to which they were attached.[35]

The changing face of post-war British society called for new patterns of theological education. One response was the work of St Paul's House, Liverpool, a training centre based in a terraced house on the edge of Sefton Park.[36] Muriel Paulden, minister of Berkeley Street Congregational Church, foresaw there would be a shortage of ministers after the war. She set about persuading the Congregational Union to let her train women as home missionaries:

> We need women who are ready to give themselves to the Home Field as for the last 150 years they have given themselves to the Foreign. I am not thinking of the ministry, – that is open to those who are called to it – but rather a lay ministry, a community; women who would live together, train for service, and then be ready to go out to the churches as they are needed.[37]

The idea was to recruit as many women as possible but, in the event, only a few applied. Women recruits had to be single and were not expected to marry within seven years of beginning their work. St Paul's House opened in August 1945 with two students, Alice Platts and Rachel Moore. Students studied for the London Certificate of Proficiency in Religious Knowledge and the London Diploma in Theology. They also undertook church placements for two days a week. Typically students would spend Sunday at Berkeley Street Congregational Church and support weekday events such as the women's meeting and youth club. Later placements included work in the new housing estates. For one month each summer the whole community visited another part of the country to gain experience and gain recruits. St Paul's House closed in 1965 due to a lack of students. In twenty years, 19 women had become home missionaries. Despite this small number the significance of the venture for future developments in community ministry would prove great. Not only did it develop diaconal ministries focused on the community but it also modelled contextual methods of training – something that is now commonly accepted.

Another long lasting and unique initiative, the ecumenical Urban Theology Unit (UTU), was founded in Sheffield in 1969 by Methodist minister, John Vincent. Still thriving in 2011, UTU became a learning institution encouraging reflection upon the work of churches, particularly inner-city ones. Vincent's 2000 book *Hope from the City*[38] gives stories of struggle, frustration, failure, joy and hope from ministry to a small community in inner-city Sheffield. UTU has provided for Christians searching for a relevant and radical model of discipleship in contemporary society, a committed community where people from different backgrounds, nationalities and traditions can discover their vocation and study theology.

As churches began to work in community, various organizations offered their support. In 1977 the British Council of Churches (BCC) published 'Work or What?', a paper expressing concern for the disadvantaged, poor and unemployed. It stressed the value of human equality and world brotherhood.[39] In the same year the BCC's Community Resource Unit challenged churches to take poverty seriously. Picking up the work of liberation theologians, it referred to God's option for the poor. Since local churches had 'a quite unique contact' with families in their neighbourhoods the unit challenged them to find ways of working with the poor.[40] These ideas were assisted by government funding changes in the 1970s and 1980s which made it possible to obtain local authority salaries for workers based in churches.

III. The Thatcher Age 1979–1997

Margaret Thatcher came to power in 1979, inaugurating almost two decades of Conservative government in Britain during which period she was re-elected twice. The Iron Lady, as she became nicknamed, expressed her views on society in a 1987 interview:

> I think we have gone through a period when too many children and people have been given to understand "I have a problem, it is the Government's job to cope with it!" or "I have a problem, I will go and get a grant to cope with it!" "I am homeless, the Government must house me!" and so they are casting their problems on society and who is society? There is no such thing! There are individual men and women and there are families and no government can do anything except through people and people look to themselves first. It is our duty to look after ourselves and then also to help look after our neighbour and life is a reciprocal business and people have got the entitlements too much in mind without the obligations.[41]

Thatcher's Conservative government advocated individual effort and voluntary action rather than reliance on the Welfare State. Its political and economic policies emphasized deregulation (particularly of the financial sector), flexible labour markets, the sale or closure of state-owned companies, and the withdrawal of subsidies to others. By 1982 the UK showed signs of economic recovery; inflation was down to just over 8 per cent from a high of 18 per cent, but unemployment was over three million for the first time since the 1930s.[42] Britain had moved away from manufacturing to a service and financial economy, with an emphasis on globalization and the market. Following monetarist economic policies, Chancellor of the Exchequer, Geoffrey Howe, lowered income tax and increased indirect taxation. He increased interest rates in order to lower inflation, capped public spending, and reduced expenditure on education and housing. Thatcher reformed local government income, including the abortive attempt to replace domestic rates with the unpopular Community Charge (or Poll Tax). These years were ones of great racial tension in Britain against a backdrop of strict immigration controls. The 1981 riots, largely sparked by racial issues, began in Brixton, the spiritual home of Britain's Afro-Caribbean community. Youths rioted amid accusations that the police were increasing stop and search procedures for young black men on the streets. Similar riots followed in Liverpool and the Midlands.

In contrast to Thatcher's views on life in 1980s Britain, and possibly in reaction against them, the churches saw a great flowering of theological reflection about conditions in society. In 1982 the ecumenical social justice charity Church Action on Poverty was founded. The next year David Sheppard, Bishop of Liverpool published his book *Bias to the Poor*, detailing the needs of the poor in inner cities, Liverpool and south London.[43] Then in 1985, the influential *Faith in the City* report was published by the Church of England.[44] Free Churches were also involved in championing the needs of the disadvantaged, especially in urban areas, and church-based community projects blossomed.

One example of this, the Bethany Christian Trust, was set up in 1983 in response to steadily increasing numbers of homeless people in Edinburgh.[45] Its initial goal was to provide hostel accommodation but this expanded to operating a van to meet the immediate needs of rough sleepers. Meanwhile in Chalfont St Peter, Buckinghamshire, Gold Hill Baptist Church set up the BeFrienders scheme as part of a family and community initiative offering a professional service in partnership with other organizations. Their long-term vision was to provide such a service throughout the UK.[46]

Some churches found their outreach focused by contemporary political events. The People's Movement in Blackbird Leys, near Oxford, was a product of the 1980s wave of public protests against the Community Charge. Various projects were set up by the ecumenical Church of the Holy Family to help those in Blackbird Leys who could not afford the new taxes. As well as a nearly new clothing shop, a credit union was established, providing affordable finance for local people and helping those who were victims of loan sharks.

On the troubled council estate at Penrhys, South Wales, churches responded to a community which had grown up with little traditional church presence by establishing Llanfair Uniting Church. Its initiators, John and Norah Morgans, believed that 'in order to understand and support a community you must live there'.[47] They moved to the hilltop estate, between the Rhondda Fawr and Rhondda Fach valleys, in 1986 when Morgans was still Moderator of the Wales Synod of the United Reformed Church. One reason for living there was that they did not believe the estate's scurrilous media reputation. It was a surprise for some when, on completing his national leadership role, Morgans chose to stay and offer incarnational ministry in this setting. By the mid-1980s Penrhys was experiencing third-generation unemployment and acceptance of a dependency culture, yet people also supported one another and could enjoy themselves on very little. Norah Morgans set up and ran a community newspaper, *Penrhys Voice*, which gave her access to many local groups. With John as its minister the church began the Llanfair project, which opened in 1992, bringing together private business, statutory authorities, churches and residents. The project team lived and worked on Penrhys in the refurbished maisonette block which also housed community projects and a small chapel. Outside support was given by larger, better resourced churches in places such as Wilmslow, Cheshire. Starting in 1991 a succession of international volunteers from the UK, Madagascar, Europe, North America and Asia helped the community work.

A project with the aim of encouraging people to understand their community was Salford Urban Mission.[48] Founded in 1983, following a variety of community work initiatives, its banner illustrated the belief that ignored, neglected people actually have deep roots in community. Training was a main focus. A key philosophy was for both trainer and trainee to be active in the local community, as well as learning from it. Salford Urban Mission was located in and understood the language, thinking and values of the community.[49] It focused on the insights of contextual theology and saw its knowledge of local issues as a hermeneutical advantage. One of the project's first tasks was to pioneer training ideas locally with the William Temple Foundation and Northern Baptist College, Manchester. It initiated community-based training patterns for students from a variety of denominations (mostly Free Church) who lived in Salford or later in other inner-city areas. In 1991 Salford Urban Mission began student exchanges with Diak Lutheran Seminary, Järvenpää, Finland. More and more people with an interest in theological education were attracted by this contextual approach to training ministers.[50] They observed how learning arose from practice and was integrated with it, while pastoral work was fundamental. This philosophy drew on work in South and Central Africa and was a major Free Church contribution to theological education. The contextual learning was grounded in Trinitarian and incarnational theology, and strongly influenced by the *Kairos Document*, a South African Christian challenge to apartheid written in 1985.[51] Training and education only comprised 40 per cent of the project's work. Representatives also established and worked in credit unions and with families, providing among other things shoes, equipment and camping holidays for disadvantaged youngsters. Camp Project Wales in 1986–87 involved over fifty trainees from United Reformed Churches throughout the country. Salford Urban Mission worked with the Salford Law Centre, using government grants to represent local people. Other groups taught needlework, supported young families at risk, created the Rough and Tumble Girls' Group and worked with the advice centre in Lower Broughton. In partnership with the Quakers the project also helped people to create a co-operative housing association in Ordsall. Wherever they felt that powerless people were being exploited, the Salford Urban Mission team tried to counter this. When an explosion in a local chemical factory blew roofs off warehouses full of blue asbestos the project helped local people to obtain compensation for the resulting health problems. Sadly Salford Urban Mission had to close in 1997.

The 1980s also saw the rise of community ministry in a style best described as Christian social entrepreneurship. Its exponents use business techniques to develop substantial community projects, often based in large, underused church buildings. Examples include the work of United Reformed Church ministers Andrew (now Lord) Mawson and Peter Southcombe. In 1984 Mawson arrived at the run-down, freezing, hundred-year-old, 200–seater Bromley-by-Bow United Reformed Church in east London.[52] After being initially daunted he began to get to know those in the local community and draw people in to the church building. One such was Santiago Bell, a dissident Chilean master craftsman and educator. In exchange for a place to sculpt statutes, he agreed to teach others in the community, proving to be a great inspiration. The main church building was redesigned. A tented shape with the Bible and a cross provides a worship focus, opportunity for plenty of space for other groups to use. A group for those with learning difficulties developed the church gardens; a visual arts degree course began; a café was opened; and later a fully-equipped health centre was built. Most of these projects required considerable sums of money, some of which has come from government and European Union grants. Large numbers of local people have also been involved.

The Methodist Diaconal Order also emerged in this period. It succeeded the Wesley Deaconess Order in 1986, after much discussion about that order's future following the Methodist Church's decision to ordain women as presbyters in 1973. By the late twentieth century the work of the Wesley Deaconess Order had become increasingly church-based. The new Methodist Diaconal Order, which was open to both men and women, regarded different forms of social work as ways of expressing Christian diaconal ministry. A Methodist deacon not only serves the local church but also makes contacts between the congregation and social services or other agencies. He or she tries to strengthen and encourage Christian faith in every aspect of people's lives, from home and neighbourhood to workplace. They support church people in their daily ministry, bring the needs of the world into the heart of worship through intercession, and challenge churches to respond to the call of the Kingdom. Deacons both represent the Church to the community and help those in the Church to live out their role as God's servants in the world.

The United Reformed Church (URC) recognized a similar community role to this in 1987 by publicly acknowledging a limited number of church related community workers (CRCW) who were 'properly trained and appropriately employed, as a new diaconal lay ministry'.[53] This programme partly evolved from the deaconess order of the former Presbyterian Church of England, which by 1975 had fallen to six members only at the formation of the URC in 1972. It was decided to cease recruiting for the order, to phase out this ministry gradually, and to recognize the need for a full-time, paid diaconal ministry open to both men and women. In 1977 it was suggested that a CRWC ministry be set up to meet the needs of areas under stress due to urban renewal, chronic unemployment, broken families and tensions caused by immigration.[54] The URC recognized that the church was often at its weakest in such areas, and embraced the principle of working 'with' rather than 'for' people.[55] It declared:

> Church Related Community Workers are commissioned to care for, to challenge and to pray for the community, to discern (with others) God's will for the well-being of the community, and to endeavour to enable the church to live out its calling to proclaim the love and mercy of God through working with others in both church and community for peace and justice in the world.[56]

Initially it was decided that churches should seek local authority, trust or ecumenical grants to fund this evolving ministry but when the availability of such funds declined the United Reformed Church itself began paying CRCWs. The first person appointed was commissioned at Bradford in September 1981 and seconded to work with Central Bradford Baptist Fellowship. By 1984 there were three CRCWs deployed, and four students in training, while a number of development locations had been identified. Each CRCW had a local church base from which to help people to reflect theologically on their congregation's ministry and mission. Such community workers can avoid the constraints of working within local authority or secular organizations but can develop partnerships with them. By 1989, five to six CRCWs were employed on the same basis as stipendiary ministers, rising by about one per year in following years. Tensions have sometimes emerged, however, between the aims of those working in community ministry and the aims of church congregations. Church related community workers prefer to get alongside people outside the church using non-directive leadership styles.[57] Church congregations, on the other hand, often seek to evangelize and thus to increase the community of worshippers.[58]

IV. New Labour and Beyond: 1997–2010

Under Tony Blair's leadership the Labour party moved away from its socialist roots for the centre ground of British politics in a process he described as becoming 'New Labour'. His governments enacted legislation on the minimum wage, human rights, freedom of information and forms of devolution for Northern Ireland, Scotland and Wales. Laws banning fox hunting, smoking in public and parental use of strong physical punishment on children were criticized by opponents as eroding personal responsibility to create a 'nanny state'. Other declared aims, such as the halving of child poverty by 2010 and its ending by 2020, were lauded by some people for their idealism but, despite some success, proved hard to implement. This period also saw the continued decline of traditional British manufacturing industries and their replacement by service industries such as accountancy and tourism.

Against this changing political and social background people's views on the nature of church life also underwent new thinking. As the twenty-first century began there was an increasing understanding that people no longer lived in one, solid community but juggled their commitments to their work and leisure communities in a liquid way.[59] Pete Ward argued that while the previous, solid model of church had focused on attendance at worship, on size, and on 'joining the club' a new 'liquid' church approach must be networked, consumer-oriented and flexible.[60]

One church whose mission to serve its surrounding neighbourhood responded by adapting to changing social patterns during this period was St Mark's United Reformed Church in Wythenshawe, south Manchester, one of the largest social housing estates in Europe. Surrounded by a deprived community, the church had sold clothing and other goods at affordable prices in a community shop since 1984. From this the Tree of Life Centre project was launched within the church building in 2002, with paid staff, volunteers and transport to collect and sell furniture, household goods and clothing. Meals and friendship were offered at the community café along with a variety of health-related projects from counselling to aerobics.

Another Christian scheme, offering quality second-hand furniture and goods to those people referred by local agencies, was the Sutton Furniture Project (later renamed the Vine Project).[61] By 2009 it employed at least ten people with funding from European grants. The achievements of such ventures as Seaforth Community Shop, run by Caradoc Mission United Reformed Church near Liverpool, Weoley Castle Community Church in Selly Oak, Birmingham, and Peaceful Solutions for Conflict Resolution, the project for children run by High Cross United Reformed Church in Tottenham, London, were also impressive.

Another factor which influenced church community work during the New Labour period was the increased funding which became available to improve areas with the highest indices of multiple deprivation. Communities were encouraged to bid for grants from local authorities, trusts and the National Lottery fund. Churches interested in finding partners and funding for projects to serve their local communities responded with interest to this favourable new climate. Contemporary British theologian Ann Morisy noted the links between contemporary church community work and the social capital ideas of Lyda Judson Hanifan, based on his observation of successful early twentieth-century rural schools in the United States.[62] Social capital theory noted the process through which people provided pathways to facilitate social networks by offering reciprocal help, building strong allegiances and neighbourliness between one another, coupled with extending friendship to strangers. Ann Morisy suggested the existence of a further type of community investment, 'brave social capital', where volunteers and workers worked in particularly difficult and often unsafe conditions so as to help others. Churches were particularly good at providing social capital in all of these ways.

As the twenty-first century began many local churches were becoming involved in Local Strategic Partnerships, where discussions between council officers and councillors, other agencies, charities and local groups centred on a local area's future planning needs. Other instances of joint working took place where government New Deal for Communities regeneration schemes were active, covering almost forty of England's most deprived neighbourhoods. In 2001, following his experience at New Addington Baptist Church in Croydon, North West Baptist Association regional minister Phil Jump researched how Baptist churches had experienced these New Deal schemes.[63] He found that 12 had expressed an interest in such involvement, 7 were in initial contact with a local partnership, 17 had received funding or were active service providers, 24 were active in local regeneration initiatives and 13 were significant leaders and policy makers. Examples of churches serving areas of social need included Tanterton Christian Fellowship near Preston, Nutley Baptist Church, Bromley Baptist Church and Mersey Street Baptist Tabernacle in Openshaw, East Manchester. Phil Jump noted how churches could reach those who might not access other provision and also provided a skills base. Tensions existed, however, as when churches had to play down their core beliefs in order to obtain grants from local authorities which were afraid of encouraging proselytizing. Nevertheless, churches which took part in the New Deal scheme found that their involvement resulted in increased church attendance. Funding for the entire New Deal for Communities project ended during 2011.

Some partnerships between churches and their community arose from providing for the needs of groups such as pre-school children in disadvantaged neighbourhoods. In Tonge Moor, Bolton, the United Reformed Church was demolished and a local authority children's centre built on the site, along with land from the neighbouring primary school. The new Church at the Centre was established in the children's centre when it opened in 2006 and a church related community worker was appointed to work from there. Agreements with other building users have to be regularized and special ad hoc arrangements have to be made when, for instance, worship space is needed for a weekday funeral.

During this period a local church that relied on central or local government funding often found that it could experience considerable insecurity. Altering patterns of government funding and the short terms and restrictions on many grants meant that some church community projects were short-lived. Thus a Baptist church in West Croydon, situated in an area where there were many asylum seekers, spent money adapting its premises to serve them but then found official funding for work with asylum seekers was reduced due to government cuts.

When such central and local government grants became less available some churches looked for alternative sources of funding. The Rainbow Haven project at St Paul's with St John's United Reformed Church in East Manchester and in Salford largely secured its future for four years when it won a National Lottery grant in 2010 for its work with migrants, refugees and asylum seekers. The Lottery in particular has created ethical problems for some Free Churches, especially if their official denominational stance was opposed to receiving money raised by any form of gambling.

There are many other examples of churches providing help to their communities. In 2004 Trinity United Church (Church of England/United Reformed) in Cheetham Hill, Manchester, set up the Welcome Centre to support asylum seekers with advice, hot food, and a crèche. The work was initially supported by a trainee URC church related community worker, together with the vicar, and later by a paid worker who had previously been an asylum seeker himself. Similarly, while making tea for asylum seekers at City United Reformed Church in Cardiff, a retired lawyer discovered that one of their key needs was for legal advice. He began to spend sixty to seventy hours a week working, with other volunteers, meeting that need. The Asylum Justice project, having extended its work to Swansea and Newport as well as Cardiff, won the 2010 United Reformed Church Community Project Award.

Levenshulme Inspire in Manchester, an example of social entrepreneurship, was officially launched on 31 October 2010. A decaying United Reformed Church building, home to a small congregation, has been transformed with Lottery and other grants into a bright new environment with a church, café, business centre, social media suite and 14 rented apartments offering social housing. In a different initiative Peter Southcombe, a United Reformed Church minister, co-founded the registered charity, Hope in the Community. This has worked

nationally with faith and voluntary sector groups to develop partnerships with regional government from which activities to regenerate local
communities would arise.[64] The charity offered help for groups as they
researched possible funding sources, wrote business plans, submitted
bids and monitored projects.[65]

However, there can be problems. Some churches have allowed their
buildings and land to be used by community projects, in partnership with
other organizations, without making proper legal agreements. They later
found they had lost their building, or failed to keep alive the relationships
that validated the presence of church representatives in the management
structure. Some churches found themselves unable to display Christian
symbols or notice boards in their own buildings. There could be tensions
between the priorities and needs of an ageing, existing congregation and
the new vision for their buildings and mission developed through adopting
a community project. Despite these difficulties the contribution of many
churches to community development projects was considerable.

The 1990s and 2000s also saw a rise in initiatives where Free Churches,
and those from other denominations, sought to make positive links with
other faith groups. The Commission on Integration and Cohesion, which
reported in 2007, received a joint submission from the Baptist Union,
Methodist Church and United Reformed Church. This document reminded
central government that the only way to build up understanding of religious
faiths was through sustained listening on the ground. It encouraged local
councils to promote opportunities for interfaith, multi-cultural, inter-racial
dialogue and to celebrate different religious festivals as a way of increasing
understanding. Local faith leaders and members were urged to see their
sacred spaces as community resources, and to foster interfaith relationships based on partnership, that would survive even at times of community
tension and pressure.[66] An example of good interfaith relations was the
work of Grassroots, a small ecumenical Christian group based in Luton.
From 1992 onwards Grassroots provided opportunities for people of
different faiths to find out about one another's beliefs, often working in
partnership with Luton Council of Faiths.

One reason for the growing importance of interfaith work has been the
recent increased multiculturalism of British society. In the years following
the fall of the Iron Curtain a wave of migration from Eastern Europe began,
with some people fleeing political persecution and others seeking a better
life. Between 1998 and 2000 there were 45,000 people who arrived from
Africa, 22,700 from the Indian sub-continent, 25,000 from Asia and almost
12,000 from the Americas. In 2000 some 125,000 people were allowed
to settle in the UK. The Labour government responded to these changing
immigration patterns by shifting attention onto the economic benefits
represented by new migrants. It also introduced tighter rules for asylum
seekers which resulted in many who failed to meet the new criteria going
underground.

A number of churches tried to counter fears that immigrant groups were 'taking over'. For example, following the Bradford race riots of 7 July 2001, Methodist minister Geoff Reid joined with other leaders of mainstream churches to help rebuild community relations. The Touchstone Centre, a Methodist project in Bradford, opposed the rise of the British National Party in the area.[67]

During the late twentieth century many Free Churches began to recognize their past failures in relating to people of other races and faiths, and adopted policies that committed them to working for racial justice. They acknowledged and challenged the existence of institutional racism in the life of Church and society. The Methodist Church has committed itself to racial justice and declared racism to be a sin that must be constantly resisted. In 2005, the United Reformed Church declared itself a multi-cultural church. It affirmed that the human family is one race consisting of people of different ethnicities and cultures, and rejoiced in all of the variety of gifts of the human family.[68]

From 1961, inheriting the work of its Presbyterian predecessors, the United Reformed Church in London collaborated with a Ghanaian minister of the Presbyterian Church of Ghana and the Evangelical Presbyterian Church, Ghana (known as the Ghanaian Chaplain). Ghanaian Presbyterians living in London were encouraged to join local churches, but they also gathered regularly to meet and worship with their chaplain. In 2011 this fifty-year ministry came to an end with a thanksgiving service in London, a sign of how relationships had come to fruition and needs altered over that period. Many Free Churches now include a range of people from different cultures worshipping among them. Some have shared their premises with other ethnic congregations, which meet at different times, enabling them to worship in their own language and style. Ethnically based congregations from Africa, Asia and the Caribbean could be found in many British towns and cities by the start of the new millennium.

Changing needs in society also encouraged fresh forms of incarnational community work. When gang violence plagued Moss Side, Hulme and Longsight in inner-city Manchester, local people organized a Gangstop march in 2002. A group of local Christians began asking why young people were attracted to gangs and what was missing from community and family life. They wondered what messages young people were receiving to make them feel left out, and where the fathers and positive role models might be. Questions were raised about the way police were eight times more likely to stop and search a black young person than a white one.[69] Then in November 2002 another local group launched the community organization Carisma (Community Alliance for Renewal, Inner South Manchester Area) to work with young people and help them discover life options other than crime and gang culture. Carisma was not a church organization as such but many of those involved in it were Christian. This initiative built on the 1970s Hideaway Youth Project run by the United People's Church in Moss

Side (Baptist and United Reformed) which had worked with many similar young people at that time.

Another example of Christian community action was The Message Trust's pioneering ministry among young people in Greater Manchester, which began in 1988. From this the Eden Project was launched in 1997 to reach children and young adults through schools, community projects and offenders groups in some of Manchester's most deprived estates, using a bus or local churches as a base. As a company limited by guarantee, with no denominational basis, The Message Trust exemplified a new missionary response to community need. Traditional churches might be bemused by this at first but often become supportive once they recognized the effectiveness of this new way of doing Christian youth work.

> Followers of Jesus are moving out of their comfort zones. Leaving old securities behind, they plant their homes and their souls in urban community. Young and old, single and married...they choose to live out their lives in the face of some of the highest rates of crime, social deprivation, drug and alcohol abuse, teen pregnancy and unemployment... Eden is about reaching young people right in the heart of forgotten communities.[70]

Other churches created new church plants, often in their neighbouring communities. Church planter and missiologist Stuart Murray Williams, an initiator of the Incarnate Network, reflected that most Baptist church plants came about when large, thriving churches set up daughter churches nearby.[71] An example of this was Rhiwbina Baptist Church, Cardiff, which planted a church in Caerphilly in 2005. This began in a home and later moved to a community centre as the congregation expanded. Similarly, the Grace Baptist Churches have set up a number of plants around the Home Counties.[72] Murray Williams argued that Baptists should work more strategically, if possible through Regional Baptist Associations, so church plants could be made in the areas of greatest need.

An important social change of recent years has been the changes in patterns of employment and leisure. This is seen most clearly in the expansion of working hours for many who had a job, the increasing number of families where both parents worked and single-parent families. This greatly reduced the time many working people had for voluntary activities. The changing pattern of family activity on a Sunday meant the Sabbath was now for shopping, sport and socializing, rather than worship and rest. To meet some of these changes, churches have experimented with new forms of worship, offered outside the church premises and not on Sundays and have tried to develop new forms of Christian community. Fresh Expressions was launched in 2004 by the Church of England and Methodist Church to support these experiments, joined in 2010 by the United Reformed Church. Worshipping communities have grown up in cafés, community centres, sports clubs, and city centres, many related closely to a particular community or group. Baptist evangelist Penny Marsh set up a worshipping group at a coffee shop in Bluewater Shopping Centre, Greenhithe, Kent. Other initiatives have worked with young adults, using film. Children and those new to worship have often been introduced through informal activities, such as arts and crafts, which has been described as Messy Church. Ways have been found of growing a new congregation where a church building no longer existed. In 1999, Methodist minister Barbara Glasson was given the task of re-discovering how to exercise ministry in Liverpool city centre, where the old Methodist Central Hall had been taken down. For a year she walked the city streets and got to know the needs of local people. Out of this came Somewhere Else, often referred to as the Bread Church, in rooms above a bookshop where people could make a loaf for themselves and one to give away. An invitation to share worship was offered to them if they wished to take it up. Reflecting on this ministry, Glasson and URC minister John Bradbury likened it to a well where vagabonds and passersby came and went for sustenance.[73] The Church has also been found on the streets of the city, especially in the city centre, involved with the club culture. The notable example has been the rise of Street Pastors, working with the police and others among the weekend revelers that are to be found at the heart of any town.

Church community outreach in modern secularized society has had a low level of public recognition. In 2003 a survey of the community involvement of faith communities in north-west England revealed the significance of their work.[74] The responses of over 2,300 faith communities across eight faith groups showed they made an important contribution to the region's social and economic life through 5,000 projects. Faith communities ran or managed schemes covering homelessness, racism, crime, drug and alcohol abuse, health skills development, art, music, and environmental improvement. They were especially involved in work with older people, children and deprived communities. Of the 3,151 volunteers nearly 28 per cent were Anglican, nearly 27 per cent were Free Churches (proportionately the highest figure in proportion to the total number of church members) and nearly 12 per cent Roman Catholic Church.

A survey in 2008, carried out by the Evangelical Alliance in Wales in conjunction with the Wales Council for Voluntary Action, uncovered similar patterns. They found that over 40,000 volunteers worked in activities organized by faith communities for 80,000 hours a week, the equivalent of 2,300 full-time workers. It also emerged that churches employed around 1,500 staff to work with the wider community, equivalent to another 650 full-time posts. The faith communities provided services such as hospital visiting, lunch clubs and coffee bars and personal support for the bereaved. In addition, they were working in areas of emerging need such as employment training, alcohol and drug awareness and personal finance. With the onset in 2008 of a serious, worldwide economic recession, there was no doubt that church-based voluntary community work would continue to have a significant value in British society.

The churches have become increasingly aware of their calling to social witness and responsibility in society. This has become part of the fabric of church life at various levels. Church education programmes have encouraged people to think about their community, as was the case in the Free Church educational and worship resource material for children, young people and adults in *Partners in Learning*.[75] Organizations such as Christian Aid and the British Council of Churches have produced study material which encouraged Christians to consider societal and justice issues.

Modern hymn books and liturgical materials offer personal and congregational resources for including these themes in worship. These include the hymns of John Bell and Graham Maule from the Church of Scotland, of Methodists Fred Pratt Green and Andrew Pratt, and of Brian Wren, Fred Kaan and John Campbell and the prayers and meditations of Baptists Clare McBeath and Tim Presswood,[76] URC minister, Jan Berry,[77] The Iona Community's Wild Goose Worship Group,[78] and the Corrymeela Community.[79]

At a more academic level there has been a growing interest in public theology. This both attempts to challenge the Christian community to wrestle with the social, economic and political realities of the age, and to feed into the national channels of debate and opinion formation something of the Christian insights that witness to the gospel. In 2004, the Manchester Centre for Public Theology was launched with conferences and seminars considering such issues as Religious Capital in Declining Communities,[80] The Work of the Northwest Development Agency,[81] The Work of Wythenshawe Voices,[82] and the significance of Community Pride.[83] There have been established similar centres in New College, Edinburgh, and Ridley Hall, Cambridge, with others, such as the Christian Institute and Kairos in London.

V. Conclusion

The period since World War II has seen major changes in British social fabric, not least in the towns and cities. There has been a continuous decline in heavy industry and manufacturing and an emerging dominance of financial, service and consumer interests. This process, however, has been made more complex and fragile by the depression induced by the banking crisis of 2008–2009. Something of this was indicated by the Commission on Urban Life and Faith in the report *Faithful Cities*,[84] issued in 2006, set up by the Church of England with ecumenical and interfaith membership. Methodist minister, Baroness Kathleen Richardson, who chaired the commission, acknowledged that the modern city is 'work-in-progress' rather than definitive.[85]

It was the notion of 'faithful capital' which the report identified as the Church's contribution by its committed involvement, through its structures and the service offered through its members, to the life of the city. This indeed offers a helpful perspective from which to reflect on the story that has been told here. Despite institutional decline, especially among the mainstream denominations, social concern, community service and community development have been a vital expression of Christian presence in the wider society. A number of different approaches to church involvement in community work have emerged. Some people have worked on a very small scale in a particular local context. Others have used a much larger community involvement model. National networks, such as Christians Against Poverty, have emerged. Community work experiments, however, have sometimes only been recognized by their denominations once they were successful. Projects have inevitably come and gone as volunteers and funding became available and then disappeared. The theological and missiological basis of many of the initiatives mentioned here was an incarnational and diaconal vision that encouraged the empowerment of the powerless and vulnerable by helping them to find their voice. Those projects based on liberal, liberationist and radical theologies are perhaps now facing competition for limited resources from more evangelical and charismatic churches doing community work with a stronger missiological style and clearer evangelical purpose. This may reflect the fact that the Church is no longer a necessary part of most people's lives and that the period of Christendom is at an end.[86] In order to overcome the fact that many people view the Church as irrelevant all traditions seek, by involving themselves in their community, to reconnect people with the Gospel.[87]

Since 1945 another characteristic of much of the Church's work in the community has been its ecumenical practice and it was usually stronger for that. Another factor has been the partnership often created between churches, government funding, local authority structure and other voluntary bodies. The value of setting up projects with the proper legal arrangements to cover church resources at the start is a lesson that can be drawn. Also, there has always been the danger that, although the aim was often for the congregation to own the project and for church members to contribute, it is clear that some projects suffered because the congregation actually expected their minister, deacon or youth worker to do all the work. Too frequently, community work has still relied on the pioneering energy of particular individuals. Again, there has been the problem that projects move away from their Christian founding aims, or original character, and sometimes it is difficult to keep those links alive. Yet it is still necessary that Christians celebrate every piece of work that builds the kingdom of God and enhances human well-being, even if a project seems to have become totally secular.

This chapter has touched on the variety and scope of recent Church engagement in neighbourhood and community and the lives of people old and young. This is a story that deserves to be told. Social activists, by their nature, are better at initiating things than at recording what has taken place. All these ventures, remembered or forgotten, successful or failed, were faithful attempts to respond to God's invitation to risk taking partnership in service of others. This has been one strong characteristic of the Free Churches down the centuries, a tradition that contemporary Christians can claim is being creatively and excitingly continued, albeit in very different circumstances.

9

Living out of History
Paul Ballard

I. Introduction

This volume offers a contribution to both the social history of Britain
and the history of the churches in these islands. It tries to set out how
a particular faith tradition, British Nonconformity, has contributed to
and been moulded by modern British society. Chapters have followed a
particular strand of that story from a time when Dissent was a marginalized and sometimes persecuted minority, as they struggled for and
benefited from the processes of liberalization and democratization that
characterized the emergence of industrialism, down to the very different
situation of the present where the churches, having been pushed more
and more to the edges of society, face the challenges of radical social
pluralization. It has been a varied and variable story: of pioneering charismatic leadership, of collective action and reforming societies, of national
campaigns and denominational initiatives, of local congregations and
charitable bodies, and the commitment of countless individuals within this
Gospel tradition.

The project, however, came out of a particular felt need. There has
been no obvious and accessible resource relating to the Free Churches that
would help those training for or engaged in socially related ministry or
action, especially church-related community workers, to root their theory
and practice within this particular tradition. Such discussion has tended
to be dominated by the establishment Anglican perspective or working-
class Catholicism. The hope, therefore, was not only to redress that
imbalance but also to explore something of the relevance of such history
to the practical work of ministers, community workers, youth workers and
others. This is the purpose of this last chapter through a brief presentation
of some key issues and practical approaches.

II. The Historical Perspective in Practical Theology

Practical theology is the theology of Christian practice. John de Gruchy summarizes this as follows:

> ... to enable the community of faith critically to understand the faith and express answers to the question: Who is God? Where is God found today and what does God require of us here and now?[1]

That is, it is about discipleship, personal and corporate. It is about seeking what God has given us to do in our own time, evaluated in the light of the Gospel imperative. It is a critical activity of discernment.

Of course this process of enquiry and evaluation can be and is carried out through the normal activities of prayer and faithful action as we go about our corporate and personal living. But there are moments when the process of reflection is engaged in more deliberately, such as a personal crisis or when a congregation is trying to explore its missional calling. This more structured and reflective activity is frequently described in terms of 'the pastoral cycle'[2] or 'critical correlation'.[3] In response to the need to explore a particular need or issue there are three moments of analysis. The first is to understand the nature and circumstances of the situation. The next is to appraise the possible responses to that situation in the light of the circumstances and resources available. The third is to set this within an understanding of the Gospel imperative, through prayerful contemplation and recourse to the Scriptures and the wisdom of the tradition, in order to determine the path of faithful obedience that is both Gospel led and realistically hopeful. This last has become known as theological reflection and is regarded as the heart of most contemporary practical theological practice.[4] At each of these points it is necessary to draw on the appropriate perspectives and skills from the social and psychological sciences, which will inevitably include the need to look at the historical dimension.

Imagine the case of a city centre Free Church, already probably a united congregation given the weakness of the Church in such a location, faced with the pressures of urban renewal plans, the problems of a binge-drinking culture and the effects of economic depression on the retail trade. The question is to know where to deploy its limited resources for mission over the next five years. Their analysis will include the history of their town: the urban and industrial expansion, the causes of the economic decline, the effects of government policies down the years and the important events and personalities that have shaped their present. Similarly they will need to understand themselves. What is their history? How do they fit into the tradition? What is their theological and community ethos? This is clearly intertwined with the wider social context within which they are set. But it also relates directly to their understanding of the Gospel because that truth has itself been mediated through the tradition of which they are a particular example and which will shape their response. Part of theological reflection, therefore, is to begin to know in depth their own story of faith and to be able to evaluate it, see its strengths and to counter its weaknesses, so as the better to be able to act creatively and perhaps boldly in stepping into the future. This will be done by setting themselves against the wider sweep of the history of the whole Church, including the specific traditions of Nonconformity such as are set out in the previous chapters, recognizing where their story both echoes and is an example of the wider story. At the same time they will discover how their tradition has shaped their perception of the Gospel as they wrestle with the guidance of the Spirit through Bible study and prayer. They will bring out treasures old and new as they learn to hear the Gospel afresh.

III. History in an Interdisciplinary Context

The historical dimension, therefore, is an essential factor in practical theology. This implies that history as an academic discipline sits alongside the more obvious disciplines such as psychology and sociology as a dialogue partner with theology in the process of pastoral and practical discernment. This inevitably raises a range of issues. Stephen Pattison,[5] in a seminal article, usefully sets out some of these in relation to the use of the human sciences in the teaching of practical theology. Broadly the same questions can be posed in relation to history as a discipline and the use made of it by the practitioner.

The teacher or the practitioner in an interdisciplinary context is at a disadvantage. They are trespassing into territories where experts hold sway. They can easily be dismissed as amateurs with little understanding of the complexities and nuances of any particular field. Moreover they tend to be there fishing, looking for a useful tool by which they can address a given problem. This need can colour their choice of theme or example, as can the attraction of the latest popular theory or approach found on the internet or in a paperback. There is also what Pattison calls 'pastoral pragmatism',[6] that is the desire to find a ready packaged model that would appear to provide the solution to a particular issue. Too often the phrase 'history teaches' or 'sociology has proved' masks the fact that this is only what some experts think or say. The practical theologian who has also studied another discipline or practised another profession may well have more than one arrow in his or her quiver, but hardly ever the full range needed. Yet it is practically inevitable that a selection must be made as to which guides to follow in the search for understanding of the human condition or of this or that historical situation. This is true for all practitioners, from the politician to the therapist, but it is always important to accept that there may be other perspectives open for consideration and to ensure as far as possible that the guides chosen stand up to scrutiny and have a good pedigree. Thus one of the arts of theological reflection is for the practitioner to understand something of and to respect the discipline being laid under contribution and to try to be in touch with recent developments so as to be able to discern the resources that mediate that which is most valuable. Two such resources that are immediately accessible are the encyclopaedia, which is intended to provide an overview of a field or topic, and the current text book, which is designed to introduce the student to the present state of a discipline. There is also, perhaps as much in history as in any subject area, a rich seam of material from leading scholars designed to inform the general reader. All this can become the informed background of pastoral and social action. However, as Pattison comments:

> There is only a thin line between a search for valid and truthful perspectives in many different disciplines and being a thorough dilettante who has no understanding of the discipline from which a particular insight might come and with which it may be ineffably tainted.[7]

Yet this is the risk that must be taken as part of the willingness to be open and receptive to fresh insights without which the creative practical wisdom being sought will be immeasurably poorer.

IV. History for Practice

Each of the social sciences and humanities is looking at the human situation from a particular standpoint. The historian is trying to make sense of the past and to understand how and why that story has played itself out in the way it has. As one of the humanities, history is fundamentally a hermeneutic process; that is, it engages in a dialogue that seeks to elicit coherence and meaning in the past whilst standing in the present.[8]

The primary data, which constitutes one partner in the dialogue, are the artefacts, documents and, sometimes, oral witnesses that come out of the past. So, the material set out in the earlier chapters was ultimately based on such evidence as chapels, graveyards, minute books, magazines, letters, diaries, reports in the media, memoires and memories handed down the generations. The historian is essentially trying to get behind the presenting evidence in order to reconstruct, with all the limitations of fragmentary data, how people, in their own time and place, understood the world and why they acted as they did, and what were the pressures and possibilities that moulded their lives and choices. History is, therefore, about the past which has its own reality and integrity that must be properly respected. The past is, in the first place, studied for its own sake, not primarily for a purpose. A purely instrumental view of history must be eschewed.

History, like other humanities, is also a critical discipline. This is seen, first, in the critical evaluation of the evidence which has to be sifted and tested. Witnesses are examined as to their intention, credibility and bias. Different voices out of the past have to be compared and contrasted. More weight will be given to some pieces of information than others. Similarly the accounts given by previous historians will be put under the micro-scope. These will then be drawn together into a fresh coherent account, both affirming and challenging what has been said previously. To this the historian brings a set of tools and skills, passed on through the profession, which have been honed and tested in experience. These include, like the practical theologian, drawing on other disciplines such as psychology and sociology.

History, however, is critical in another sense because the account of the past is always under review. Not only is new evidence coming to light but the discussion as to how to present and interpret that evidence is constantly shifting. There is also the tradition of historical understanding and presen-tation through which this story has been understood down the generations, the various received versions both of scholarship and of popular under-standing. Thus the understanding of the past is always, to some extent, being re-evaluated as historians strive the better to come to grips with their subject matter and to interpret it more adequately. History, therefore, is an ongoing conversation in which the participants question, correct and enrich each other. This means that the appeal to history can be a somewhat slippery thing. Accepted assumptions and beliefs can be undermined in the light of new evidence or a more critical or revised understanding. An example of this can be the way the perception of the modern missionary movement has frequently been revised in the light of revised understandings of the nature and effect of western colonial and economic imperialism.[9] But it does not stop there. Each such revision itself has to be placed under scrutiny as we seek an ever more nuanced and realistic appraisal of this important phase, or any other phase in Christian history.

History is about the past but it is impossible to ignore the other pole of the hermeneutic circle. The historian too is inevitably part of the equation because he or she will bring to the task their own interests and perspec-tives; so that, for example, someone interested in feminist issues will have a very different take from the historian of technology. More important, however, are the underlying values that inform the interpretive stance of each historian; for example, the progressive Whig view or a Marxian view of history. The historian endeavours to deal with the past with integrity but can only do so within the perspectives of how he or she understands the world to work.[10]

If, however, history is to make sense, if we are to understand the past at all, then there must in fact be some common ground, some continuity, between the past and the present. This is provided, in the first place, because part of the coherence of the historical narrative is that it, in one

way or other, relates to our present. It is how we make sense of our lives
today. We draw on a common story, inherited language and culture, on
ways and habits that have been passed on down the generations. There is,
second, the common humanity which is shared with those of former times.
The past is indeed in a very real sense a distant world. Those living earlier
saw things very differently from ourselves and such differences must be
respected. Yet their experience was, in so many ways, also similar to ours.
There is, therefore, both discontinuity and continuity. It is indeed because
of the common ground that the past can speak to us, but only critically
and obliquely because of the differences which force us to pause and to ask
how their witness actually illuminates ours. To read history, therefore, is
to explore another's dwelling place in expectation that it will be interestingly different. Yet it will be curiously familiar as we see how they faced the
same problems, but in their own way. It will, also, be to come away excited
and refreshed, with new perspectives on familiar issues and seeing the old
familiar places differently.

Another fairly usual scenario would be a congregation in, for example, a
late Victorian industrial inner-city suburb which has been rapidly changing
in recent decades under the impact of both new immigrant and culturally
diverse communities and 'gentrification' by young professionals, wanting
to rediscover its mission or planning to set up a new project. Such a
congregation is likely to have a long and possibly complex history that
overshadows its present, most obviously in the form of the grandiose and
substantial plant. For some members there will be sadness and grieving for
the glories of the past. Old traditions will die hard, of which much will
still be within memory, especially of those brought up on the stories of the
heady days before World War II, not least among those who have moved
away but who still look back with nostalgia to their families' spiritual
roots. For others this is all a burden to carry and an irrelevance in the vastly
changed circumstances of the present. There is, indeed, need to recall the
past: how the founding members caught a vision, the 'great' ministries of
previous ministers, the pioneering work of deaconesses in the working-class
streets nearby at times of recession and unemployment, especially in the
Great Depression, the Sunday School and youth work; but alongside all
this there are also rumours of division and controversy, the reality of class
distinctions and patronising church leadership and, since the war, the years
of struggle and decline, of wandering in the wilderness, and the bewildering
impact of the new-comers, frequently from other immigrant traditions. This
recall, however, can be one of rediscovery and critical re-evaluation that
may be strange and even painful, yet also full of surprises as the creativity
of former members suggest the possibility of release from slavish tradition
and boldness in the face of challenge, while regretting and learning from
the failures and less fortunate episodes.[11] And this church's story has also
to be seen as part of the wider development of the neighbourhood as it
has moved through various phases from the carriage-lined avenues of the

first occupants through the decline into multi-occupancy and the impact of diverse ethnic groups from radically different cultures and faiths, to the signs of another twist in the story with the return of the new professional classes and the problems of the new multi-culturalism. Hopefully, they will be able to discern both the continuities and the discontinuities from the past and to be able to be freed to discard the unnecessary burdens of the past and to rejoice in being enabled to face the future.

V. Engaging with Historical Resources

In order to do this it is necessary to have the resources. A major resource is naturally to be found in the writings of the historians, providing both, as in this volume, the background of the broader sweep of relevant history and the more immediate and local histories. However, more often than not, this latter needs to be supplemented in a particular situation. It may be that there is little or nothing on a specific issue or neighbourhood or that more recent events have not yet been recorded. Nor do many churches boast an amateur historian. It can, therefore, be necessary, in order to do the historical part of the community audit, to engage in some modest historical research for which some of the skills and resources used by historians may be required.

This community audit, properly devised, will analyse the local social structures, the hopes and fears of the residents, the way the neighbourhood relates to the wider city and the public, private and voluntary resources to hand. Similarly, the strengths and weaknesses of the congregation will be assessed, part of the evidence for which is the inherited tradition. The first call will be to any published historical accounts. Beyond this, however, there are other sources of information. In the community this will include the local press, the county archives, census data, the registers of births, marriages and deaths, and so forth. Within the church the research team will turn to minute books, magazines, correspondence, registers and even sermons. Importantly, both in the community and in the church, the memories of families and individuals, as well as the experience of key figures, will provide an oral record of the collective memory.[12]

The knack is to know how to retrieve this information and how to sift it out and assess it. This will include agreeing as to methods, such as questionnaires, interviews or focus groups, which need to be set up and administered. Statistics may have to be read. All this has to be gathered into a coherent narrative which people will recognize is about themselves and their place but which can also spotlight convincingly the unpalatable or surprising truth that has now to be taken into account. The results may be presented in one or more of a variety of ways. The most usual is the formal printed report; but, alternatively or as a supplement to the report, through, for instance, oral presentation, an exhibition or even a 'history-fest' which can draw on old documents, photos and other memorabilia supported by talks and other events.

Not many congregations will have a wealth of talent that can undertake such a task, though there may well be teachers or local history enthusiasts to be discovered. Community workers and ministers, too, should have developed considerable relevant experience through their dealings with the local authorities and other organizations as well as through their work with people. It is also possible to seek help from outside. This can be done as part of a professional, commissioned feasibility study; or members of the local history group or teachers in the local FE or HE colleges may well welcome the opportunity to engage in what is tantamount to fieldwork or even supervise some students on a project. There are courses on becoming engaged in local historical research and resources in print and on the web. It is best, however, to ensure that all the members of the project group or congregation be fully involved even if this means a steep learning curve. As with all community work, participating in the learning and researching is part of the process of community development.[13]

VI. The Relevance of the Project for Mission

This project is about mission. Earlier chapters have shown the long concern within the Free Churches with and for the wider society that continues to this present day. They remain widely active and are, not infrequently, leading partners in community-based initiatives across the country. How then does an understanding of the past, as set out in these pages, provide a valuable grounding for those presently working from within this tradition, not least at a time of profound change within the life of the churches and society?

First, there is a perennial tension often found within both congregations and the denominations. To be in engaged in community work or to be caught up with the wider neighbourhood entails working on or sometimes beyond the normal boundaries of church life. It can involve collaboration with statutory and voluntary bodies of many kinds, including people of other faiths. Those in such work can find themselves on the fringes of their own community of faith, having interests and concerns that may differ from those of their fellow disciples. This may lead to marginalization and isolation. The story in these pages provides something of a counter to any assumptions that what they are engaged with is either incidental or new to the tradition. It says to the practitioner that they are not odd but can claim to be in a strong succession. It provides the church related community worker with a pedigree and will help other people to understand where they are coming from. It will be easier to stake a claim to be part of the mainstream of Christian witness.[14]

Second, the rapid decline of the mainstream churches in recent decades has resulted, almost inevitably, in an anxious turning inwards. Tight budgets have produced a nervousness concerning any activity that seems to be draining the resources of the churches without any visible returns. There has, therefore, been a significant withdrawal from activities regarded as peripheral, including specialist ministries in community and economic life. It is good, therefore, to be reminded that to withdraw from these areas is to deny a strong element in the tradition that must not be lost.[15]

Third, however, the pattern of British church life has been widely transformed. The ecumenical imperative, sometimes stimulated by economic circumstances, has produced, not least in the inner city, a plethora of Local Ecumenical Projects (LEPs). These have brought together the older traditions to create new and often very innovative local patterns of church life. This hiatus has also been accentuated by the influx of new members from the Caribbean, Africa and Europe. To a large extent the old denominational boundaries have been blurred. Such enterprises have produced many community initiatives as the LEPs have sought to find their mission in their new configurations. There are two reasons, therefore, to welcome the witness set out in these pages. It can give credibility and depth to what some of the key partners can bring to such situations; and it may mitigate the loss of memory as the older traditions merge and evolve in radically new ways.[16]

Fourth, there has been an upsurge of evangelicalism, charismatic Pentecostalism and independency in recent times. This has both changed the ethos of the older denominations, sometimes radically, and produced many new ecclesiastical groupings, from mega-churches to small fellowships. In this can be included churches based on immigrant ethnic and cultural ties.[17] Incidentally a somewhat similar influx has affected Catholicism. This has brought with it a new, vigorous concern with social issues, superseding the personalistic quietism that has tended to dominate modern evangelicalism. Characteristically this new energy has been expressed both through locally based, often small responses, created by individuals who have perceived a need and national networks such as Street Pastors. The emphasis has tended to be on working with people in personal difficulty such as the mentally distressed, detached youth or the homeless. It has, however, increasingly been seen as integral to the 'mission mandate' that is incumbent on every congregation and is now widely described in terms of 'holistic mission' or 'community ministry'.[18] One of the effects of such a shift has been a renewed interest in the earlier tradition of social evangelicalism, embodied in such figures as William Wilberforce and Lord Shaftesbury, that came out of the Evangelical Revival of the eighteenth century.[19] This is a tradition that spans across denominations and has profoundly shaped the Free Churches. So their story can be seen as woven into that greater story.

VII. Faith-works in British Society

Alongside this, one of the unexpected social phenomena of our time has been the resurgence of religion onto the public arena. The widely presumed progressive secularization of modern society has at least been put on hold. Commentators, for instance, point to the rise of militant Islam, the rapid spread of Pentecostalism in Latin America, Africa and elsewhere and the renewal of Orthodoxy after the collapse of Leninist communism. From being the supposed norm ultra-secular Europe now appears to be the exception.[20] This has, too, affected the United Kingdom, but in its own way. There seem to be three strands that need to be noted here.

First, there is the rise of a more militant humanism. This is seen in the reinvigoration of the science versus religion debate.[21] Strident voices attack the plausibility of religion. This has spilled out into the political realm where much public debate starts from the premise that religion is irrelevant and socially divisive. Any public support for religion should be resisted. Thus the establishment, faith schools, chaplaincies and other perceived entrenchments of faith-based activity come under attack. This has been fuelled by the rise of fundamentalism, Christian as much as Islamic or Hindu, and other areas of religious conflict.

Second, however, and somewhat paradoxically, there has been a growing interest in spirituality. Its popularity is clearly shown in any bookshop. Spirituality is clearly separated from religion and has a larger and more prominent display. It is coupled with 'wellbeing' and books on counselling and psychotherapy. It is often associated with the interest in neo-paganism, such as Wicca and Druidism. It arises from a desire to counter the mechanization of our understanding of the human person and to allow the possibility of responding to the feeling of transcendence and the mysterious. It could be termed as a recovery of Romanticism. But it is also highly personal and individual as each seeks their own path to meaning and wholeness. Religion, by contrast, is seen as externally imposed and authoritative, even though some may (still) find religion useful. Spirituality is increasingly seen as a factor in a 'holistic' view of healthcare and counselling.[22]

Thirdly, British society has become religiously and culturally diverse in ways that have not been previously experienced in modern times. Post-war immigration, dramatically enhanced in recent decades, has seen the cityscape radically transformed. Physically it is seen in the appearance of mosques and temples and gurdwaras as well as new Christian churches. On the streets it is seen in the range of ethnic shops, in the festivals that break out throughout the year, in clothing, in schools and in other ways. This has brought new patterns of communal living, sometimes closed and fearful but elsewhere open and joyfully mixed. Politically there are the tensions of the street gangs and the hard right.

This clearly has implication for the churches' social mission. Most immediately is the imperative to explore the challenges of working in a multi-faith and multi-cultural situation. Especially is this so in the inner city where the churches are often at their weakest, though, at the same time it is here that some of the largest churches, usually based on immigrant groups, are to be found. The traditional churches, therefore, find themselves simultaneously located within the older established but increasingly fragile communities and yet, at the same time, seeking to build bridges across the sometimes fractious and even violent divides between different groups. This thrusts them into the socio-political arena as they try in different ways to respond to economic, cultural and social needs. This will entail a long process of discovering not only how to live creatively in this new context but what it means to witness to the Gospel alongside others with integrity. It will take a generation or more before this will begin to find a recognizable form both theoretically at the theological level and in terms of day-to-day living in the neighbourhood.[23]

The problems of migration and the inner city are a key factor in the search for greater social cohesion that has preoccupied recent governments.[24] Under Labour this was thought of in terms of 'social capital' while David Cameron uses the rhetoric of 'the big society'. At the heart of the initiatives undertaken under these programmes is the idea of a partnership between the public, the private and the voluntary sectors. Whatever this may mean in practice, especially in the context of a recession, it must imply that the churches and other Christian agencies are going to continue to be caught up in this process. They are, as has been strongly pointed out through various studies, already one of the major providers of voluntary service.[25] There is, however, something of a confusion at this point. The public sector wants to deal with 'faith communities', for which the model is the immigrant group that has its own fairly clear boundaries. The most obvious expressions of this are the Muslim communities based on a mosque. However the churches tend not to conform to this model, being much more diffusely dispersed through the society. They are also caught up in the other debates about the secular society noted above. It is, thus, not always easy for the churches. What does it mean to be a faith community in these circumstances? One response is to harden the boundaries, to become much more conscious of one's identity. But what if the immigrant communities move in the other direction and, as they become increasingly part of the host society, become more and more diffuse? Nevertheless the new situation can and has opened up fresh opportunities for the churches to exercise their social and community ministry.[26]

There is also, however, another challenge. The Church has, over the past century, been edged out of the central ground of ethical and cultural debate and practice. It has lost its monopoly as the religious ground of society. It is now but one of the competing voices in the market place of ideas. The Church, therefore, needs to learn how to speak relevantly and creatively out of the Gospel to the contemporary social and political debate. This is the impetus behind the new search for ways to do 'public theology'. There are not a few national 'think tanks', such as Theos, Ecclesia, the London Institute for Contemporary Christianity and the Centre for Theological and Public Issues, Edinburgh, as well as individual thinkers trying to analyse the 'signs of the time' in the light of Christian understanding, to speak to both Church and nation.[27] This is, however, also the task of the activist practitioner and the local congregation. It is necessary, first of all, to embed Christian practice in an adequate and realistic theological bedrock, whether this faith is to be expressed in word or in deed, in faithful action or silent witness. But the local is also theologically important in its own right. It is in and through that local exploration, service, collaboration and receiving that the Gospel is appropriated and expressed relevantly. This suggests there is also an imperative for the local experience to be fed into the wider, collective understanding of the faith. Ways should be found to share our stories with others. We are, after all, all on a journey, moving into a new phase of British communal life. This is a pilgrimage, a road of discovery, taking us more fully into that reality which is the Kingdom of God, to which Christ has called us.

These are exciting and possibly creative days for the Christian community. The danger is that the extent and rapidity of the changes in our society, and indeed throughout the world will overwhelm and snap the chain of memory that links us to the experience and wisdom of the past where others have, in their turn, struggled with radical cultural, social and economic sea-changes. To lose that memory would be greatly to impoverish our resources when facing our own crisis. It is important, therefore, that we recall the way Christians, not least among the Free Churches, strove to be faithful to the Gospel in face of the intellectual, industrial, political and social revolutions that produced the modern world.

VIII. Reading History Faithfully – a Theological Coda

This chapter has, so far, been concerned with three facets of the part played by the historical dimension in the reflective processes employed by those engaged in church related community work. The first was some of the issues around the interdisciplinary nature of practical theology. The second was how such resources might be deployed. The third suggested the relevance for today's Church in mission. There is, however, another facet undergirding these. At the outset it was pointed out that the primary task of the practical theologian was to ask the question about, to use a common formulation, 'Where is God in this situation?' and 'What is God asking us to do?' This implies that, in some sense, it is possible to discover God's leading and to be faithful to it in and through the historical reality within which we find ourselves. So the further question arises as to how to exercise this discernment. It is to some limited aspects of this in relation to the theological importance of history that we now, briefly, turn.

Christianity is, in a profoundly and unique way, an historical faith. Not only does it, like other major religious traditions, look to certain foundational figures and events but it also claims that God has been and, in a direct way, still is involved in and known through events in history. Supremely this has happened in and through the life, death and resurrection of Jesus Christ. This special revelation is embedded in and claimed to be the culmination of the Hebraic tradition traced from Abraham through Moses and the prophets. This covenant tradition is complemented by and informs the general revelation of God through nature and in history. That is the ordinary history of the world is the arena in which the God of Abraham, Isaac and Jacob, the God and Father of our Lord Jesus Christ, is present and active. This is the reality that lies behind the practical theological question of how the events of human history, critically investigated by historical and other disciplines, can carry theological meaning.[28] From a theological point of view it can only be approached through the mystery of Christ and that is best done through the Bible which is the primary witness to God's action in Christ.

First, it is necessary to recall that the story of Jesus, as presented in the Gospels, is, inevitably, written from faith to faith. This is explicitly stated at the end of the Fourth Gospel:

> ... these [things] are written so that you [the reader] may come to believe that Jesus is the Messiah, the Son of God, and that through believing may have life in his name. (John 20:31 NRSV)

The story is so shaped therefore, especially in relation to the miracles, to underline the Christological beliefs of the Church. But there is also another and equally important strand of historical realism. The story, firmly set in his time, is also one of scepticism, puzzlement and rejection. Jesus is an ambiguous character. His preaching was of the challenge of the Kingdom of God. Yet when John the Baptist sent his disciples to ask: 'Are you the one who is to come or are we to await another?' (Luke 7:19 NRSV) the answer was in effect, 'you decide'. Jesus is often shown refusing to prove himself (cf. Matt. 16:1–4; Mark 8:11–13). This is at the heart of the cross. Luke underlines in that event what has happened at many points during Jesus' life, the mockery of the people, the soldiers and the impenitent thief (23:32–43). There was always a wide range of responses to Jesus public ministry and who the people crowding round Jesus said that he was. When the disciples replied to Jesus' question: 'But who do you think I am?' by calling him the Christ, not only were they caught floundering as to what that meant but Jesus attributed even their stumbling faith to the Holy Spirit. The theological reality that lies within and gives meaning to the event of the Messiah is only grasped through the creativity and sensitivity that perceives the hidden meaning and opens up the possibility of faith (Mark 8:27–9:1).

The turning point of the New Testament is the resurrection. It was this experience that transformed and filled with meaning the life, teaching and death of Jesus.

> The gospel concerning his Son, who was descended from David according to the flesh and was declared to be the Son of God with power according to the Spirit of holiness by the resurrection from the dead. (Rom. 1:3–4 NRSV)

The resurrection, however, was actually a quiet and private affair, restricted to those who already, in some sense, had committed themselves. The demonstration of God's power was hidden and restrained, only discernible by faith (Luke 24:13–35; John 20:11–18). So also was it in the mission of the Church. The resurrection faith is passed on by word of mouth, in the fellowship of believers, through the deeds of care and compassion. The discernment of God's love is always to see the beckoning presence behind the stark reality of the world. Historical events do not unambiguously declare God's presence or will. We, too, like Christ himself, can only point to the Kingdom in word and deed and offer the gift.

At the heart of the Gospel story we see that Jesus proclaimed the Kingdom of God. This was the heart of his message: that, with him, this Kingdom had broken in afresh. This is the framework within which we can understand how to live by faith in our place in the stream of history.

First, God is king. The creator has not left the creation to be alone but holds it within a providential will. Behind the vicissitudes of historical existence, hidden and mysterious, yet hinted at, lies God's good purpose (Psalm 47; Isaiah 40:12–31).

Second, Jesus brings the Kingdom (Mark 1:14–15). Round him cluster the signs of this Kingdom in the gathering of the New Israel, in the welcoming of the poor and outcast, in the healing of the diseased and broken of spirit. The power of the Kingdom, its resistance to the wiles of the Devil and evil powers, is seen in love and compassion, in service and humility, in companionship and inclusiveness. All this is rooted in Jesus' dependence on and obedience to the Father. It comes to its climax and triumph in the cross and resurrection.

Thirdly the Kingdom is to come. It is for this that the disciples are told to pray and for which they require the pilgrim's rations of daily bread (Matt. 6:10–11). Christianity is an eschatological faith in that it looks to the future consummation. It is, therefore, a faith that lives in hope and trust, that there is more to come, things that we have not yet seen nor even imagined (1 Cor. 2:9). Change is, therefore, possible. What has been hitherto is not the last word. We are not stuck in the round of endeavour and futility but can struggle and suffer, rejoice and create in hope (Rom. 5:2–5; Heb. 6:18).

So, fourthly, what of the present? The Kingdom is still hidden but its shape has been disclosed and inaugurated in Christ. Thus it is possible to live in and for the Kingdom, albeit in a fragmented way, often seemingly in frustration, yet with joy and success. The enemy is still strong but the gates of hell can be broken down (Matt. 16:18). Thus, in word and action, signs can be erected. This is done in the worship and loving bonds of the Church. It is also found in and through that proclamation and those deeds that draw from faith to point to faith. But this is done in the ambiguities of our social, economic, personal and historical existence, in the midst of birth and death, of flourishing and destruction, of all that makes for the greatness and misery of being human. Signs point to a deeper reality which they also begin to create but they have to be recognized and accepted and participated in.

Christian faith affirms the resurrection. In the first instance that is the resurrection of Jesus Christ but it is also of the whole creation (1 Cor. 15:20–28). This means that Jesus died. There was indeed a separation from God. But there was a new creation, a coming into existence again. It was 'this Jesus whom you crucified' (Acts 2:22) whom God brought back. He was recognized by the disciples in the breaking of bread (Luke 24:35). There was a continuity. The resurrection affirmed and began to make sense of all that he 'began to say and do' (Acts 1:1) as it was seen in the new light. At the same time there was something radically new. Jesus had entered into his Kingdom and is Lord and Christ. He is in a new relationship, through the Holy Spirit, with his people (Rom. 8:4). The past, the life and the death, have all been caught up into a new dimension. The miscarriage of justice, cruel torture, rejection and mockery and fear and weeping have become the work of the Kingdom. So it is with our living of the Kingdom. We can work in faith and hope because what is of the Kingdom is not lost, even if it seems transitory, because resurrection means the bringing together by God's power and in God's perfection all that makes for beauty, truth and goodness. Nothing that is worthwhile, that is of the Kingdom's values, will be lost in God (Phil. 4:8–9).

It is against this background, therefore, that it is possible to begin to suggest what it means to ask the theological practical question as to what God is doing and how we ought to respond in faith. When John the Baptist's disciples posed their question Jesus upbraided them and their generation with a challenge to 'discern the signs of the times' (Matt. 16:3). In doing this Jesus was following the tradition of the great prophets of Israel. Their ministries, too, were conducted in the midst of the political, social and economic realities of their day, often in the turmoil of the great dramas of their times, such as the march of imperial armies. The fate of their own people leading to the destruction of Jerusalem, exile and return which so concerned them would have been trivial in the councils of the great empires of the day. So our local issues of today may seem comparatively trivial but we too are caught up in wider movements across the world. This broad perspective should not be lost as we busy ourselves in our immediate concerns. Nor should we 'despise the day of small things' (Zech. 4:10).

The first point to be made is that the prophets, too, were rejected and ridiculed and even persecuted. Nor was theirs the only voice of the time. There were other prophets as well as the great and the good thronging the court trying to influence policy and get a cut of the action. In terms of their aims many of the prophets were failures. The various power games were played out without them. Only in retrospect were their insights valued and their words incorporated into the Scriptures. They were marginal, only a few listened, though they had the 'words of life' (John 6:67). They were willing to 'cast their bread upon the waters' (Eccles. 11:1).

This, however, leads to the second point. In the Hebrew Scriptures the second section, the prophets, can be seen as the story of how the people worked out, mostly through failure, their covenant obligations and as a commentary, a midrash, on the Torah, interpreting the demands of the Law for a new situation. There is a hermeneutic, a dialogue, between the normative foundation event and what was happening in their own society. The shape of the covenant was clear: Israel, rescued from slavery, had been given its existence by God, therefore the life of the nation should be one of justice, peace and respect, especially for the poor, widow, stranger and even enemy, and power, wealth and talent should be exercised for the common good. By reflecting on this the prophets would discern afresh in and for their own time what it meant to live out the covenant. This is the continuing pattern of working. The Bible does not primarily lay down definitive rules and regulations. Rather it draws us into the history of a particular human tradition, which it asks to be taken with utmost seriousness through a continuous process of creative imagination. Then it is possible to ask, if that is how they in their time saw things, how are we to act in our own time in the service of the God of Abraham, Isaac and Jacob, of Moses or Amos or Jeremiah, the God and Father of our Lord Jesus Christ.[29]

Thirdly the prophet suffers in and for the people. This is the attraction of Jeremiah (8:18–9:1) and the Servant of Second Isaiah (49:1–7; 53). Judgement and calamity are not wished upon the nation. God's will is for the people's good. God is seen as longing over Israel (Hosea 11:1–2). So for the modern practitioner, community development arises from the concrete suffering of real people. The practitioner will, therefore, be closely identified with and involved in their experience. But this is more than empathy. It includes knowing about and understanding the pressures and opportunities in this or that situation and how it meshes in with the wider social context.

Fourthly, the prophets were always operating in a politico-social setting – the Philistine invasion, imperial threats and the affairs of the nation. God was always understood as being involved in these historical events (e.g. Isaiah 43). What comes across consistently is a profound sense of crisis which, in biblical terms, is both challenge, a critical situation, and opportunity, a place of choice that opens up the possibility of a new start. This is the key to 'reading the signs of the times' (Matt. 16:3): to have a profound and thankful sense of the gift of this time and this place. To remain embattled is to invite destruction but to accept release allows for fresh beginnings. So it should be when entering into a new project or closing an old one. This is a time of thanksgiving, of renewed energy or even of solemn relief. There is a sense that it feels right and that it is possible to face God in comfort. But time will not stand still. There will be other challenges occasioned by external and internal changes as the People of God continue on their pilgrimage.

Fifthly, a significant prophetic theme is that of the faithful remnant (e.g. Isaiah 6–7). After the winds of change that might have been like a tornado, there is left a small residue. The point of the remnant is that it is a sign of hope. The story has not stopped but will continue, albeit that the link has almost snapped. God has not left himself without witness. The small, tentative expressions of faith in action can have immense value. The churches may be comparatively weak but they remain as pointers to an alternative set of values. They can lend support to others who find themselves asking the awkward question or living on in the wilderness in straitened circumstances. The Christian presence in society may be marginal, though there are signs that its voice is being heard again in the public arena, but it persists through prayer and faithful action. There is a dawn breaking on the horizon.

So the hermeneutic process goes on. Jesus himself was engaged in it as he read the Law in the light of his situation. The Law stands and yet it is radically recast (Matt. 6). The New Testament can be seen as a Midrash on the Old, taken by Christians as the definitive witness to the coming of the promised Kingdom as found in Christ. This flows down the years as each generation both receives it and passes it on coloured by the light of their new situation. It is in this multi-layered conversation, enriched by 'the great cloud of witnesses', that we are called to be citizens of the City of God on pilgrimage, seeking and yet living under the shelter of the city to which the nations will bring their riches (Heb. 11:8–12; 12:1; Rev. 21:24).

NOTES

Notes to Chapter 1

1   R. Mudie-Smith ed., *The Religious Life of London* (London: Hodder and Stoughton, 1904).

2   Christopher Driver, *A Future for the Free Churches?* (London: Living Church Books, 1962).

3   George Eliot, *Middlemarch* (Harmondsworth: Penguin Classics, 2003 [1871–72]).

4   John Taylor and Clyde Binfield (eds), *Who They Were in the Reformed Churches of England and Wales 1901–2000* (London: United Reformed Church, 2007).

5   Charles Kingsley in *Congregational Praise* No 671 (London: Independent Press, 1980).

6   Tim Rice and Andrew Lloyd Webber, *Joseph and the Amazing Technicolour Dreamcoat*, first performed at Colet Court, 1968.

7   John Gray, *Dictionary of Methodism and Pastoral Care* (Highgate: Westminster Pastoral Foundation).

Notes to Chapter 2

1   Milton Congregational Church, *Year Book* (1881), p. 10, quoted in Clyde Binfield, *So Down to Prayers: Studies in English Nonconformity 1780–1920* (London: J. M. Dent, 1977), p. 159.

2   Milton Congregational Church, *Year Book* (1883–84), pp. 12–13. Quoted in Binfield, *So Down to Prayers*, p. 159.

3   Binfield, *So Down to Prayers*, p. 159, records that the new church 'bore all the signs of success – a readymade Sunday School of 520, most of whom had followed their teachers from Ramsden Street, and a church membership which had reached 253 by May 1882 and included most of the families who had made Ramsden Street notable'.

4   'E. W.', 'Yr Eglwys a'r Byd', *Y Drysorfa* (1862), p. 406.

5   See E. G. Rupp and R. G. Davies, *A History of Methodism in Great Britain* (London: Epworth, 1965), I, p. xxxvi.

6   'The Examination of Certain Londonders before the Ecclesiastical Commission, June 20, 1567', in William Nicholson, *The Remains of Edmund Grindal DD* (Cambridge: Parker Society, 1843), quoted in R. Tudur Jones, *Congregationalism in England* (London: Independent Press, 1962), p. 14.

7   Champlin Burrage, *Early English Dissenters in the Light of Recent Research: 1550–1641* (Cambridge: Cambridge University Press, 1912), II, pp. 9–11; see Tudur Jones, *Congregationalism in England*, p. 14.

8   Burton (1641) (d. 1648) declared: 'Surely Gods people must be separatists from the world and from false churches, to become a pure and holy people unto the Lord.' *The Protestation Protested*, quoted in Geoffrey, F. Nuttall, *Visible Saints: The Congregational Way, 1640–1660*, 2nd edn (Weston Rhyn: Quinta Press, 2001), pp. 52–53.

9   Bartlet claimed that the church was 'A visible segregation from the world, and a visible aggregation to Christ, is necessary to Church union and communion'. Quoted in Nuttall, *Visible Saints*, p. 53.

10   '[T]he true Church of Christ,' claimed Rogers, is '1. A society of Believers sanctified in Christ Jesus; 2. Separate from the world, false-ways, and worships ...' Quoted in Nuttall, *Visible Saints*, p. 73.

11   After 14 August 1662, around two thousand of them were ejected from their livings because they held such views.

12   See the entry for 'community' in *The Oxford English Dictionary*.

13   Jacob (*c.*1563–1624) had been in exile in Holland where he had come under the influence of John Robinson. Neither man advocated total separation and Robinson wrote in justification of continued communion with the established church where it enjoyed 'godly ministers as could expound the faith and doctrines of Christianity in an edifying manner'. Nevertheless, they continued to oppose 'the formal church order of the Established Church'. See Tudur Jones, *Congregationalism in England*, p. 22.

14   Daniel Neal, *A History of the Puritans*, abridged in two volumes by Edward Parsons (London, 1811), I, p. 371, quoted in Alan P. F. Sell, *Saints: Visible, Orderly and Catholic: The Congregational Idea of the Church* (Geneva: World Alliance of Reformed Churches, 1986), pp. 23–24.

15   He described the testing of the faith and character of those gathered, the seeking of approval from neighbouring churches and local ministers, the appointment of a 'day of submission' where the members gave testimony to their spiritual experiences and then bound themselves together in covenant. See Vavasor Powell, *Spirituall Experiences of Sundry Beleevers*, 2nd edn (London, 1653); see also R. Tudur Jones, *Congregationalism in Wales*, ed. Robert Pope (Cardiff: University of Wales Press, 2004), pp. 37–38.

16   R. Tudur Jones, Arthur Long and Rosemary Moore (eds), *Protestant Nonconformist Texts*, vol. 1 (Aldershot: Ashgate, 2007), pp. 130–31.

17   Alan P. F. Sell, David J. Hall and Ian Sellers (eds), *Protestant Nonconformist Texts*, vol. 2 (Aldershot: Ashgate, 2006), pp. 384–85.

18   Isaac Chauncey (1697), who later became a tutor at the Hoxton Academy,

expanded briefly on the responsibilities of believers one to another: 'A Visible Church is a particular Assembly of Professing Believers, visibly embodied in Christ, for a stated and holy Communion in one place, with God and one another, in all instituted Ordinances, appertaining to themselves and their immediate need, for God's glory in Christ, and their mutual Edification ...'. *The Divine Institution of Congregational Churches, Ministry and Ordinances etc.* (London: Nathaniel Hiller, 1697), pp. 38–39.

19   See the Covenant signed by the Baptists of Oakenshaw in Lancashire in Sell et al., *Protestant Nonconformist Texts*, vol. 2, p. 386, and the covenant made at Bluntisham, Huntingdonshire, on 28 December 1786 in Sell, *Saints: Visible, Orderly and Catholic*, p. 13.

20   Puritan and Congregational theologian John Owen noted that church members were to show 'affectionate sincere love' and 'vigilant watchfulness over each others conversation', 'mutual to bear with each others infirmities' and 'bearing each others Burthens', with 'frequent spiritual Communication for Edification' and 'free Contribution, and communication of temporal things'. John Owen, *Eschol ... Or, Rules of Direction, for the Walking of the Saints in Fellowship*, quoted in Nuttall, *Visible Saints*, p. 74.

21   See E. D. Bebb, *Nonconformity and Social and Economic Life, 1660–1800: Some Problems of the Present as they Appeared in the Past* (London: Epworth, 1935), p. 130.

22   See Bebb, *Nonconformity and Social and Economic Life*, pp. 130–32. Firmin consistently recorded financial losses: £214 in 1682; £400 in 1683; £763 in 1684 and £900 in 1685.

23   See Henry D. Rack, 'Societies and the Origins of Methodism', *Journal of Ecclesiastical History* 38 (1987), pp. 582–95; also L. Tyerman, *The Life of the Rev. George Whitefield* (London: Hodder and Stoughton, 1876), I, pp. 317–19.

24   Quoted in Bebb, *Nonconformity and Social and Economic Life*, p. 11.

25   Ibid., p. 170.

26   Kenneth Young, *Chapel: The Joyous Days and Prayerful Nights of the Nonconformists in their Heyday, c.1850–1950* (London: Eyre Methuen, 1972), p. 115.

27   Ibid., p. 117.

28   Bebb, *Nonconformity and Social and Economic Life*, p. 68.

29   Of the disciplinary measures exercised by Coventry Baptists in the nineteenth century, 'What is remarkable about these cases is not their frequency, it is not even the evidence which they provide of an habitual intervention in private life and conduct which not one of these stiffnecked individualists would have tolerated for a moment on the part of government; it is that the church was steadied by them. Its members did not vote with their feet. The church's high standards of right living were accepted, and the church's continued oversight was taken as a matter of course'. Clyde Binfield, *Pastors and People: The Biography of a Baptist Church: Queen's Road Coventry* (Coventry: Queen's Road Baptist Church, 1984), p. 34. The same can be

said *mutatis mutandis* of other dissenting churches as they strove to establish their alternative societies.

30   James Munson, *The Nonconformists: In Search of a Lost Culture* (London: SPCK, 1991), p. 38.

31   Munson, *The Nonconformists*, p. 39.

32   K. S. Inglis, *Churches and the Working Classes in Victorian England* (London: Routledge and Kegan Paul, 1963), p. 3.

33   Munson, *The Nonconformists*, p. 39.

34   Binfield, *So Down to Prayers*, p. 9. Binfield bases his conclusion on an assessment of A. D. Gilbert, 'The Growth and Decline of Nonconformity in England and Wales with Special Reference to the Period Before 1850: An Historical Interpretation of Statistics of Religious Practice', unpublished DPhil Thesis, University of Oxford, 1973. Cf. A. D. Gilbert, *Religion and Society in Industrial England 1740–1914: Church, Chapel and Social Change* (London: Longman, 1976) .

35   See Philip Jenkins, *A History of Modern Wales, 1536–1990* (Harlow: Longmans, 1992), pp. 236ff.

36   See Ieuan Gwynedd Jones and David Williams (eds), *The Religious Census of 1851: A Calendar of the Returns Relating to Wales*, vol. 1 (South Wales, Cardiff: University of Wales Press, 1976); also Ieuan Gwynedd Jones ed., *The Religious Census of 1851: A Calendar of the Returns Relating to Wales*, vol. 1, North Wales. (Cardiff: University of Wales Press, 1981).

37   See K. S. Inglis, 'Patterns of Religious Worship in 1851', *Journal of Ecclesiastical History XI* (1960), pp. 74–86.

38   See John Davies, *Hanes Cymru* (Harmondsworth: Penguin, 1992), p. 377.

39   Young, *Chapel*, p. 132.

40   Ibid., p. 133.

41   Tudur Jones, *Congregationalism in England*, p. 316.

42   R. Tudur Jones, *Faith and the Crisis of a Nation: Wales, 1890–1914*, ed. Robert Pope (Cardiff: University of Wales Press, 2004), p. 90.

43   Tudur Jones, *Faith and the Crisis of a Nation*, p. 89.

44   Ibid., p. 88.

45   Ibid., p. 114.

46   Young, *Chapel*, p. 16.

47   Binfield, *So Down to Prayers*, p. 19; E. Luscombe Hull, *Sermons Preached at Union Chapel, Kings Lynn* (1869), 2nd series, p. 193.

48   *Religious Worship in England and Wales* (1854), p. 93; Inglis, *Churches and the Working Classes*, p. 1.

49   George Sails, *At the Centre: The Story of Methodism's Central Missions* (London: The Methodist Church, 1970), p. 8.

50   Ibid., p. 4.

51   Ibid., p. 7.

52 Ibid., p. 7.

53 Christopher Oldstone-Moore, *Hugh Price Hughes: Founder of a New Methodism, Conscience of a New Nonconformity* (Cardiff: University of Wales Press, 1999). Also, John Kent, 'Hugh Price Hughes and the Nonconformist Conscience', in G. V. Bennett and J. D. Walsh (eds), *Essays in Modern English Church History* (New York: Oxford University Press, 1966), pp. 181–205; D. W. Bebbington, *The Nonconformist Conscience: Chapel and Politics, 1870–1914* (London: Allen and Unwin, 1982).

54 Robert Moore, *Pit-men, Preachers and Politics: The Effects of Methodism in a Durham Mining Community* (Cambridge: Cambridge University Press, 1974), p. 9.

55 D. Miall Edwards, 'Neges Gymdeithasol yr Efengyl', in D. Miall Edwards ed., *Efengyl y Deyrnas* (Bala: Evans and Son, 1927), p. 23.

56 *Wesleyan Conference Minutes* (1884), p. 282; Inglis, *Churches and the Working Classes*, p. 83.

57 Sails, *At the Centre*, pp. 12–13.

58 Ibid., p. 26.

59 Ibid., pp. 27, 29.

60 Ibid., p. 30.

61 David M. Thompson, J. H. Y. Briggs and John Munsey Turner (eds), *Protestant Nonconformist Texts. IV: The Twentieth Century* (Aldershot: Ashgate, 2007), p. 21.

62 The Pleasant Sunday Afternoon was first established by John Blackham, a deacon at Ebenezer Congregational Church, West Bromwich. His aim was that they be 'brief, bright and brotherly'. Tudur Jones noted that the men who attended would 'enjoy the mixture of orchestral music, community hymn-singing and man-to-man talking'. Tudur Jones, *Congregationalism in England*, p. 317; Inglis, *Churches and the Working Classes*, pp. 79–82.

63 Hence the oft-quoted remarks of Thomas Binney from the chair of the Congregational Union that 'the special mission is neither to the very rich nor to the very poor. We have a work to do upon the thinking, active, influential classes ... which ... gathered into cities ... are the modern movers and makers of the world.'

64 See Munson, *The Nonconformists*, p. 108. Also, J. W. Dixon, *Pledged to the People: A Sketch of the Rev. Richard Westrope* (London: H. R. Allensen, 1891).

65 *Westminster Record* (1905), vol. 1, no. 6, p. 141, quoted in John Brencher, *Martyn Lloyd-Jones (1899–1981) and Twentieth-Century Evangelicalism* (Milton Keynes: Paternoster, 2002), p. 59.

66 Brencher, *Martyn Lloyd-Jones*, p. 60.

67 Ibid., p. 62.

68 Young, *Chapel*, p. 136.

69 Ibid., pp. 134–35.

70 From the *ODNB*, article on Charles Silvester Horne.

71 Munson, *The Nonconformists*, p. 57.

72 *ODNB*.

73 Tudur Jones, *Congregationalism in England*, p. 318.

74 H. J. S. Guntrip, *Smith and Wrigley of Leeds* (London: Independent Press, 1944), pp. 96–97, quoted in Binfield, *So Down to Prayers*, p. 212.

75 *Y Tyst* (11 March 1926), p. 9; Tudur Jones, *Faith and the Crisis of a Nation*, p. 247.

76 The information on the Revd Leon Atkin comes from a collection of newspaper cuttings loaned by his family. None are dated.

77 W. Cathcart, *Baptist Encyclopaedia* (1881), quoted in Faith Bowers, *A Bold Experiment: The Story of Bloomsbury Chapel and Bloomsbury Central Baptist Church, 1848–1999* (London: Bloomsbury Central Baptist Church, 1999), p. 46.

78 Bowers, *A Bold Experiment*, pp. 138–39.

79 Bloomsbury Chapel, *Year Book* (1854), in Bowers, *A Bold Experiment*, p. 139.

80 Ibid., p. 459.

81 Ibid., p. 145.

82 Faith Bowers, 'For God and the People: Baptist Deaconesses, 1901–1905', *Baptist Quarterly* 43 (October 2010), p. 475.

83 Quoted in Mark Hopkins, *Nonconformity's Romantic Generation: Evangelical and Liberal Theologies in Victorian England* (Milton Keynes: Paternoster, 2004), p. 174.

84 Munson, *The Nonconformists*, p. 56. See also 'A Travelling Correspondent', in *The Rev. William Cuff in Shoreditch* … (London: James Clarke and Co., 1878); Henry J. Cowell, *These Forty Years, 1900–1940* (London: Baptist Union, 1940), p. 4.

85 Munson, *The Nonconformists*, p. 56.

86 Asa Briggs, *Victorian Cities* (London: Odhams, 1963), pp. 157–58; Young, *Chapel*, p. 136.

87 Young, *Chapel*, p. 137; See Binfield, *Pastors and People*.

88 Young, *Chapel*, p. 136.

89 Adolf Harnack, *What is Christianity?* (London: Williams and Norgate, 1901).

90 See Elaine Kaye, *Mansfield College Oxford: Its Origin, History and Significance* (Oxford: Oxford University Press, 1996), pp. 134–48.

91 See Will Reason, *The Issues of Personal Faith in Social Service* (London: Congregational Union, 1916), p. 7.

92 T. Rhondda Williams, *The Church and the Labour Cause* (London, 1911), p. 1; A. E. Garvie, *Can Christ Save Society?* (London: Hodder and Stoughton, 1935), p. 197; A. E. Garvie, *The Fatherly Rule of God: A Study of Society, State and Church* (London: Hodder and Stoughton, 1935), p. 215; S. E. Keeble, *Towards the New Era: A Draft Scheme of Industrial Reconstruction* (London, 1917), p. 7.

93 T. Rhondda Williams, *Faith Without Fear* (London: Hodder and Stoughton, 1933), p. 33; Garvie, *Can Christ Save Society?*, p. 104; Garvie, *The Fatherly Rule of God*, p. 215; S. E. Keeble ed., *The Social Teaching of the Bible* (London: Charles H. Kelly, 1909), p. 15; Keeble, *Towards the New Era*, p. 4; S. E. Keeble, *Christian Responsibility for the Social Order* (London: The Fernley Lecture Trust, 1922), p. 239.

94 T. Rhondda Williams, *The Working Faith of a Liberal Theologian* (London: Williams and Norgate, 1914), p. 236.

95 T. Rhondda Williams, *Making the Better World* (London: The Congregational Union of England and Wales, 1929), p. 3; Reason, *Issues of Personal Faith*, p. 3.

96 A. E. Garvie, *The Christian Ideal for Human Society* (London: Hodder and Stoughton, 1930), p. 348; Garvie, *Can Christ Save Society?*, p. 222; Keeble, *Towards the New Era*, p. 4.

97 The 'Social Gospel' is often seen as an import from the United States, and there were prominent American ministers at the forefront of the movement such as Washington Gladden, Robert T. Ely and, most importantly, Walter Rauschenbusch. In fact the Free Church theologians advocated social work as a result of insights of European thought. For the Social Gospel in America, see Robert Handy ed., *The Social Gospel in America, 1870–1920* (New York: Oxford University Press, 1966).

98 See Robert Pope, *Building Jerusalem: Nonconformity, Labour and the Social Question in Wales, 1906–1939* (Cardiff: University of Wales Press, 1998), pp. 198–99; also Robert Pope, *Codi Muriau Dinas Duw: Anghydffurfiaeth ac Anghydffurfwyr Cymru'r Ugeinfed Ganrif* (Bangor: Centre for the Advanced Study of Religion in Wales, 2005), pp. 165–81; G. A. Edwards, 'A North Wales Housing Experiment', *The Welsh Outlook* 15.2 (February 1928), pp. 37–38.

99 Tudur Jones, *Congregationalism in England*, p. 315.

100 For example, Charles Garrett, minister at the Liverpool Mission, was quoted as saying 'of course we have helped thousands of people who have been in distress but never until we have assured ourselves that their religious professions or intentions were sincere'. *Methodist Times* (28 April 1886), p. 278. See also Inglis, *Churches and the Working Classes*, p. 293.

101 Moore, *Pit-men, Preachers and Politics*, p. 113.

Notes to Chapter 3

1 D. W. Bebbington, *Congregational Members of Parliament in the Nineteenth Century* (Cambridge: United Reformed Church History Society, 2007).

2 See Chapters 3 and 6 of this book.

3 H. P. Hughes, *Ethical Christianity* (London: Sampson Low, Marston & Co, 1892). *The Sword and the Trowel* (April 1880), p. 191.

4 See Chapter 5 of this book.

5 Hughes, *Ethical Christianity*, pp. 76, 169.

Notes to Chapter 4

1   Adam Smith, *Wealth of Nations* (London, 1776), volume II, Book V, part III, article III, 'Of the Expence of the Institutions for the Instruction of People of all Ages'.

2   *Evangelical Magazine* 6 (1798), pp. 15–18, 52–59. Other similar accounts of early Sunday Schools are to be found in Philip B. Cliff, *The Rise and Development of the Sunday School Movement* (Redhill: National Christian Education Council, 1986).

3   *Evangelical Magazine* 13 (1805), p. 57.

4   Ibid., p. 59.

5   Further information in *ODNB*. Fox had worked with Jenner on inoculation. When Fox died Brougham told the House of Commons that he had been the saviour of the Lancastrian system.

6   *BFSS Annual Report 1815*, p. 58.

7   James Tennant: Further information in ODNB.

8   *ODNB*.

9   *ODNB*.

10 *Derby Mercury*, 3 May 1843.

11 The proceedings of the Committee are recorded in *The Congregational Year Book* for 1844.

12 John Campbell, *David Nasmith, His Labours and Travels* (London: John Snow, 1844), p. 96.

13 T. Lewis, *The Christian Triumphant in Death: a sermon occasioned by the decease of David Nasmith, founder of City Missions, and Honorary Secretary of the 'British and Foreign Mission' delivered in Union Chapel, Islington, on Lords) Day Dec. 1 1839* (London: Houlston and Stoneman, 1840), p. 29.

14 John William Adamson, *English Education, 1789–1902* (Cambridge: Cambridge University Press, 1930), p. 349.

15 *Derby Mercury*, January 1871.

16 Ibid.

17 Stephen Orchard and John H. Y. Briggs (eds), *The Sunday School Movement* (Milton Keynes: Paternoster, 2007), pp. 109–123.

18 More information in John Taylor and Clyde Binfield (eds), *Who they Were: In the Reformed Churches of England and Wales 1901–2000* (United Reformed Church, Church History Society, Donnington, Dyas, 2007).

19 D. W. Bebbington, *The Nonconformist Conscience* (London: George, Allen & Unwin, 1982), p. 147, drawing on contemporary reports in *The Christian World*.

20 Henry Bryan Binns, *Century of Education; Being the Centenary History of the British and Foreign School Society, 1801–1908* (London: J. M. Dent, 1908), p. 235.

Notes to Chapter 5

1   H. Mann, *Census of Great Britain 1851: Religious Worship in England and Wales*, revised edn (London: George Routledge and Co, 1854). The attention of historians was alerted by K. S. Inglis, *Churches and the Working Classes in Victorian England* (London: Routledge and Kegan Paul, 1963). It was pursued by D. M. Thompson, 'The 1851 Religious Census: Problems and Possibilities', *Victorian Studies*, XI,1 (1967), 87–97; W. S. F. Pickering, 'The 1851 Religious Census – a Useless Experiment?' *British Journal of Sociology*, II (1967–68), 383–407; and has informed continuing debate, e.g. R. Gill, *The Myth of the Empty Church* (London: SPCK, 1993).

2   C. Mullin, *Decline and Fall: Diaries 2005–2010* (London: Profile Books, 2010), p. 12.

3   N. Jackson, J. Lintonbon and B. Staples, *Saltaire: The Making of a Model Town* (Reading: Spire Books, 2010), p. 29.

4   H. Escott, *A History of Scottish Congregationalism* (Glasgow: The Congregational Union of Scotland, 1960), pp. 26–30.

5   *Who Was Who 1897–1916* (London: A & C Black, 1920), p. 485; B. Meakin, *Model Factories and Villages: Ideal Conditions of Labour and Housing* (London: T. Fisher Unwin, 1905).

6   Meakin, *Model Factories and Villages*, p. 7.

7   Ibid., esp. pp. 475–80.

8   P. Unwin, *The Publishing Unwins* (London: Heinemann, 1972); S. Unwin, *The Truth About a Publisher* (London: George Allen & Unwin, 1960).

9   Meakin, *Model Factories and Villages*, p. 479; P. Unwin, *The Printing Unwins* (London: Heinemann, 1976).

10 Meakin, *Model Factories and Villages*, p. 17. For Robert Forman Horton, see C. Binfield and J. Taylor (eds), *Who They Were in the Reformed Churches of England and Wales 1901–2000* (Donington: Shaun Tyas, 2007), pp. 107–109.

11 Meakin, *Model Factories and Villages*, p. 9.

12 Binfield and Taylor, *Who They Were*, pp. 3–5.

13 Meakin, *Model Factories and Villages*, pp. 296–97, 318; W. Arthur, *The Successful Merchant: Sketches of the Life of Mr. Samuel Budgett, Late of Kingswood Hill*, 43rd edn (London: William Mullan and Son, 1878); John A. Vickers ed., *A Dictionary of Methodism in Britain and Ireland* (Peterborough: Epworth Press, 2000), p. 47.

14 J. Reynolds, *The Great Paternalist: Titus Salt and the Growth of Nineteenth-Century Bradford* (London: Maurice Temple Smith, 1983).

15 [Rehoboth Chapel] Book 57. Baptismal Register: New Independent Chapel, Morley 1765–1967. In care of St. Mary's United Reformed Church, Morley, when consulted. See also: J. G. Miall, *Congregationalism in Yorkshire: A Chapter of Modern Church History* (London: John Snow and Co., 1868), pp. 320–24.

16   Miall, *Congregationalism in Yorkshire*, pp. 236–37.

17   Conveyance and Declaration of Trust of Salem Chapel, Bradford, 2 January 1836. Bradford City Archives 53080/1/2.

18   N. Chapman, 'Saltaire United Reformed Church. Historical Notes. Titus Salt Centenary Year 1876–1976', typescript, 1976.

19   Miall, *Congregationalism in Yorkshire*, pp. 270, 344, 247, 310–11; R. Balgarnie, *Sir Titus Salt, Baronet: His Life and Its Lessons* (London: Hodder and Stoughton, 1877), pp. 195–99; D. H. Mason, *Ten Thousand Sermons 1871–1971: The People, Parsons, and Praise of Lightcliffe Congregational Church* (Lightcliffe: Lightcliffe Congregational Church, 1971), p. 66.

20   Philip Barlow and Dave Shaw, *Balgarnie's Salt. With Commentary and Additions* (Saltaire: Nemine Juvante Publications, 2003), pp. 287–311.

21   J. Reynolds, *Saltaire: An Introduction to the Village of Sir Titus Salt* (Bradford: Bradford Art Galleries and Museums City Trail No. 2, 1976), p. 5.

22   J. Roberts, 'The Development of the Industry', in R. W. Suddards ed., *Titus of Salts* (Idle: Watmoughs Ltd., 1976), p. 25; W. Cudworth, *Round About Bradford* (Bradford, 1878), p. 313.

23   J. C. G. Binfield, 'Salt, Sir Titus, 1st Baronet (1803–1876)', in J. O. Baylen and N. J. Gossman (eds), *Biographical Dictionary of Modern British Radicals, Vol. 2. 1830–1870* (Brighton: Harvester Press, 1984), pp. 446–50.

24   Balgarnie, *Sir Titus Salt*, p. 122

25   J. Waddington-Feather, *A Century of Model-Village Schooling: The Salt Grammar School, 1868–1968* (Bingley, n.p., 1968), p. 11.

26   J. Bailey ed., *The Diary of Lady Frederick Cavendish*, Vol. II (London: John Murray, 1927), pp. 223–24. Entry for 30 September – 6 October 1878.

27   Reynolds, *Saltaire*, p. 22.

28   Ibid., p. 7.

29   Ibid., p. 28.

30   W. L. Creese, *The Search for Environment: The Garden City Before and After* (New Haven: Yale University Press, 1966), p. 31.

31   J. Tempest, 'The Making of the Village', p. 49, and J. Ayers, 'The Face of the Place', p. 55 in Suddards, *Titus of Salts*; Jackson et al., *Saltaire: The Making of a Model Town*, pp. 49–58.

32   Jackson et al., *Saltaire: The Making of a Model Town*, pp. 76–77, 84, 86, 92.

33   *Bradford Observer*, 22 August 1884.

34   *In Memory of William Evans Glyde*, [Bradford], n.d. [1884], unpag. [pp. 41–43].

35   J. Roberts, 'The Development of the Industry', p. 35, and D. Hanson, 'The Growth of the Company', p. 40, in Suddards, *Titus of Salts*.

36   Meakin, *Model Factories and Villages*, pp. 32, 416–17.

37 Jackson et al., *Saltaire: The Making of a Model Town*, pp. 186–87; Barlow and Shaw, *Balgarnie's Salt*, pp. 342–43.

38 E. Hampden-Cook, *The Register of Mill Hill School 1807–1926* (London [priv.]: Mill Hill School, 1926), p. 98.

39 Typed transcripts of John and Martha Crossley's reminiscences, in the possession of Mrs Mary Crossley when consulted.

40 J. A. Hargreaves, 'Religion and Society in the Parish of Halifax, circa 1740–1914', unpublished PhD, Huddersfield Polytechnic, 1991, p. 173.

41 Creese, *The Search for Environment*, p. 16.

42 'On show around the world – since the Great Exhibition of 1851', *Face to Face: Crossley Carpets Magazine*, Summer 1969, p. 4; E. Webster, *Dean Clough and the Crossley Inheritance* (Halifax: Dean Clough Publications, 1988), pp. 9–11.

43 M. Girouard, 'A Town Built on Carpets', *Country Life*, 24 September 1970, p. 757.

44 Hargreaves, 'Religion and Society in the Parish of Halifax', p. 174; G. P. Wadsworth, *S.S.S. Square Sunday School: A Short History* (Halifax, 1903), p. 17.

45 *Congregational Year Book*, 1858, pp. 264–66.

46 J. Browne, *History of Congregationalism and Memorials of the Churches in Norfolk and Suffolk* (London: Jarrold and Sons, 1877), p. 546.

47 S. Hadland, *Annals of Milton Mount College* (London: Mackie & Co., n.d.), p. 52.

48 'Failure of Alderman Allott', *Sheffield Telegraph*, 24 November 1876; 'The Failure of Mr. Allott. Meeting of Creditors', *Sheffield and Rotherham Independent*, 4 January 1877; with gratitude to Richard A. Frost.

49 Girouard, 'A Town Built on Carpets', p. 757.

50 Ibid., p. 758.

51 Creese, *The Search for Environment*, pp. 46–50; Hargreaves, 'Religion and Society in the Parish of Halifax', p. 340; K. Powell, *People's Inheritance: The People's Park Conservation Area of Halifax* (Calderdale, unpaginated, 1984); J. N. Tarn, *Five Per Cent Philanthropy: An Account of Housing in Urban Areas between 1840 and 1914* (Cambridge: Cambridge University Press, 1973).

52 *Congregational Year Book* 1867, pp. 370–71.

53 I. J. Shaw, *High Calvinists in Action. Calvinism and the City. Manchester and London, c.1810–1860* (Oxford: Oxford University Press, 2002), pp. 314–20.

54 A. T. Mitchell, *Rugby School Register 1842–74*, vol. II (Rugby, 1902), p. 275.

55 Hargreaves, 'Religion and Society in the Parish of Halifax', p. 342; Powell, *People's Inheritance*.

56 Powell, *People's Inheritance*.

57 Girouard, 'A Town Built on Carpets', p. 759.

58   Miall, *Congregationalism in Yorkshire*, p. 269; Girouard, 'A Town Built on Carpets', pp. 758–59.

59   Powell, *People's Inheritance*; Creese, *The Search for Environment*, pp. 48–55; Girouard, 'A Town Built on Carpets', pp. 758–59.

60   E. Hodder, *The Life and Work of the Seventh Earl of Shaftesbury, K.G.*, vol. III (1886), p. 71.

61   Creese, *The Search for Environment*, pp. 51–52.

62   Ibid., pp. 54–55; Powell, *People's Inheritance*.

63   *Somerleyton: An Illustrated Guide* (c.1994). P. L. Cottrell, 'Peto, Sir Samuel Morton', in D. J. Jeremy and C. Shaw (eds), *Dictionary of Business Biography*, vol. 4 (London: Butterworth, 1985), pp. 644–53.

64   R. Bretton, 'Crossleys of Dean Clough, Part IV. John Crossley MP', *Transactions, Halifax Antiquarian Society*, February 16–17, 1953; Creese, *The Search for Environment*, p. 58.

65   W. H. G. Armytage, *A.J. Mundella 1825–1897* (London: Benn, 1951), pp. 132–36, 145, original emphasis.

66   O. J. Whitley, 'Giulio Marchetti 5th June 1843 – 4th January 1931', typescript, 1988. I am indebted to J. P. Whitley for this reference.

67   Binfield and Taylor, *Who They Were*, pp. 242–43.

68   Webster, *Dean Clough and the Crossley Inheritance*, p. 17.

69   *Halifax Courier*, 31 August 1891.

70   F. A. Freer, *Edward White* (London, 1902), p. 169.

71   D. Johnson, 'Eric Lawrence, Edward Crossley, and the Conflict at Square Church, Halifax', typescript, 1990, p. 60. Hargreaves, 'Religion and Society in the Parish of Halifax', pp. 342–43; Webster, *Dean Clough and the Crossley Inheritance*, p. 18.

72   *Somerleyton: An Illustrated Guide*, pp. 6, 13.

73   'The Country Life Interview: Lord Somerleyton, Master of the Horse', *Country Life*, 4 May 1995, p. 78.

74   T. H. Green, *Works*, III, pp. CX–CXI, quoted in M. Richter, *The Politics of Conscience: T. H. Green and His Age* (London: Routledge, 1964), pp. 356–57.

75   Binfield and Taylor, *Who They Were*, pp. 129–31.

76   For Philip, 3rd Viscount Leverhulme (1915–2000) see *The Times*, 6 July 2000. I am indebted to Anthony Clinch for further information, 1 June 2004.

77   Leverhulme, 2nd Viscount, *Lord Leverhulme* (London: George Allen and Unwin, 1927), p. 272.

78   *Declaration of Faith by James Lever on being Admitted to Membership of Grosvenor Street Chapel, Manchester, February, 1845*. n.d., no publisher. 1845 should read 1835, as the text makes clear.

79   J. S. Drummond, *Charles A. Berry: a Memoire* (London, Cassell, 1899), p. 246.

80 Ibid., p. 33.

81 Ibid., p. 124.

82 Ibid., p. 139.

83 Leverhulme, *Lord Leverhulme*, p. 274.

84 Ibid., p. 106. C. Binfield, ' "A tradition handed on by preaching": the Allure of Broad Sermons – William Page Roberts of Vere Street', in Anna M. Robbins ed., *Ecumenical and Eclectic: The Unity of the Church in the Contemporary World* (Milton Keynes: Paternoster, 2007), pp. 86–128.

85 Leverhulme, *Lord Leverhulme*, p. 106; E. Kaye, *The History of the King's Weigh House Church: A Chapter in the History of London* (London: George Allen & Unwin, 1968), pp. 106–14, 118–40.

86 F. W. Peaples, *History of the St. George's Road Congregational Church and Its Connections* (Bolton: Tillotson & Son Ltd., 1913), p. 289.

87 Ibid., p. 288.

88 H. A. Hamilton to C. Binfield, 5 May 1997.

89 J. A. Pugh, *A History of Christ Church, Port Sunlight* (Unpublished dissertation, Sheffield, n.d.), p. 4.

90 In the possession of Christ Church United Reformed Church, Port Sunlight, when consulted: Port Sunlight Divine Services Committee Minute Book 1899–1914; Christ Church Port Sunlight Minute Book 1914–1925; Christ Church Port Sunlight Minute Book 1925–1937.

91 W. Atherton to C. Binfield, 24 March, 10 April 1977.

92 Minute Book 1914–1925, 5 July, 6 September, 11 October, 6 December 1915.

93 Minute Book 1925–1937, 16 April 1929.

94 Cutting in ibid., 1929–30.

95 Ibid., 27 February, 22 March 1930.

96 F. J. Powicke, *A History of the Cheshire County Union of Congregational Churches* (Manchester: Thomas Griffiths & Co., 1907), pp. 266–67; Information about Neston from A. R. Connell, H. W. Foote and the Revd. R. W. Kidd; Pugh, *A History of Christ Church*, p. 26.

97 J. Lomax-Simpson (25 February 1977) and Mr and Mrs G. Jellicoe (17 March 1977) to C. Binfield.

98 Powicke, *A History*, p. 267.

99 St. George's Thornton Hough, Church Roll, in possession of St. George's United Reformed Church, Thornton Hough, when consulted. D. Stewart, *St. George's United Reformed Church, Thornton Hough, The First Hundred Years 1907–2007* (Thornton Hough, 2007).

100 W. P. Jolly, *Lord Leverhulme: A Biography* (London: Constable, 1976), p. 126.

101 J. Marchal, *Lord Leverhulme's Ghosts: Colonial Exploitation in the Congo* (London: Verso, 2008).

102 A. Watson, *My Life: An Autobiography* (London: Ivor Nicholson and Watson, 1937), pp. 140–44.

103 Ibid., p. 143.

104 Leverhulme, *Lord Leverhulme*, p. 275.

105 *Progress*, vol. 25 (1925), pp. 85, 98–105.

106 Ibid., p. 93.

107 Leverhulme, *Lord Leverhulme*, p. 30.

108 Ibid., p. 31.

109 Ibid., p. 38.

110 Ibid., p. 290.

111 Jolly, *Lord Leverhulme*, p. 188.

112 'In memoriam: William Hesketh Leverhulme. Born 19 September, 1851; died 7 May, 1925', *Progress*, vol. 25 (1925), pp. 154, 141.

113 W. J. Reader, 'Lever, William Hesketh', *Dictionary of Business Biography*, vol. 3 (1985), p. 748; Jolly, *Lord Leverhulme*, p. 8.

114 Quoted in Leverhulme, *Lord Leverhulme*, p. 142.

115 Reader, 'Lever, William Hesketh', pp. 748–49; C. Wilson, *The History of Unilever*, vol. I (London, Unwin, 1954), p. 147.

116 Wilson, *History of Unilever*, pp. 154, 151.

117 Leverhulme, *Lord Leverhulme*, pp. 84, 198.

118 Ibid., p. 202.

119 Ibid., pp. 118–20, 177.

120 Jolly, *Lord Leverhulme*, p. 72.

121 *Progress, op. cit.*, pp. 151–52.

122 Leverhulme, *Lord Leverhulme*, p. 254.

123 H. Stafford, *A History of Caterham School* (Shrewsbury: Wilding & Son Ltd., 1945), pp. 89, 92, 100, 109; E. De C. Blomfield to C. Binfield, 17 March, 26 March 1980.

124 Leverhulme, *Lord Leverhulme*, p. 139; Hubbard and Shippobottom, 'Lord Leverhulme', in *Architecture* (London: Royal Society of Arts, 1980), pp. 192–93.

125 *ODNB*.

126 A. G. Gardiner, 'Sir William Lever', in *The Pillars of Society* (London: J.M. Dent & Sons, n.d.), pp. 191, 184, 186, 188, 189.

127 Creese, *The Search for Environment*, p. 109.

128 Ibid., p. 111.

129 Ibid., p. 125; Meakin, *Model Factories and Villages*, pp. 426–33.

130 Meakin, *Model Factories and Villages*, pp. 413–12.

131 Creese, *The Search for Environment*, p. 133.

132 Ibid., pp. 133–34; T. H. Mawson, *The Life and Work of an English*

Landscape Architect: An Autobiography (London: The Richards Press, *c*.1927), esp. pp. 115–17, 125–29, 190–91, 207–208.

133 Creese, *The Search for Environment*, p. 108.

134 Watson, *My Life*, p. 138.

135 Creese, *The Search for Environment*, pp. 139–40.

136 Ibid., pp. 141–43, 202.

137 Marchal, *Lord Leverhulme's Ghosts*, pp. 15–16, 23, 27, 34, 86–88, 95–98, 134, 165–66, 170–71.

138 See R. Hutchinson, *The Soapman, Lewis, Harris and Lord Leverhulme* (Edinburgh: Birlinn Ltd., 2003).

139 Wilson, *History of Unilever*, p. 272.

140 Binfield and Taylor, *Who They Were*, pp. 219–21; D. Newton, *Sir Halley Stewart* (London: George Allen and Unwin, 1968).

141 E. Crittall, 'Crittall, Francis Henry', in *Dictionary of Business Biography*, vol. I, 1985, pp. 831–34.

142 N. Chapple, 'C.H. James (1893–1953)', unpublished Postgraduate Diploma Thesis in Building Conservation, Architectural Association, 2011, p. 11.

143 Meakin, *Model Factories and Villages*, p. 433.

144 D. Macfadyen, *Sir Ebenezer Howard and the Town Planning Movement* (Manchester University Press, 1970).

145 J. R. Edwards, 'Cooper, Sir Francis D'Arcy', in *Dictionary of Business Biography*, vol. I, 1985, pp. 781–85.

146 W. Blackshaw, *The Community and Social Service* (London: Sir Isaac Pitman & Sons, 1939).

147 *Congregational Year Book*, 1954, pp. 505–506.

148 *Sheffield Congregational Year Book*, 1908, frontispiece.

149 W. Blackshaw, Institutional Churches. A Paper read before the Congregational Union of England and Wales at Leeds, October 11, 1905 (London: Examiner Office, 1905), pp. 3, 6, 8. I am indebted to Professor John Roach.

150 I am indebted to Dr J. H. Thompson for this information.

151 Blackshaw, *Community and Social Service*, pp. v, vii.

Notes to Chapter 6

1 *Christian World*, 10 October 1929.

2 *Methodist Times*, 19 June 1924.

3 A. D. Gilbert, *Religion and Society in Industrial England: Church, Chapel and Social Change 1740–1914* (London: Longman, 1976), chaps. 2–5.

4 David Hempton, *The Religion of the People: Methodism and Popular Religion c.1750–1900* (London: Routledge, 1996), pp. 101–102, 118–19.

5   Cited in Timothy Larsen, *Friends of Religious Equality: Nonconformist Politics in Mid-Victorian England* (Woodbridge: Boydell Press, 1999), p. 19.

6   Michael R. Watts, *The Dissenters*, vol. II (Oxford: Clarendon, 1995), pp. 597, 718–76.

7   Donald M. Lewis, *Lighten their Darkness: The Evangelical Mission to Working-Class London 1828–1860* (Westport, CT: Greenwood, 1986), p. 127.

8   A view questioned in Hempton, *Religion of the People*, p. 64.

9   Cited in Lewis, *Lighten their Darkness*, p. 50.

10   Martin Gorsky, *Patterns of Philanthropy: Charities and Society in Nineteenth Century Bristol* (Woodbridge: Boydell Press, 1999), p. 147.

11   Trygve R. Tholfsen, *Working Class Radicalism in Mid-Victorian England* (New York: Columbia University Press, 1977), p. 136.

12   Alan J. Kidd, 'Charity Organisation and the Unemployed in Manchester, *c*.1870–1914', *Social History* 9/1 (1984), pp. 45–66.

13   Tholfsen, *Working Class Radicalism*, pp. 37–39.

14   Betsy Rodgers, *Cloak of Charity: Studies in Eighteenth Century Philanthropy* (London: Methuen, 1949), p. 13.

15   Cited in Frank Prochaska, *Women and Philanthropy in Nineteenth Century England* (Oxford: Clarendon, 1980), p. 99; see also Gorsky, *Patterns of Philanthropy*, p. 116.

16   David Turley, 'The Anglo-American Unitarian Connection and Urban Poverty', in Hugh Cunningham and Joanna Innes (eds), *Charity, Philanthropy and Reform from the 1690s to 1850* (Basingstoke: Macmillan, 1998), pp. 230–31.

17   Francis Bishop cited in Anne Holt, *A Ministry to the Poor, being the History of the Liverpool Domestic Mission Society 1836–1936* (Liverpool: H. Young & Sons, 1936), p. 53.

18   Lewis, *Lighten their Darkness*, p. 129.

19   Kathleen Heasman, *Evangelicals in Action: An Appraisal of their Social Work in the Victorian Era* (London: Geoffrey Bles, 1962), chap. 6.

20   Holt, *A Ministry to the Poor*, p. 36; C. A. Piper, *A Century of Service* (Liverpool: Liverpool North End Domestic Mission Society, 1959), p. 11.

21   See Holt, *A Ministry to the Poor*, pp. 55–58; Andrew Mearns, *The Bitter Cry of Outcast London* (London: London Congregational Union, 1883), p. 27; Gorsky, *Patterns of Philanthropy*, p. 193.

22   *Norwich Mercury*, 26 April 1902.

23   Seth Koven, *Slumming: Sexual and Social Politics in Victorian London* (London: Princeton University Press, 2004), pp. 8–15.

24   Heasman, *Evangelicals in Action*, pp. 97–99, shows that this technique was also imitated subsequently in other orphans' charities.

25   Philip S. Bagwell, *Outcast London: A Christian Response* (London: Epworth Press, 1987), p. 25.

26   Gorsky, *Patterns of Philanthropy*, p. 169.

27   Prochaska, *Women and Philanthropy*, p. 109.

28   Ibid., pp. 149–50.

29   Benjamin Waugh, *The Gaol Cradle, Who Rocks It?* (London: Strahan, 1912).

30   Cited in George Railton, *General Booth* (London: Hodder & Stoughton, 1912), p. 188.

31   The Baptist Edward Smith, cited in Sarah Wise, *The Blackest Streets: The Life and Death of a Victorian Slum* (London: Vintage, 2009), p. 208.

32   *The Times*, 26 January 1882.

33   Cited in T. Rhondda Williams, *How I Found my Faith: A Religious Pilgrimage* (London: Cassell, 1938), pp. 127–28.

34   Gorsky, *Patterns of Philanthropy*, p. 146.

35   Prochaska, *Women and Philanthropy*, pp. 188–90.

36   Congregational and Baptist conferences also passed supportive resolutions.

37   Cited in Christopher Oldstone-Moore, *Hugh Price Hughes: Founder of a New Methodism, Conscience of a New Nonconformity* (Cardiff: University of Wales Press, 1999), p. 147.

38   Ibid., p. 144.

39   Disputed between Andrew Mearns and William C. Preston.

40   Mearns, *Bitter Cry*, pp. 11–13.

41   Ibid., p. 24.

42   Cited in J. W. Wolfenden, 'English Nonconformity and the Social Conscience 1880–1906', Unpublished Yale PhD Thesis, 1954, p. 19.

43   Cited in Heasman, *Evangelicals in Action*, p. 87.

44   Cited in Oldstone-Moore, *Hugh Price Hughes*, p. 142.

45   Cited in David M. Thompson, 'R. W. Dale and the "Civic Gospel"', in Alan P. F. Sell ed., *Protestant Nonconformists and the West Midlands of England* (Keele: Keele University Press, 1996), p. 103.

46   Mearns, *Bitter Cry*, p. 24.

47   Ibid., p. 27.

48   Cited in Oldstone-Moore, *Hugh Price Hughes*, p. 114.

49   Cited in John Banks, *The Story so Far: The First 100 Years of the Manchester and Salford Methodist Mission* (Manchester: Manchester and Salford Methodist Mission, 1986), p. 22; see also S. J. D. Green, *Religion in the Age of Decline: Organisation and Experience in Industrial Yorkshire 1870–1920* (Cambridge: Cambridge University Press, 1996), pp. 115–16.

50   Cited in John D. Beasley, *The Bitter Cry Heard and Heeded: The Story of the South London Mission 1889–1989* (London: South London Mission, 1990), p. 14.

51   Cited in Alan Tuberfield, *John Scott Lidgett: Archbishop of British Methodism?* (Peterborough: Epworth Press, 2003), p. 35.

52 Liverpool Record Office: Liverpool Free Church Council, Advisory Board minutes, 16 June 1911: Report on Netherfield and South Toxteth districts.

53 Cited in Tuberfield, *John Scott Lidgett*, p. 36.

54 Wilfrid J. Rowland, *The Free Churches and the People: A Report of the Work of the Free Churches of Liverpool* (Liverpool: Arthur Black, 1908), p. 40.

55 Ian Sellers, 'Nonconformist Attitudes in Later Nineteenth Century Liverpool', *Transactions of the Historic Society of Lancashire and Cheshire* 114 (1962), p. 216.

56 Robin Gill, *The Myth of the Empty Church* (London: SPCK, 1993).

57 Rowland, *The Free Churches and the People*, pp. 98–99.

58 J. C. Carlile, *My Life's Little Day* (London: Blackie, 1935), p. 82.

59 *British Weekly*, 8 March 1928.

60 William Ward, in W. Forbes Gray ed., *Non-Church Going: Its Reasons and Remedies* (Edinburgh: Oliphant, Anderson & Ferrier, 1911), p. 181.

61 Banks, *The Story so Far*, pp. 22–29.

62 See Green, *Religion in the Age of Decline*, p. 152.

63 Further information in H. C. G. Matthew, and Brian Harrison; see ODNB.

64 W. F. Lofthouse, 'The Warden of the Bermondsey Settlement', in Rupert E. Davies ed., *John Scott Lidgett: A Symposium* (London: Epworth Press, 1957), p. 51.

65 Percy Alden, 'That Reminds Me', *Congregational Quarterly* 11 (1933), pp. 197–200.

66 *Mansfield House Settlement*, undated brochure in the British Library, pp. 22–23.

67 Cited in Paul Rowntree Clifford, *Venture in Faith: The Story of the West Ham Central Mission* (London: Carey Kingsgate, 1950), p. 63.

68 Following the pioneering work Frank Tillyard started at Mansfield House in 1891.

69 Cited in Bagwell, *Outcast London*, p. 42.

70 Sir Josiah Stamp, *The Christian Ethic as an Economic Factor* (London: Epworth Press, 1926), p. 66. For an expression of such beliefs by a prominent early nineteenth-century Baptist, see Olinthus Gregory ed. *The Works of Robert Hall A.M.*, vol. VI (New York: J & J Harper, 1932), p. 458.

71 Gorsky, *Patterns of Philanthropy*, p. 228.

72 *Methodist Recorder*, 30 March 1905.

73 *Methodist Times*, 21 December 1922.

74 R. J. Barker, *Christ in the Valley of Unemployment* (London: Hodder & Stoughton, 1936), pp. 34–48, 93–112.

75 Brian Frost with Stuart Jordan, *Pioneers of Social Passion: London's Cosmopolitan Methodism* (Peterborough: Epworth Press, 2006), p. 18.

76 See Chapter 4.

77 *Daily Herald*, 20 March 1933.

78 *Methodist Times*, 20 June 1929.

79 Sir Geoffrey Shakespeare, *Let Candles be Brought in* (London: Macdonald, 1949), pp. 144–59.

80 *Free Churchman*, July 1934.

81 Thomas Tiplady, *Spiritual Adventure: The Story of 'The Ideal' Film Service* (London: United Society for Christian Literature, 1935), p. 17.

82 Frost, *Pioneers of Social Passion*, pp. 21–24.

83 Green, *Religion in the Age of Decline*, chap. 9.

84 *Free Church Year Book*, 1923, p. 35.

85 *Congregational Year Book*, 1934, p. 149.

86 *Hope Street Monthly Calendar*, 21/212, April/May 1922, pp. 2–3.

87 Margaret R. Pitt, *Our Unemployed: Can the Past Teach the Present?* (privately printed, 2nd edition, 1985), p. 47.

88 *London Yearly Meeting* (1936), p. 154.

89 John Storer, 'Social Responsibility to our Neighbours', in Alan Rushton and John Storer (eds), *Church and Society: Some Unitarian Views for Discussion* (London: Social Services Department, General Assembly of Unitarian and Free Christian Churches, 1969), p. 17.

90 See Malcolm Brown and Paul Ballard, *The Church and Economic Life: A Documentary Study: 1945 to the Present* (Peterborough: Epworth Press, 2006), chapters 1 and 2.

91 Frank Prochaska, *Christianity and Social Service in Modern Britain* (Oxford: Oxford University Press, 2008), p. 149.

92 Tom Stephens cited in John Mcnicol, 'From "Problem Family" to "Underclass", 1945–95', in Helen Fawcett and Rodney Lowe (eds), *Welfare Policy in Britain: The Road from 1945* (Basingstoke: Macmillan, 1999), p. 74.

93 Pat Starkey, 'Can the Piper Call the Tune? Innovation and Experiment with Deprived Families in Britain, 1940s–1980s: The Work of Family Service Units', *British Journal of Social Work* 32/5 (2002), pp. 573–87.

94 Frost, *Pioneers of Social Passion*, pp. 25–26. Infant welfare also ceased to be largely the preserve of voluntary societies.

95 Phyllis Thompson, *The Midnight Patrol* (London: Hodder & Stoughton, 1974), pp. 42–106.

96 Andrew Mawson, *The Social Entrepreneur: Making Communities Work* (London: Atlantic Books, 2006).

97 Frost, *Pioneers of Social Passion*, pp. 40–41, 84–98.

98 Storer, 'Social Responsibility to our Neighbours', p. 16.

99 Author's interviews at Eastbrook Hall, Bradford, 14 July 1986. See also Frost, *Pioneers of Social Passion*, p. 149.

100 Banks, *The Story so Far*, p. 150.

101 Author's interview: 22 May 1992.

102 Cited in Frost, *Pioneers of Social Passion*, p. 104.

103 Ermal B. Kirby, 'At the Heart of the City: New Patterns Emerge in Birmingham', in *Changing Times: Annual Review for 1990* (London: Methodist Church Home Mission, 1990), p. 8.

104 Cited in Anne Wilkinson-Hughes and Paul Mortimore (eds), *Belonging: A Resource for the Christian Family* (London: Baptist Union of Great Britain, 1994), p. 104.

105 John Vincent, *Five Pillars of Christianity* (Sheffield: Urban Theology Unit, 1989), p. 11.

106 John Morgans, *Journey of a Lifetime* (privately printed, 2008), p. 441.

107 Mission-Shaped Working Group, *Mission-Shaped Church: Church Planting and Fresh Expressions of Church in a Changing Context* (London: Church House Publishing, 2004). Also see Chapter 8 in this book.

108 Ibid., p. 462.

109 John Kirkby, with Marianne Clough, *Nevertheless: The Incredible Story of One Man's Mission to Change Thousands of People's Lives* (Bradford: CAP Books, 2003), p. 84.

110 See Steve Chalke and Anthony Watkiss, *Intelligent Church – a Journey Toward Christ-centred Community* (Grand Rapids: Zondervan, 2006).

111 See, for instance, the Bradford Town Mission reports of the decade.

Notes to Chapter 7

1 See, for example, *Nonconformity and Politics* by a Nonconformist Minister (London, 1909).

2 Karl Marx, *Capital: A Critique of Political Economy*, 4th edn (Harmondsworth: Penguin, 1976), pp. i, 619.

3 W. C. Braithwaite, *The Second Period of Quakerism* (London: Macmillan, 1919), pp. 565–87.

4 See Peter Clark, *British Clubs and Societies 1580–1800: The Origins of an Associational World* (Oxford: Oxford University Press, 2000).

5 M. Southwood, *John Howard Prison Reformer* (London: Independent Press, 1958); D. L. Howard, *John Howard: Prison Reformer* (London: C. Johnson, 1958).

6 Rational Dissent (i.e. Unitarians) also played a key part in this mass movement. For the general under-estimate of the role of Rational Dissent in anti-slavery, see A. Page, 'Rational Dissent, Enlightenment, and Abolition of the British Slave Trade', *Historical Journal* 54.3 (September 2011), pp. 741–72, especially pp. 750–54.

7 B. Stanley, *The History of the Baptist Missionary Society* (Edinburgh: T & T Clark, 1992), pp. 76–80.

8 See e.g. Roger Anstey, *The Atlantic Slave Trade and British Abolition,*

1760–1810 (London: Macmillan, 1975); Howard Temperley, 'Anti-slavery', in Patricia Hollis ed., *Pressure from Without* (London: Edward Arnold, 1974), pp. 27–51.

9   For Baines, see Derek Fraser, 'Edward Baines', in Hollis, *Pressure from Without*, pp. 183–209; Edward Baines, *The Social, Educational, and Religious State of the Manufacturing Districts* (London: Woburn, 1843, 1969 edn).

10   See H. U. Faulkner, *Chartism and the Churches* (New York: Columbia University Press, 1916); Eileen Groth Lyon, *Politicians in the Pulpit* (Aldershot: Ashgate, 1999).

11   See Michael Watts, *The Dissenters Volume II: The Expansion of Evangelical Nonconformity, 1791–1859* (Oxford: Clarendon, 1995).

12   http://www.johnlewispartnership.co.uk/.

13   Bill Lancaster, *Radicalism Co-operation, and Socialism: Leicester Working-class Politics, 1860–1906* (Leicester: Leicester University Press, 1987).

14   This section is heavily dependent on C. D. Field, 'Safe as Houses: Methodism and the Building Society Movement in England and Wales', in P. Forsaith and M. Wellings (eds), *Methodism and History: Essays in Honour of John Vickers* (Oxford: Oxford University Press, 2010), pp. 91–139. This essay actually covers more than Methodism.

15   See Brian Harrison, *Drink and the Victorians* (London: Keele University Press, 1971).

16   It was anonymous, and various authors were initially suggested, but the scholarly consensus today is that Mearns was the author.

17   See also Chapter 5 section IV in this book.

18   Seebohm Rowntree, *Poverty: A Study of Town Life* (London, 1902), p. viii.

19   B. F. Westcott, *Social Aspects of Christianity* (London: Macmillan, 1887), pp. v, 96.

20   R. J. Campbell, *Christianity and the Social Order* (new edn, London, Chapman and Hall, 1912), p. 117.

21   T. Rhondda Williams, *How I Found my Faith* (London: Cassell, 1938), pp. 98–101, 106–10, 188–89.

22   I have discussed this question in more detail in 'The Emergence of the Nonconformist Social Gospel in England', in K. Robbins ed., *Protestant Evangelicalism: Britain, Ireland, Germany and America, c.1750–c.1950* (Oxford: Ecclesiastical History Society, 1990), pp. 275–79.

23   C. Ensor Walters ed., *The Social Mission of the Church* (London: National Council of Free Evangelical Churches, 1906), p. xiii.

24   Williams, *How I Found my Faith*, p. 98.

25   R. Pope, *Building Jerusalem: Nonconformity, Labour and the Social Question in Wales, 1906–39* (Cardiff: University of Wales Press, 1998), pp. 123–64; R. Moore, *Pit-men, Preachers and Politics: The Effects of Methodism in a Durham Mining Community* (Cambridge: Cambridge University Press, 1974), pp. 169–90. E. T. Davies, *Religion in the Industrial*

Revolution in South Wales (Cardiff: University of Wales Press, 1965), pp. 160–61, dates the division earlier from 1898.

26 W. Paynter, *My Generation* (London: Allen and Unwin, 1972), p. 110, quoted in Pope, *Building Jerusalem*, p. 92.

27 See *ODNB* for more details.

28 John Harvey, J. St. G. C. Heath, Malcolm Spencer, William Temple and H. G. Wood, *Competition: A Study in Human Motive* (London: Macmillan, 1917), p. viii.

29 M. Lawson, *God's Back-Room Boy* (London, 1952), p. 35; John Taylor and Clyde Binfield, *Who They Were in the Reformed Churches of England and Wales 1901–2000* (Donington: Dyas, 2007), pp. 213–14.

30 D. Killingray, *Race, Faith and Politics: Harold Moody and the League of Coloured Peoples* (London: Goldsmiths College, 1999), p. 5.

31 Killingray, *Race, Faith and Politics*, passim; *ODNB*: Harold Moody, 38:886–7; Taylor and Binfield, *Who They Were*; E. Kaye, J. Lees and K. Thorpe, *Daughters of Dissent* (London: United Reformed Church, 2004), pp. 108–109; D. A. Vaughn, *Negro Victory: The Life Story of Dr Harold Moody* (London: Independent Press, 1950).

32 See Chapter 8 of this book.

33 Kaye et al., *Daughters of Dissent*, pp. 109–21; D. M. Thompson, *Protestant Nonconformist Texts, IV: The Twentieth Century* (Aldershot: Ashgate, 2007), pp. 56–58.

34 F. K. Prochaska, *Women and Philanthropy in Nineteenth-Century England* (Oxford: Clarendon, 1980), pp. 171–73. For a critique of traditional approaches to the history of prisons, and in particular the effects of ignoring gender, see L. Zedner, *Women, Crime and Custody in Victorian England* (Oxford: Clarendon, 1991); Zedner's book is, however, relatively negative about the effect of religious motivation in this area.

35 L. Fox, *The English Prison and Borstal Systems* (London: Routledge and Kegan Paul, 1951), pp. 89–90, 201–205; J. D. Broadbent, 'The Church and the Prisoner', *The Howard Journal*, x, 4 (1961), pp. 320–25.

36 A. F. Young and E. T. Ashton, *British Social Work in the Nineteenth Century* (London: Routledge, 1956), pp. 172–82; Fox, *English Prison*, pp. 340–42.

37 *ODNB*: 'Susanna Meredith' (37:873–4) and 'Mary Carpenter' (10:237–9); Young and Ashton, *British Social Work*, pp. 163–72; David Owen, *English Philanthropy 1660–1960* (Cambridge, Mass.: Belknap, 1965), pp. 154–55; Henry Richard, *Memoirs of Joseph Sturg* (London, 1864), pp. 555–61; L. Radzinowicz, Introduction to the re-issue of S. and B. Webb, *English Prisons under Local Government* (London: Cass, 1963). Lionel Fox's study, *English Prison*, pp. 327–34, spends very little time on Reformatories, and concentrates on those penal institutions funded solely by the state.

38 *ODNB*: 'Andrew Reed' (46:292–3), 'George Müller' (39:711–2); D. M. Lewis ed., *Dictionary of Evangelical Biography* (Oxford: Blackwell, 1995), 'Andrew Reed' (ii, 921–92), 'George Müller' (ii, 803–804); A. T. Pierson,

George Müller of Bristol (London: James Nisbet, 1899); Owen, *English Philanthropy 1660–1960*, pp. 158–62.

39 *ODNB*: 'Thomas John Barnardo' (3:970–3); Owen, *English Philanthropy 1660–1960*, pp. 157–58.

40 *ODNB*: 'Henry Solly' (51:835–6). His last initiative was the establishment of the Society for the Promotion of Industrial Villages in 1884, which despite its failure was one inspiration for Ebenezer Howard's Garden City Movement.

41 C. L. Mowat, *The Charity Organization Society 1869–1913* (London: Methuen, 1961), pp. 1–18, 63–70.

42 Young and Ashton, *British Social Work*, pp. 223–58.

43 Thompson, *Protestant Nonconformist Texts*, pp. 39–41.

44 Stanley, *History of the Baptist Missionary Society*, pp. 439–58; the quotation is from p. 456.

Notes to Chapter 8

1 Gustavo Gutiérrez, *A Theology of Liberation: History, Politics and Salvation* (Maryknoll: Orbis, 1973).

2 Leonardo Boff, *Jesus Christ, Liberator* (Maryknoll: Orbis, 1978); Clodovis Boff, *Theology and Praxis: Epistomological Foundations* (Maryknoll: Orbis, 1987).

3 Paulo Freire, *Pedagogy of the Oppressed* (Harmondsworth: Penguin, 1970).

4 See, for example, James Cone, *A Black Theology of Liberation* (Philadelphia: Lippencott, 1970).

5 See Ann Loades, *Feminist Theology: A Reader* (London: SPCK, 1990).

6 See Stephanie Y. Mitchem, *Introducing Womanist Theology* (Maryknoll: Orbis, 2002).

7 British Council of Churches, *Community Work and the Churches* (London: British Council of Churches, 1975), p. 5.

8 Ibid., p. 7.

9 Ibid., p. 16.

10 Andrew Marr, *A History of Modern Britain* (Basingstoke: Pan Macmillan, 2007–2009), p. 73.

11 Manchester City Council, *Manchester Trends 2000* (Manchester City Council, 2000); Planning Studies, p. 35 (Pamphlet published by the Manchester City Council); Manchester City Council, *New East Manchester: A New Town in the City Regeneration Framework* (Manchester City Planning Office, 2001), pp. 10–12; Manchester City Council, *The Manchester Plan: The Unitary Development Plan for the City of Manchester: Deposit Draft* (Manchester City Council, 1992).

12 Hulme Study Information, *Hulme Views Project, Hulme, Manchester* (Hulme Views, 1991).

13   Joan B. Miller, *Casework Ministry* (London: SCM, 1972).

14   Christopher Baker, 'From the Land of the Concrete Cow: Milton Keynes', in John Vincent ed., *Faithfulness in the City* (Hawarden: Monad Press, 2003), p. 90.

15   Ministry of Housing and Local Government, People and Planning: Report of the Committee on Public Participation in Planning ('The Skeffington Report') (London: HMSO, 1969).

16   Mark K. Smith, 'Community Work'. *Encyclopaedia of Informal Education* (1996, 2006), http://www.infed.org/community/b-comwrk.htm

17   M. Loney, *Community Against Government: The British Community Development Project 1968–78. A Study of Government Incompetence* (London: Heinemann, 1983).

18   Calouste Gulbenkian Foundation, *Community Work and Social Change: A Report on Training* (London: Longman, 1968).

19   David N. Thomas, The Making of Community Work (London: George Allen and Unwin, 1983), p. 9.

20   Smith, 'Community Work' (2006).

21   Malcolm Brown and Paul Ballard, *The Church and Economic Life: A Documentary Study. 1945 to the Present* (Peterborough: Epworth, 2006), p. 60.

22   Peter Sharrocks, 'The Story of a Youth and Community Centre', in Wendy Godfrey ed., *Down to Earth: Stories of Church Based Community Work* (London: British Council of Churches, 1985), pp. 33–43.

23   Graham Cook, 'South Leeds: The Story of a Team Ministry', in Godfrey, *Down to Earth*, p. 4.

24   Kate McIlhagga, 'St Ives', in Godfrey, *Down to Earth*, pp. 45–56.

25   Joan Miller, *Aberfan: A Disaster and its Aftermath* (London: Constable, 1974), p. 42. On 21 October 1966, one of the coal tips on Merthyr Mountain above Aberfan started to move and engulfed Pantglas Junior School and some houses killing 144 people, 116 of them children.

26   Brown and Ballard, *The Church and Economic Life*, p. 66. Barbara Castle, in Harold Wilson's government, published 'In Place of Strife', an abortive attempt to rebalance the relationship between management and unions. Under the Heath government, in 1973–74, miners' strikes led to the three-day week. Despite an economic recovery in the late 1970s, the Labour government faced a series of damaging strikes during the winter of 1978–79, popularly dubbed the 'Winter of Discontent'.

27   Brown and Ballard, *The Church and Economic Life*, p. 62.

28   Home Mission Dept. Occasional Paper 5, 'The Methodist Approach to Industrial Mission' (1968), in Brown and Ballard, *The Church and Economic Life*, pp. 137–39.

29   Brown and Ballard, *The Church and Economic Life*, p. 62.

30   Prime Minister Harold Macmillan at a Conservative rally in Bedford (1957)

to mark 25 years' service by Mr Lennox-Boyd, the Colonial Secretary, as MP for Mid-Bedfordshire.

31   Even so, some 83,000 immigrants from the Commonwealth settled in the UK between 1968 and 1975, largely through gaining work permits or obtaining permission to join relatives. The most significant immigration of the decade began in 1972 when the Ugandan dictator, Idi Amin, expelled 80,000 African Asians from the country, families who had been encouraged to settle there during the days of Empire. Many held British passports and the UK admitted 28,000 in two months.

32   Michael Eastman and Steve Latham (eds), *Urban Church: A Practitioner's Resource Book* (London: SPCK, 2004), pp. 74–77.

33   Interview with Janet Lees, December 2009.

34   David Sutton-Jones ed., *Full Circle: A Journey for Justice* (Sheffield: St James' United Reformed Church, 2002); Elaine Kaye, Janet Lees and Kirsty Thorpe, *Daughters of Dissent* (London: United Reformed Church, 2004), pp. 112–15, 119–20, 126, 150–51.

35   Kaye et al., *Daughters of Dissent*, p. 151.

36   Muriel Paulden had already set up a Training Scheme for her Liverpool churches called 'The Congregational Training Fellowship'. This had also supported holiday clubs for children in deprived parts of Liverpool. I am indebted to Brenda Willis for information about St Paul's house (February 2009).

37   Muriel Paulden, quoted in Derek Watson, *Angel of Jesus: The Life and Work in Liverpool 8 of the Rev'd Muriel Olympia Paulden MA (1892–1995)* (Wimbourne: Minster Press, 1994), p. 50.

38   John Vincent, *Hope from the City* (Peterborough: Epworth, 2000).

39   British Council of Churches, 'Work or What?' and 'Understanding Inequality' (1977), in Brown and Ballard, *The Church and Economic Life*, pp. 85–88.

40   British Council of Churches, 'Understanding Inequality' (1977), in Brown and Ballard, *The Church and Economic Life*, pp. 87–88.

41   Interview with Margaret Thatcher in *Women's Own*, 23 September 1987.

42   By 1983 inflation and mortgage rates were at their lowest levels since 1970, although manufacturing output had dropped by 30 per cent since 1978; unemployment remained high, peaking at 3.3 million in 1984.

43   David Sheppard, *Bias to the Poor* (London: Hodder and Stoughton, 1983).

44   The Report of the Archbishop of Canterbury's Commission on Urban Priority Areas, *Faith in the City: A Call for Action by Church and Nation* (London: Church House Publishing, 1985). This report was followed by a number of edited volumes under the auspices of the Commission, including: Peter Sedgwick ed., *God in the City: Essays and Reflections from the Archbishop's Urban Theology Group* (London: Mowbray, 1995); and by a second report from the Commission on Urban Life and Faith, *Faithful Cities: A Call for Celebration, Vision and Justice* (London: Methodist Publishing House and Church House Publishing, 2006).

45   Steve Chalke, with AnthonyWatkis, *100 Proven Ways to Transform your Community* (Eastbourne: Great Ideas, 2003), pp. 50–51.

46   Ibid., pp. 28–29.

47   John Morgans, *Journey of a Lifetime from the Diaries of John Morgans* (Llanidloes: John and Nora Morgans, 2008), p. 435.

48   Interview with Revd Keith Argyle, 3 August 2010.

49   Ibid.

50   Charles Brock ed., *Sightings of Hope: World Church and Mission* (London: United Reformed Church, 1994), p. 98.

51   http://www.thatreligiousstudieswebsite.com/Ethics/Applied_Ethics/Race_Racism/kairos_document.php

52   Andrew Mawson, *The Social Entrepreneur: Making Communities Work* (London: Atlantic Books, 2008).

53   Michael Diffey, *Church Community Work and the URC* (undated). www.urc.org

54   This was set out in a Supplementary Ministries Paper (unpublished) of the United Reformed Church (London, 1977): 'The purpose of a CCW is to lead and strengthen the local church's mission to the community through caring service. The title will apply where the church accepts and commissions the person for a defined role in the community, working alongside a minister in some local church context with the approval and authorization of the District Council and the Supplementary Ministries Committee.'

55   United Reformed Church, *Report to General Assembly* (London: United Reformed Church, 1980).

56   United Reformed Church, *Basis of Union of the United Reformed Church* (London: United Reformed Church, 2011).

57   T. R. Batten, *The Non-Directive Approach to Group and Community Work* (Oxford: Oxford University Press, 1965); Fred Milson, *Community Work and the Christian Faith* (London: Hodder and Stoughton, 1975), p. 28.

58   Paul Ballard, 'Why Community Work? The Issues', in Paul Ballard ed., *Issues in Church Related Community Work: Holi 6* (Cardiff: University of Wales College, 1990), p. 11.

59   Christopher Richard Baker, *The Hybrid Church in the City: Third Space Thinking* (Aldershot: Ashgate, 2007), pp. 53–56; Eddie Gibbs and Ryan K. Bolger, *Emerging Churches: Creating Christian Community in Postmodern Cultures* (London: SPCK, 2006), pp. 113–15.

60   Pete Ward, *Liquid Church* (Carlisle: Paternoster, 2002).

61   Chalke and Watkis, *100 Proven Ways*, pp. 180–81.

62   Ann Morisy, *Journeying Out: A New Approach to Christian Mission* (London: Continuum, 2004), chap. 3.

63   Phil Jump, *Community Regeneration and Neighbourhood Renewal: Towards a Baptist Response* (Didcot: Baptist Union of Great Britain, 2001).

64   http://www.hitc.org.uk/cms/index.php?option=com_content&task=view&id=2&Itemid=3

65 Andrew Mawson, Peter Southcombe and Donald Findley, *One Church – 100 Uses: The National Agency for the Creative Transformation of Churches* (London: Bromley-by Bow Centre, undated).

66 http://www.jointpublicissues.org.uk/jpit_COIC_submission_0107.pdf

67 Eastman and Latham (eds), *Urban Church*, pp. 100–101.

68 United Reformed Church, *Reports to General Assembly* (London: United Reformed Church, 2005). See also: United Reformed Church, *Supplementary Ministries Paper* (1977); United Reformed Church, *Report to General Assembly* (1980, 1986, 1989, 1990, 1991, 2002): sections on 'Ministries'; United Reformed Church, General Assembly, *Records of Assembly* (1978, 1980, 1987, 1989): sections on 'Ministries'.

69 Paul Keeble, 'Gang Violence', in Eastman and Latham, *Urban Church*, p. 104.

70 Matt Wilson, *Eden: Called to the Streets* (Manchester: The Message Trust, 2005), frontispiece.

71 Stuart Murray ed., *Planting Churches: A Framework for Practitioners* (2009); www.incarnateministries: web page no longer available but see: *Church Planting: Strategic Pathways* (Mission Files; Baptist Union of Great Britain, 2011), p. 8. http://www.baptist.org.uk/crossingplaces. html; Baptists and Church Planting History: http://churchplanting.org.uk/ church-plants-and-baptists-in-uk-where-are-we-at

72 Including The Angel, London; Chatteris; Chelmondiston; Edlesbrough in Aylesbury; North Watford; Richings Park, Iver, Bucks.; Southall; Thamesmead; Wood Green as at 2010.

73 Barbara Glasson and John Bradbury, 'Liverpool: The Lived Example of Culture', unpublished paper given at Core Cities Theology Network conference: 'Cities of Culture: Whose Vision? Which Agenda?', Scargill House, 12–14 September 2008.

74 Northwest Development Agency, *Faith in England's Northwest: The Contribution Made by Faith Communities to Civil Society in the Region* (Manchester: Northwest Development Agency, 2003).

75 A joint publication by the Methodist Church Division of Education and Youth and the National Christian Education Council: a Church Community Education programme from the 1980s until the end of the twentieth century.

76 Clare McBeath and Tim Presswood, *Crumbs of Hope: Prayers from the City* (Peterborough: Inspire, undated).

77 Jan Berry, *Ritual Making Women: Shaping Rites for Changing Lives* (London: Equinox, 2009); Jan Berry, 'Whose Threshold? Women's Strategies of Ritualization', *Feminist Theology* 14/3 (May 2006), pp. 273–88; Jan Berry, 'The Worship and Action of the Local Church: Theological Strand', in H. Cameron, P. Richter, D. Davies and F. Ward, *Studying Local Churches: A Handbook* (London: SCM, 2005); Jan Berry, 'Passion for Justice', in H. Walton and S. Durber (eds), *Silence in Heaven: A Book of Women's Preaching* (London: SCM, 1994).

78   For example: Kathy Galloway ed., *The Pattern of our Days: Liturgies and Resources for Worship* (Glasgow: Wild Goose Publications, 1996).

79   For example, Jaycinth Haymill, *Travelling the Road of Faith: Worship Resources from the Corrymeela Community* (Belfast: The Corrymeela Community, 2001).

80   Elaine Graham and Chris Baker, *Religious Capital in Regenerating Communities* (Manchester: William Temple Foundation and North-West Development Agency, 2004), p. 4.

81   Helen France, in Graham and Baker, *Religious Capital*, p. 22.

82   Claire Kerfoot, in Graham and Baker, *Religious Capital*, p. 24.

83   Anne Stewart, 'About Community Pride', in Graham and Baker, *Religious Capital*, p. 32.

84   The Archbishop's Council, *Faithful Cities: A Call for Celebration, Vision and Justice* (London: Methodist Publishing House and Church House Publishing, 2006).

85   Ibid., p. iv.

86   Stuart Murray, *Church After Christendom* (Carlisle: Paternoster, 2004) .

87   Philip Richter and Leslie J. Francis, *Gone but Not Forgotten: Church Leaving and Returning* (London: Darton, Longman and Todd, 1998); Department of Research and Training in Mission and P. A. Jump, *Community Regeneration and Neighbourhood Renewal: Towards a Baptist Response. A Report* (Didcot: Baptist Union of Great Britain, 2001).

Notes to Chapter 9

1   John de Gruchy, *Theology and Ministry in Context and Crisis* (New York: Harper and Row, 1966), p. 55.

2   Paul Ballard and John Pritchard, *Practical Theology in Action: Christian Thinking in the Service of Church and Society* (London: SPCK, 2006), pp. 81–95.

3   Don S. Browning, *Practical Theology: The Emerging Field in Theology, World and Church* (New York: Harper and Row, 1983).

4   Cf. Elaine Graham, Heather Walton and Frances Ward (eds), *Theological Reflection – Methods* (London: SCM Press, 2005); Laurie Green, *Let's Do Theology: Resources for Contextual Theology* (London: Mowbray, 2009); Judith Thompson, *SCM Study Guide to Theological Reflection* (London: SCM Press, 2008); Richard R. Osmer, *Practical Theology – an Introduction* (Grand Rapids: Eerdmans, 2008).

5   Stephen Pattison, *The Challenge of Practical Theology* (London: Jessica Kingsley, 2007), pp. 253–60.

6   Ibid., p. 257.

7   Ibid., p. 256.

8   Cf. John H. Arnold, *History: A Very Short Introduction* (Oxford: Oxford

University Press, 2000); John Vincent, *An Intelligent Person's Guide to History* (London: Duckworth, 1996); W. H. Walsh, *An Introduction to the Philosophy of History* (London: Hutchinson, 1967).

9   Brian Stanley, *The Bible and the Flag: Protestant Missions and British Imperialism in the Nineteenth and Twentieth Centuries* (Leicester: Apollo, 1990).

10 John Burrow, *A History of Histories: Epics, Chronicles, Romances and Inquiries from Herodotus and Thucidides to the Twentieth Century* (London: Allen Lane, 2007), pp. 467–519.

11 Cf. Ballard and Pritchard, *Practical Theology in Action*, pp. 145–60.

12 Paul Ballard and Lesley Husselbee, *Community and Ministry: An Introduction to Community Development in a Christian Context* (London: SPCK, 2007), pp. 65–80, together with further resources listed.

13 Ballard and Husselbee, *Community and Ministry*, pp. 65–80; Helen Cameron, Philip Richter, Douglas Davies and Frances Ward (eds), *Studying Local Churches: A Handbook* (London: SCM Press, 2005); Paul Henderson and David N. Thomas, *Skills in Neighbourhood Work* (London: Unwin Hyman, 1980), pp. 54–91.

14 Ballard and Husselbee, *Community and Ministry*, pp. 26–41, 151–57.

15 Cf. Giles Legood ed., *Chaplaincy* (London: Cassell, 1999); Miranda Threlfall-Holmes and Mark Newitt (eds), *Being a Chaplain* (London: SPCK, 2011).

16 Cf. Paul Ballard, 'Requiem for Ecumenism? Some Personal Reflections', in *Expository Times* 120/5 (2009), pp. 225–30; Laurie Green, *Urban Ministry and the Kingdom of God* (London: SPCK, 2003); Laurie Green and Christopher R. Baker, *Building Utopia? Seeking the Authentic Church for New Communities* (London: SPCK, 2008).

17 Eddie Gibbs and Ryan K. Bolger (eds), *Emerging Churches: Creating Christian Community in Post-modern Cultures* (London: SPCK, 2006).

18 Ann Morisy, *Journeying Out: A New Approach to Christian Mission* (Harrisburg: Morehouse, 2004).

19 David Hilborn, *Movement for Change: Evangelical Perspectives on Social Transformation* (Milton Keynes: Paternoster, 2004).

20 Cf. Grace Davey, *Religion in Modern Europe – a Memory Mutates* (Oxford: Oxford University Press, 2000); K. Moelendijk, L. Arie, Justin Beaumont and Christoph. Jedan (eds), *Exploring the Post-secular: The Religious, the Political and the Urban* (Leiden: Brill, 2010).

21 Cf. Alistair McGrath, *Why God Won't Go Away: Engaging the New Atheism* (London: SPCK, 2011).

22 Cf. Pattison, *The Challenge of Practical Theology*, pp. 132–43; Stephen G. Wright, *Reflections on Spirituality and Health* (London: Whurr, 2005).

23 Ballard and Husselbee, *Community and Ministry*, pp. 81–97.

24 Malcolm Brown, 'Marx, Methodism and Mayhem', *Practical Theology* 1.2 (2008), pp. 155–58.

25   E.g. Gweini, *Faith in Wales: Counting for Communities* (Cardiff: Evangelical
     Alliance Wales, 2008); Cardiff City Centre Churches, *Spiritual Capital
     Cardiff* (Cardiff: City Centre Churches, 2008).

26   Cf. Christopher Baker, *The Hybrid Church in the City: Third Space Thinking*
     (Aldershot: Ashgate, 2007); Chris Shannahan, *Voices from the Borderland:
     Re-imaging Cross-cultural Urban Theology in the Twenty-first Century*
     (London: Equinox, 2010).

27   Cf. Duncan Forrester, *Truthful Action: Explorations in Practical Theology*
     (Edinburgh: T & T Clark, 2000), pp. 107–160.

28   Cf. Herbert Butterfield, *Christianity and History* (London: G. Bell, 1950);
     David Bebbington, *Patterns in History* (Leicester: Inter-Varsity Press, 1979);
     Rowan Williams, *Why Study the Past? The Quest for the Historical Church*
     (London: Longman, Darton and Todd, 2005).

29   Paul Ballard, 'The Bible in Theological Reflection: Indications from the
     History of Scripture', *Practical Theology* 4.1 (2011): 35–47.

SELECT GENERAL
BIBLIOGRAPHY

This bibliography aims to provide a list of key and reasonably accessible resources that can be used to set the discussion offered in this volume in a wider context. To follow up more closely any particular topic or theme, recourse may be had to the notes provided for each chapter.

Anstey, Roger (1975), *The Atlantic Slave Trade and British Abolition, 1760–1810*. London: Macmillan.

Ballard, Paul and Pritchard, John (2006), *Practical Theology in Action: Christian Thinking in the Service of Church and Society*. London: SPCK.

Ballard, Paul and Husselbee, Lesley (2007), *Community and Ministry: An Introduction to Community Development in a Christian Context*. London: SPCK.

Bebbington, D. W. (1979), *Patterns in History*. Leicester: Inter-Varsity Press.

—(1982), *The Nonconformist Conscience – Chapel and Politics, 1870–1914*. London: George Allen and Unwin.

—(1989), *Evangelicalism in Modern Britain: A History from 1730s to 1980s*. London: Unwin Hyman.

—(2005), *The Dominance of Evangelicalism*. Downers Grove: Inter-Varsity Press.

Binfield, Clyde (1977), *And so Down to Prayers: Studies in English Nonconformity*. London: Dent.

Bowden, John (2005), *Christianity, the Complete Guide*. London: Continuum.

Briggs, J. H. Y. (1994), *The English Baptists of the Nineteenth Century*. Didcot: Baptist Historical Society.

Brown, Malcolm and Ballard, Paul (2006), *The Church and Economic Life: A Documentary Study, 1945 to the Present*. Peterborough: Epworth.

Chadwick, Owen (1966), *The Victorian Church*. London: Adam and Charles Black.

Coutts, John (1977), *The Salvationists*. London: Mowbray.

Dandelion, Pink (2007), *An Introduction to Quakerism*. Cambridge: Cambridge University Press.

Fawcett, Helen and Lowe, Rodney (eds) (1999), *Welfare Policy in Britain: The Road from 1945*. Basingstoke: Macmillan.

Gilbert, A. D. (1976), *Religion and Society in Industrial England, 1740–1914: Church, Chapel and Social Change*. London: Longman.

Gill, Robin (1993), *The Myth of the Empty Church*. London: SPCK.

Goodall, N. (1954), *History of the London Missionary Society, 1895–1945*. London: Oxford University Press.

Harrison, Linda ed. (2011), *Religion and Change in Modern Britain*. London: Routledge.

Heasman, Kathleen (1962), *Evangelicals in Action: An Appraisal of their Social Work in the Victorian Era*. London: Geoffrey Bles.

Hempton, David (1984), *Methodism and British Society, 1750–1850*. London: Hutchinson.

—(1996), *The Religion of the People: Methodism and Popular Religion c. 1750–1900*. London: Routledge.

Hilborn, David (2004), *Movement for Change: Evangelical Perspectives on Social Transformation*. Milton Keynes: Paternoster.

Hughes, M. (2008), *Conscience and Conflict: Methodism, Peace, and War in the Twentieth Century*. Peterborough: Epworth.

Inglis, K. S. (1963), *Churches and the Working Classes in Victorian England*. London: Routledge and Kegan Paul.

Jacobs, Sidney and Popple, Keith (eds) (2007), *Community Work in the 1990s*. Nottingham: Spokesman.

Jenkins, Philip (1992), *A History of Modern Wales, 1536–1990*. Harlow: Longmans.

Jones, R. Tudur (1962), *Congregationalism in England*. London: Independent Press.

—(2004), (ed. Pope, Robert) *Faith and the Crisis of a Nation – Wales, 1890–1914*. Cardiff: University of Wales Press.

Koss, S. (1975), *Nonconformity in British Politics*. London: B.T. Batsford.

Larsen, Timothy (1999), *Friends of Religious Equality: Nonconformist Politics in Mid-Victorian England*. Woodbridge: Boydell Press.

Morisy, Ann. (2004), *Journeying Out: A New Approach to Christian Mission*. London: Continuum.

Munson, James (1991), *The Nonconformists: In Search of a Lost Culture*. London: SPCK.

Pope, Robert (1998), *Building Jerusalem: Nonconformity, Labour and the Social Question in Wales, 1906–1939*. Cardiff: University of Wales Press.

—(1980), *Women and Philanthropy in Nineteenth-Century England*. Oxford: Clarendon.

Prochaska, Frank (2006), *Christianity and Social Service in Modern Britain: The Disinherited Spirit*. Oxford: Oxford University Press.

Randall, Ian M. (2005), *The English Baptists of the Twentieth Century*. Didcot: Baptist Historical Society.

Rupp, E. G. and Davies, R. G. (1965), *A History of Methodism in Great Britain*. London: Epworth.

Sell, Alan P. F., Hall, David J. and Sellers, Ian (2006), *Protestant Nonconformist Texts*, vol. 2. Aldershot: Ashgate.

Stanley, Brian (1990), *The Bible and the Flag*. Leicester: Inter-Varsity Press.

—(1992), *The History of the Baptist Missionary Society*. Edinburgh: T & T Clark.

Tholfsen, Trygve R. (1977), *Working-class Radicalism in Mid-Victorian England*. New York: Columbia University Press.

Thompson, David M. ed. (1972), *Nonconformity in the Nineteenth Century*. London: Routledge and Kegan Paul.

—(1995), *Where Do We Come From? The Origins of the United Reformed Church*. London: United Reformed Church.

Thompson, David M., Briggs, J. H. Y. and Turner, John Munsey (eds) *Protestant Nonconformist Texts. vol. 4: The Twentieth Century*. Aldershot: Ashgate.

Vickers, John A. ed. (2000), *A Dictionary of Methodism in Britain and Ireland*. Peterborough: Epworth.

Watts, Michael (1995), *The Dissenters: Vol. II. The Expansion of Evangelical Nonconformity, 1791–1859*. Oxford: Clarendon.

Young, A. F. and Ashton, E. T. (1956), *British Social Work in the Nineteenth Century*. London: Routledge.

Young, Kenneth (1972), *Chapel – The Joyous Days and Prayerful Nights of the Nonconformists in their Heyday, 1850–1950*. London: Eyre Methuen.

INDEX OF PEOPLE

INDEX OF PLACES

Churches and other institutions are given under their locality

GENERAL INDEX